Praise for *HeartSourcing*

"Ramgiri blends psychological insight and spiritual mastery into a delicious, accessible elixir. Separation is an illusion. Oneness is our birthright, and the way to claim it is effortless: drop into the heart, again and again. With clear instructions and entertaining personal stories, *HeartSourcing* reminds us that "you are the lover and all of life is the Beloved."

> – Mirabai Starr, author of *God of Love*, translator of the mystics

"*HeartSourcing* is a way to Love. Take it easy, but take it."

> – Arlo Guthrie

"Reading *HeartSourcing* you will pass through the valley of the shadow of death – *not* the valley of death and become fully alive."

> – Roshi Bernie Glassman, founder Zen Peacemakers

"Ramgiri's heartfull writing serves the One Love within us all."

> – Krishna Das, chantmaster, author of *Chants of A Lifetime and Flow of Grace*

"From his own eventful life, Ramgiri shares precious jewels of insight and wisdom. *HeartSourcing* is beautifully written and of great value for all who aspire to gain the choicest blessings of life, true happiness, peace, and success."

> – Swami Jyotirmayananda, author of over 40 books on Yoga and Vedanta

"If you journey on a path of spiritual devotion – *HeartSourcing* is for you. Ramgiri writes brilliantly of war-torn Germany and the resurrection of the human spirit into a world of Gurus and saints. He travels from horror to bliss, always seeking for truth."

> – Ma Jaya Sati Bhagavati, founder of Kashi Ashram

"In HeartSourcing Ramgiri has written an enlightened-Self help guide. His mixture of personal history and universal teaching opens doors for the novice and encourages those who have already begun to continue their journey. All this he accomplishes in a simple, clear narrative. It takes hutzpah to attempt such a work, and great humility to complete it.

> – Rabbi Mitchell Chefitz, author of *The Seventh Telling* and *The Curse of Blessings*.

"As a holocaust survivor, I am touched that Ramgiri shows us in his Auschwitz experience that love can be found even in the greatest darkness. To embrace that love is freedom itself. Ramgiri gives us the wisdom and courage to make this great journey into the heart."

> – Rabbi Zalman Schachter-Shalomi, author of *Jewish with Feeling*.

"Ramgiri is devoted to love, to what works, to peace and all the people on this earth."

> – Byron Katie, best-selling author of *Loving What Is*

"Ramgiri shares "HeartSourcing" which is a masterful road-map for accessing the love, compassion, and wisdom inherent in your own heart…your own Soul."

> – John E. Welshons, author, *One Soul, One Love, One Heart and Awakening From Grief*

"Ramgiri's touching — and often gut-wrenching — story spans from Nazi Germany to the sages of modern India. Seeking surrender, devotion, and contentment within, his saga is a potent reminder to seekers of truth everywhere that expansive love can only be found in a boundless heart."

> – Sankara Saranam, author of *God Without Religion, Questioning Centuries of Accepted Truths*

"There is a clear 'before' and 'after' HeartSourcing in my life. Through the practice I've become more present and open to love…it opens a door that guides you to become what we truly are: Love. By opening the door to that path, a strong "love wind" hits you that will amaze and even shock you."
– Sol Alonso, Miami, FL

"With the daily practice of HeartSourcing I have gone through the tunnel of my suffering to an enlightening liberation. It fell off of me like an old snakeskin. And yet it was not the technique of Heart-Sourcing, as you teach it, which has led me through, but the power of your love and your confidence in me."
– Christa Van Bracht, Germany

"Ramgiri's way of presenting the wisdom of the heart made me FREE. I do not need to search for truth anymore; I have had it in me all the time!"
– Kate Barbour, Florida

"Ramgiri has been invaluable in teaching me how to keep my thinking clear and aligned with my passion. This helps me get free of stress and communicate the great excitement I feel about my company."
– Bill Rowland, CEO

HeartSourcing

Ramgiri

HeartSourcing

Finding Our Way to Love and Liberation

Ramgiri Braun, Ph.D.

Foreword by Ram Dass

Cover design by Mayapriya Long of Bookwrights
Interior Design by Dan Frank Digital Design
Edited by Parvati Markus

HeartSourcing: Finding Our Way to Love and Liberation
by Ramgiri Braun, Ph.D.

ISBN 978-0-9858740-0-1
First Edition

1. Spirituality. 2. Memoir.

This Yearning for You

This yearning for you
Brings tears to my eyes again and again.
You who live in all beings, I offer my heart to you,
I offer my heart to you.

In your sacred presence all my fear melts away,
All my troubles dissolve. Let your loving gaze fall on me
So I can serve you in all beings, everywhere,
And bow to your feet again and again.

You are my mother and father, lover and friend.
I am here, outside your door, waiting for you.
Reveal yourself to me. Let me be what I am,
Let me be one with you.

–Ramgiri

Contents

Foreword
Ram Dass

T HIS IS THE STORY OF ONE person's inner exploration into the spiritual heart, and his lifelong process of learning to share the tools and concepts of that journey. Ramgiri, born Andreas Braun in the dark shadow of the Holocaust and World War II in Germany, had to deal with depression, fear, low self-esteem, with everything that stood in the way of his yearning for freedom and love.

That yearning led to our first meeting in London in 1972. After that he traveled to the small temple in the Himalayan foothills to be in the extraordinary presence of our guru, Neem Karoli Baba Maharajji. As it did for me, that encounter changed him in the depth of his being. Maharajji helped him realize that pure, unconditional love can and does exist in this world.

From that experience Ramgiri committed his life to sharing this love with others. From Maharajji's example of serving others, and his association with Hanuman, the Hindu god of service and devotion, Ramgiri has never grown tired of helping others on the way. Through decades of study in psychology and the wisdom traditions he has created a map that others can also follow to find fulfillment in one's own heart. Gathering the best practices, he shares with us how we can aspire to peace of mind, emotional harmony and a loving heart.

These skills have the power to awaken in us the love and wisdom that are the true qualities of each soul. Ramgiri calls these techniques HeartSourcing, and has worked to make them a direct and powerful route to the well of unconditional love inside of each of us. Rather than search in vain for fulfillment from external sources, Ramgiri takes us home into our own heart. HeartSourcing is a wonderful way to nurture yourself from your own inner core, so your love can shine into the world. Ramgiri's loving soul shines through this book.

January 2014, Maui, Hawaii

RAMGIRI WITH RAM DASS, MAUI HI 2004

HeartSourcing

Finding Our Way to Love and Liberation

Introduction

The Heart

HAVE YOU KNOWN MOMENTS WHEN YOU were down on your knees, speechless in the presence of wonder, tasting the greatness of the world in profound gratitude, awash in pure bliss and a love so vast it can embrace everything?

These moments revealed what you truly are and that your soul is free beyond measure. Perhaps it was when you were awed by a sunrise, looked at the eyes of a newborn child or felt the heart of a saint and were shaken to your very core by the depth of what you saw that was a reflection of you. During such glimpses you knew that all you wanted is to be one with this wonder, this enormous compassion, this boundless joy and tranquility. Perhaps you were praying for surrender, praying that it would last. And after a while, sure enough, the everyday reality swallowed you again with its worries and stress, its many challenges and the unrelenting search for a higher reality you *could* enjoy, if....

Well, what if, exactly? And how? What is missing, what keeps going wrong, why do you fall out of love and peace into trouble? And how can you live permanently in this great harmony, this vast love you instinctively know must exist?

The purpose of this book is to inspire your heart and mind, for unless we love there is no happiness. It is to support your invincible power to overcome any hardship on the road to enlightenment. You will find within these pages profound inspiration that can enable you to dissolve the causes of fear and suffering through some of the most practical and effective means: stillness, cultivating self-love and devotion, releasing emotions, and clearing the mind. This is the cumulative process of HeartSourcing—to elevate our consciousness by the power and purity of the heart.

> Our heart and the heart of the world are one.

Fear and struggle are characteristics of the life of the ego, but deep in the core of our being—unknown to most—a timeless peace and supreme clarity can be found. It is the only true Source of lasting happiness, and it is always present in the depth of the heart. What I call "Heart" is not the physical organ. I also do not mean the heart chakra, although both of these are representative of the true Heart. The heart I speak of is the absolute core and origin of our being. Before time and space it was what we are. It is the presence of the Absolute in us and in all things. It is beyond time and space and yet we can access it intimately in the core of our chest, the *hridayam*, the cave of the Heart.

Here the expression of the great wisdom of India, *tat tvam asi*, "You Are That," becomes a tangible, real experience. It is from here that all true contentment, joy and freedom arise. It is always pure and untouched by all obstructions and problems. It is unshakable, the seat of the ever-pure soul, the *Antaryami*, the divine essence of what we are, the true Self. It is the inner guru who can guide us with unfailing wisdom and profound compassion. It is the manifestation of Supreme Consciousness – the God of our understanding – in us. And our heart and the heart of the world are one.

This book can guide you to that heart and the absolute freedom it brings. It has been said that the journey from the ego-dominated mind (which we locate in the brain) to the heart is the longest journey in existence. This may have been so in the past, but it is no longer true today. We live in a different time. The gates of heaven are the gates of the heart, and they open to those who are willing to knock, and knock with some persistence. Freedom is a permanent state beyond all conflict and duality. It is the glorious destiny of every soul.

There are three things we must have for this journey. The first is a clear view of the goal. Since everyone has had a different taste of that ultimate goal, we call it by many names. We call it enlightenment, freedom, pure love, Self-realization and many more things. What's important is this: that our goal is permanent and outside of time. Everything that is ruled by time, everything external, will disappear. If we place our hope there, we will fail. But our essence, our true being, is timeless. It is already and always what we are - and that is what we seek. If we can relax enough, we can taste it, and we have tasted it already many times. It may have come as a grand experience or as a very simple one, hardly noticeable because it feels so natural. It is natural to be happy, to be at peace and at home in the heart.

> Freedom is to recognize who or what we really are.

This goal becomes most tangibly real for us when we have the grace to know someone in whom it is fully alive. What is it like when someone lives in continuous peace? That is why I am sharing with you my experience with my guru, which was an encounter with absolute love, a love not known in the world where I came from. It completely transformed my view of who I am as a human being; it showed me beyond any doubt that love is the foundation of being.

The second ingredient we need for a successful journey home is the knowledge of *what we can do* to find freedom. It comes through the practice of skills, given to us by those who went before us, the methods to peel away the delusions and the suffering that keep us imprisoned. I will share with you precise instructions for some of the most effective practices available today. They can help you in substantial ways to overcome fear and confusion, the roots of all suffering. The self-effort we make to calm the turbulent mind, to find emotional harmony and to open the heart is important. It enables us to receive grace, and it is the grace already inherent in our being that will set us free. Freedom is to recognize who or what we really are.

We are not on this journey alone. In fact the most important ingredient to our success – second only to grace – is the company of others who are traveling that same road. We learn and are encouraged by their experience, by the way we come to know that they have struggled just like us, and what they have done and experienced. For this I offer you my personal story that has led me from much darkness and pain into a close relationship with several enlightened teachers and the abundant love they showered on me.

This love is not for sale. It is free to all, because it does not come from outside, it arises from our very own heart and it can certainly awaken in you. It is what we are searching in everything we do. It brings the blessings of life and guides us to our true being.

Surrender to Peace

At any moment a bullet from down on the street could have snuffed out her life and the one she carried in her womb, but my mother disregarded the danger. The madness was finally coming to an end and she had to act. The end could come as an avalanche of death and destruction—or through a merciful act of surrender. Surrender was now the sweetest word in her mind. Surrender out of madness into a new life, a life of peace. So she shook off the stifling veil of fear and powerlessness that had oppressed her for twelve long years and went into action.

From the attic window of her house, she heard the muffled sounds from the street below. Since the recent bombing attacks, cars could no longer drive on the rubble-strewn streets. Although it held such hidden danger, the relative silence came as a relief to her. For days the nerve-racking wail of sirens and the growl of approaching artillery fire had been constant—the background sounds of her daily struggle for survival. They had numbed her mind and tightened the knot of fear in her belly that competed with the constant presence of hunger. Now it was almost over. The nightmare was about to end and a strange mixture of agitation and euphoria washed though her. She also knew that at this moment her life was hanging by a very thin thread.

The Americans had dropped leaflets from the sky that threatened complete destruction of the city in a matter of hours unless there was unconditional surrender. "The American army stands before Halle," she read. "American artillery is aimed at Halle. American Jabos and heavy bombers are ready to lift off to completely raze Halle to the ground, if need be. The city will be taken by us—the way it is standing now, or, after ruthless annihilation, as a heap of rubble."

Everyone knew these were no idle threats. Just days earlier the great old city of Dresden had been obliterated. Uncounted thousands had burned and suffocated to death in a firestorm the likes of which had never been seen before. My mother knew the deadly seriousness of the moment. The leaflet ended with the ominous words:

SURRENDER OR ANNIHILATION!

The "enemy" who stood before the city brought the liberation she had awaited for so long, but there were still the Nazis to contend with. Yes, the real enemy was within. The remaining SS men who had not been able to flee with their comrades patrolled the city streets and would shoot to kill any of their own people who dared to show signs of surrender. The word *surrender* was not in their vocabulary. They acted in a state of mass madness with collective suicide as their policy. The scattered gunshots she heard from different parts of the city were chilling proof of their presence. But the time had come; it was time to surrender to freedom; it was time to act.

She climbed out on the roof. At mid-April there was a chill in the air and the roof was slippery from the morning dew. Despite the cold, she slipped out of her shoes to get a better grip on the tiles. Carefully keeping herself and her pregnant belly in balance, she climbed over the steep part of the roof toward a flat area. She froze in terror when a tile came loose under her feet and crashed noisily down into the street, but to her great relief no one paid any attention. On the flat part of the roof, she spread the white linens she had gathered up from the beds and fastened them down as best as she could. Then she looked out over the rooftops. She could see white sheets here and there. On a tower in the distance a white flag was waving in the light breeze. As the day progressed, roofs all over the city would turn increasingly white. The people were bone-tired of war.

True happiness is our birthright. We have within us the capacity to end our internal and external wars and live in peace of mind and unconditional love.[1] How can we make that a reality? We want to keep our attention on pleasant things, we want to experience happiness and contentment and we deserve no less. But in reality we cannot ignore that we carry in us traces of ignorance, egoism, attachment, hatred, and fear, and harbor the potential for violence. To be free, we must not hide from these inner afflictions, but face and overcome them. Their most visible manifestations are the great catastrophes we have brought upon ourselves. In our modern era, the foremost among them is the Holocaust. Whether or not you have a personal connection to this historical tragedy, like I do, along with every other human being you carry within your deep unconscious mind your own version of tragedy, large or small. It may manifest in your individual pain, or as the collective memory of the violence we humans have inflicted on ourselves and each other for millennia. I invite you to become free of it. Free of pain on all levels of your being. To become free of the dark subconscious view of ourselves as members of a human race that is capable of committing such violence and such atrocities. The task before us is to transform this stifling self-image into the realization of our enlightened potential.

> True happiness is our birthright.

I was born in 1951 into the first generation in Germany after World War II and the Holocaust, the systematic extermination of six million Jews and other "undesirables" during the rule of the Nazis. In my case it was clear what particular manifestations of terror I had to overcome. Whatever our own hidden pain may be, its dark seed-memories conceal the brilliance and joy of what we actually are. As long as these buried mental impressions are ignored and not fully released, they invariably will manifest as trauma, aggression, or pain. We must end this karmic chain reaction of suffering, in order to live in the peace and joy of the here and now. This—and nothing short of this—can bring us the real happiness we seek and the freedom that is our birthright.

As long as our private terror burdens us, we will inevitably pass on our anxiety and sorrow to others and to future generations. Because of the pain and fear that are buried in our unconscious mind, we have work to do to stop spreading the inevitable burden of shame, insecurity, hatred, and fear by awakening out of our trance of pain.

How do you do that?

The solution lies in the very core of your being, *in your spiritual heart*. Here, life-giving wisdom and unconditional love are present in everyone. Here, in the depths of the heart, resides the reality of unending peace, profound generosity, and absolute safety: the divine Self.

But our natural ability to live in the spiritual heart is obstructed. The daily barrage of stressful thoughts, negative emotions, and hurtful behaviors locks us out of the inner sanctum and creates illness, addiction, conflicts in relationships, and deficiencies of all kinds. Because of these layers of obstructions, we fill our world with suffering. Pain from the past and fear of the future, as well as ignorance of the enlightened Self, keep us imprisoned within our minds, but our yearning for freedom and peace always beckons.

My deep anguish, confusion, and shame called me to a life-long journey seeking spiritual liberation—the quest for the end of suffering. I could never have imagined what awaited me. While I slowly found the means to free mind and heart, grace came pouring into my life, showered on me by an old man in India, my guru, who burst the doors of my heart wide open. When such profound love is awakened by a great *mahasiddha*, a perfected being of unlimited compassion, our inaccurate perception of who we are is destroyed at the root.

> Through HeartSourcing you have only your suffering to lose and complete love to gain.

Courage and an unwavering commitment to Self-realization begin to replace confusion and fear, and allow us to triumph over anything standing in the way of attaining complete freedom. Toward the end of my time in India, in my early 20's, I contracted an untreatable cancer. When I regained my health in a miraculous manner, I committed my life to sharing with you the gift of this immense love, and how we can remove what stands in the way of it.

HeartSourcing and the Skills for Awakening—among them Stillness, Devotion, Open Attention, and Self-inquiry—have an exceptional ability to set us free. They work seamlessly together, complementing each other. All essential aspects are covered in the intertwining paths of the heart and the mind. This practice can be seamlessly combined with yoga, spiritually-based therapy, exercise, ritual, study, healthy diet, conscious living practices, and so on. It does not conflict with any belief system or religious tradition. By practicing HeartSourcing, you empower everything else you do. Each one of these remarkable skills is in itself a complete path to liberation. Some people focus only on one skill, while others employ different combinations at different times. Go towards the skill that attracts you the most and see if you can build it into a genuine and steady practice.

Awakening into enlightenment is not a matter of collecting as many abilities or as much knowledge as possible. An attitude of acquisition stands in the way. Freedom is found by shedding obstructions and judgments, by becoming increasingly simpler. This is true sophistication. When we are internally free, we live in the unlimited clarity and love hidden in us. It comes through the pure intention of the heart, through the effort to engage in spiritual practice, and the loving support of our spiritual friends. The light in the heart melts away all obstructions to the bliss of the Self.

The goal of all yearning is the peace that passes all understanding, true happiness, divine bliss, unconditional love. It's what Jesus called the Kingdom of God. It's the Buddha mind. In that state, everything is known to be grace. My hope is that sharing the story of waking up from my personal Holocaust can imbue you with a sense of confidence in your own journey. The aspiration toward enlightenment will profoundly enhance your life and mold you into a vessel of grace. Through HeartSourcing you have only your suffering to lose and complete love to gain.

If you want to go deeper into this process, you can find additional information, free training, inspiration, and personal support and mentoring at **ramgiri.com**. This website is for your freedom.

WAKING UP

1

Playing in Bomb Craters

A S A CHILD, MY PLAYGROUNDS WERE bomb craters. They were everywhere, visibly in the landscape and concealed deep in the mind of the people. Germany, this gifted and capable nation, had lived through a catastrophic suicide mission. The defeat of the Germans in the Great War had reduced them to stunned victims of their own folly. After my mother's first pregnancy had ended in a stillbirth, I came along a bit later. Even then signs of the collective trauma were still everywhere: men with missing limbs, women with vacuous stares, children with fear etched in their faces—and they were the lucky ones; they had survived. Sometimes, when I needed to hide from the harsh world around me, I would climb down into one of these gaping scars in the earth where I could hide and feel safe for a little while. It was very quiet in those bomb craters. I learned to relax in that stillness. And they taught me something else: whenever you find yourself deep down in a hole, the only way out is to go up.

The adults around me seemed grateful that they had no time for reflection. Disoriented and in shock, they were fighting for their survival. The bombed, burned-out, and rubble-strewn cities were being rebuilt, but as the visible scars of the war disappeared one by one, the invisible wounds continued to bleed and to fester. It was a hidden but relentless hemorrhaging of the soul, an utter exhaustion of spirit. The inner landscape of the people was a minefield of craters filled with fear, anger, and powerlessness. The icy grip of shame choked everyone. It would take much more than bricks and mortar to repair the damage from this internal war.

Paradoxically, as these things go, it was an amazing gift to be born into such a difficult circumstance, but it took me a long time to appreciate that. A world of pain was all I knew. To my child's mind, this was simply the way the world was; it seemed completely normal for everyone to be tormented all the time. Most were cold, angry, and distant. Others seemed to be dangerous. I never knew what would explode next. I learned to be on my guard, to withdraw, to protect myself. Of course, it didn't work. The harshness depressed me. It invaded me. I became increasingly fearful and miserable.

Like a fish in water, I lived in a nameless and formless ocean of dread. I did not know that there was an alternative. Only rarely did I have fleeting glimpses of a fearless state, but they would never last, like a fish jumping into the air only to fall immediately back again into the water. Unable to make sense of an existence so filled with pain, I naturally came to the conclusion that I was to blame, that there had to be something seriously wrong with me. I had no idea how to be happy.

Through dangers and famine and fear, the Germans focused on trying to survive the war as best they could. For 12 years they had breathed the heady fumes of being the "master race" at the cost of unyielding brutality and oppression. They had indeed become masters—masters of self-deception. They had ignored the concentration camps and burning synagogues that heralded what Hitler had called his empire, the "1000-year Reich." Now their bodies were exhausted, their minds at the breaking point, and their hearts constricted. But even after the bombs stopped falling, there was still no relief. When they were down on their knees, at their weakest, with their illusory superiority destroyed and discredited, it was then that the full horror of the Holocaust was revealed to them.

So *that* was what had happened to their friends and their neighbors! *We—the German people—had perpetrated such unbelievable carnage!* This was far more than most people could handle. It was much easier to react with resignation, repression, and escape, to plead amnesia and bury your conscience.[1] The nameless, invisible dread that filled the land was the belief that *since it happened to them, it can at any time also happen to me.*

The mind could not process cruelty on this scale and so it had to shut down, and when the mind shuts down, the heart shuts down as well to protect against the unbearable pain. They had to escape from their nightmarish thoughts, from the ghastly images that secretly terrorized them. They had to repress the piercing accusations in the hollow eyes of the prisoners and the suffocating stench of millions of burning corpses that continued to choke the collective mind.

How could it be that we, people of such exceptional character, precision of mind, and immense inner depth had fallen into such hubris, delusion, and murderous madness? How could we have allowed such carnage to happen in our name?

There was no answer.

Both my parents were burdened and traumatized. My mother came from an upper-middle-class family and had many Jewish friends before the war. Germans and Jews had lived in an integrated society, and my mother's interest in the arts and her intellectual pursuits brought her close to many Jewish artists and writers. Then she had to stand by powerlessly as they disappeared one by one. Some emigrated early on; others vanished in the dark of night, having been "relocated" somewhere toward the east.

Later it was said, and often affirmed, that nobody knew exactly what had happened to those who had disappeared, only that it wasn't good. The truth, of course, was that the vast majority of decent citizens could have known much more, and most likely did know much

WITH DAD IN THE FORESTS OF BAVARIA

more than they later admitted to themselves and each other. The signs of discrimination, suppression, brutality, and destruction were everywhere. But they did not want to know about things they felt powerless to change, and so they remained silent and denied what they knew. Then, as now, state-sponsored propaganda, spin, misinformation, and fear-mongering are designed to dampen social and moral awareness. But we can hurt people not only through our action but also our inaction. The most widespread poison is human indifference. It cripples the heart and the mind, and it cripples human society.

My father was a kind man, a Black Forest farmer's son with a big heart. Conscripted into the army, his life was at risk many times during the war and he nearly died of starvation and illness in a POW camp in France. Often he spoke of the slow death of his best friend on the cot next to him, only a day before the arrival of a group of American Quakers, who snatched my father from the jaws of death. I'll never forget his gratitude to them for saving his life when it hung by such a thin thread. His faith in humanity was restored when they brought such goodness and caring into the dark hell of his suffering. He was also profoundly grateful that in all the years he served in the German army, he never had to kill anyone. He was a warm man, a pacifist at heart, and a mystic. Yet his stories of the war led me to believe that despite his pure heart and good intentions, he had endured almost unbearable pain. It made me even more insecure and increased the general fear and mistrust I felt for the world.

My parents had been horrified at what was going on around them, and paralyzed by their inability to change anything. Those not deluded by the collective madness around them were always in danger. No one survived an attempt at open dissent. The Nazis were extremely effective in brutally suppressing any and all opposition. Real danger was everywhere.

One of my father's most painful memories stemmed from his offer to help an old woman who was struggling with a heavy bag. The woman wordlessly shook her head no and pointed to the Jewish star on her coat. They both knew that he, a young soldier, could get into serious trouble simply for helping her carry her bag, so he handed it back to her and left. The image of this woman and his self-betrayal haunted him for the rest of his life. Another impression he couldn't shake came from something he witnessed at the outskirts of the Warsaw ghetto. Whatever he saw there before an SS man made him move on—and he never spoke of it in detail—disturbed him profoundly for the rest of his life.

My young heart was often in darkness and pain. Why was I so impacted by events that happened years before I was born? Instinctively I was looking for love in my environment and found very little. I felt completely out of place, as though I had been dropped here by mistake, in this strange and hostile world. Later I met many deeply spiritual people who had a similar experience during their childhood, although they were born into different countries and circumstances. It seems we share a deeper need for love which is not fulfilled. Like an alien who somehow had forgotten to grow skin, it seemed that every angry and hostile emotion of others went directly through me. I felt lost and was seeking the cause of my pain.

The terrors and the wars of the past are over in fact, but not in the mind. The endless list of human brutalities is our common inheritance, our shadow. They live on for generations in the collective mind, in our social and personal myths, even in our genes, and continue to sow fear and shame into our minds. This doesn't have to concern you greatly, unless you have an aspiration to become free of all fear and all suffering, unless you want to know a love that is all encompassing and universal. Then you have to shed light into that darkness and become light.

Whether we're aware of it or not, in the deeper layers of our being we have a profound sense of compassion and identification with all suffering beings. This compassion is pure love; it is the noblest of human traits, but instinctual identification with other's pain is a problem. Suffering with another is not true compassion. It does not help anyone; it simply spreads pain. To be effective, compassion has to be informed by wisdom. This wisdom has to mature the heart and it is gained by being exposed to suffering and by transcending it.

We feel terrified when we see what we humans are capable of. Our ability to harm others is surpassed only by the unconscious ways we hurt ourselves. This is inescapable when we do harm, because by harming others we first of all hurt ourselves. Then habits of injuring and of self-injury become deeply ingrained in us. And so, through my unconscious identification with the shadow side of humanity, I filled myself with fear and shame. I became a master of causing my-self pain about the pain in the world. None of this makes sense, but unconsciousness doesn't make sense; it is the sign how far we have lost touch with our true Self.

The human inheritance of violence weighed heavily on me. Why? I was not alive during the war, and experienced it only second hand, through the people around me. Certainly I cannot compare my situation to the suffering of those who personally went through war or persecution. And yet there was a direct link in my mind to the past, like a sharp knife, which I had to remove if I wanted to know real peace. I had to reconcile myself with the existence of evil. How is it possible to live in peace in a world filled with violence? For that I had to come to grips with the existence of evil and overcome its root in me.

We come into this world with soul lessons to learn. From former lives we bring with us *samskaras*, impressions from past experiences, karmic patterns, concealed deep in the unconscious mind. These deep unconscious tendencies manifest more superficially as subconscious habits (*vasanas*), experiential patterns or complexes, of which we can become aware. These old tendencies direct our thinking, and through our thoughts, desires and reactions we create our personal experience of the world. That is why children of the same parents often develop very differently: their reactions to what happens in the family are different. Clearly I had samskaras that urged me to find peace and freedom from a young age. Samskaras are never an unalterable fate. Understand them as a lesson plan: by causing you to react to your world in specific ways they give you the potential to encounter and overcome negative tendencies and to strengthen positive ones. Finding freedom from these deep-seated internal tendencies through regular spiritual practice gives us peace. Blaming our parents, our past, or our environment for our troubles is not at all effective. At best it can give us a momentary release of tension without truly addressing the unconscious patterns we carry in us. If we take responsibility for our own reactions, it takes us out of the victim position.

Meanwhile my ego did what egos do: it milked my story for drama. I got enormous mileage out of my sense of injustice and personal tragedy. Wasn't I interesting in all my suffering? Wouldn't it move someone, perhaps even God, to help me? I did this for years, until I realized that anger and self-pity only brought more pain. The truth is that the darkness of those years was a powerful gift: it created in me an intense desire for light, for love, for freedom from suffering. I would not want to change anything about my past. I am grateful. There are blessings in everything, blessings far more important than the pain we sometimes experience.

Our struggle to come to grips with the existence of evil and suffering and to find our freedom from them cannot be solved by the thinking mind. The archetypal initiation into the mystery of life is a descent into darkness and apparent annihilation, into hell, always followed by an ascent into the light of a new wholeness. It is through repeated experiences of death and rebirth that we elevate our consciousness into ever-expanding dimensions of being. But just a few short years after the war, the darkness was still all too palpable and intense.

The ascent of a new consciousness is inevitable, but it takes time for an individual and it takes time for a nation. The war was followed by a long dark night of the soul in which hope was scarce, the shadows long and ominous, and the silences haunted by the voiceless screams of the dead. Although most people had played no direct part in the atrocities, they felt implicated simply by being German. Unconsciously, they couldn't help but identify with both the victims and the perpetrators, and so the Holocaust raged on inside them. Their very identity was their shame. Being German meant that somewhere deep inside there was a monster, a heartless killing machine, unfeeling, depraved, insane—as though they had done the killing themselves. What horrifying inhumanity lurked deep inside them that could commit such an abomination?[2]

No answers came because it was too fearful to ask the questions. Below the stifling denial, there was the secret fear that it was true, that they were warmongers, torturers, inventors and perpetrators of a demonic culture of evil. The sub-human characteristics they had projected onto the Jews and so many others now were revealed to be their very own. They managed to keep their shame at bay through numbness, unceasing work, and the pretense that everything was okay. Underneath the superficial distractions of everyday life, there was a deadness and icy silence where love and joy had once been.

There were three types of people around me. Some, like my parents, desperately tried to free themselves from their shame, but by and large lacked the skills and guidance to do so effectively. Then there was the majority who simply couldn't deal with the past, and so they repressed their pain by escaping into ceaseless activity, distracting or numbing themselves between outbursts of anger and fear. It was a grand time for materialism: the whole country had to be rebuilt—a perfect way to avoid the chaos inside. And finally there were those who clung to their Nazi views, perpetually living in yesterday in their denial and anger, dinosaurs waiting to die out. The vast majority of the people knew only too well what an absolute disaster the Nazis had been, and so these diehards could not voice their views and opinions in public; they remained a hidden toxic presence in the body of the nation.

My interactions with people outside the family were usually painful and scary. By comparison, my parents were relatively sane and good-hearted, but they were penniless refugees and their past silence gave them a deep sense of guilt, of having betrayed their own values. My mother had been so malnourished for years that she barely managed to carry me near term. Again and again, she told me how hunger had driven her out of the city to scavenge for food, eating nettles and weeds, digging through fields after the harvest to uncover a few leftover potatoes. These stories sent a chill through my young heart, especially when I saw the naked fear still in her eyes.

> The world is revealed to us as the dance of the divine in all things.

Before I was born my parents had retreated to a one-room wooden shack in the country where they tried to weave back together the frayed threads of their lives. They had a deep love for each other, cared greatly for me, and dedicated themselves to creating the warmth and security in our family that they so missed in their world. But I, their only child, didn't make it easy. From the start I was sick. I couldn't breathe. I fought for my survival for years, while at the same time not wanting to live in this uncaring world. In and out of hospitals, I was separated from my mother for long periods of time. I grew angry at her for abandoning me to the sterile sheets and white coats, and closed myself off from the love and nurturing she could provide. I only knew that I felt frail and powerless and that life was unsafe.

Along with my mother's milk I had swallowed the women's chilling tales of endless nights spent in bomb shelters and the men's frozen silence. In my mind I heard the wail of sirens, the shots fired point blank, the screech of airplanes, the jaw-clenching calm, and then the exploding bombs, the screams, and the earth-shaking growl of heavy artillery just a few miles away. I could feel the heat and smell the fires and the cold sweat of fear. It took many decades before I could enjoy fireworks for the first time. Neurotic, fearful, and depressed, I was isolated and had few friends—the perpetual outcast, the butt of other kids' malice. I felt like a born loser.

Imagination is powerful. If it's negative, it can weave a web of illusions that holds us prisoner like no physical jail ever can, and this imprisonment can continue life after life. But while our judgments and stressful beliefs can be a deep and terrible hell, they can be dispelled in an instant by the ray of truth. When the mind clears, we awaken to the actual reality, to 'what is,' the world in pristine purity. Without judgments, it turns out we can love the world as it is and ourselves and each other as we are. And when our perception deepens and we look with the eye of wisdom and understand with the heart, the world is revealed to us as nothing less than the dance of the divine in all things.

> It is merely the clouds of stressful thoughts and emotions that confuse the mind and burden the heart. Suddenly, a ray of pure sunshine breaks through and the darkness is gone.

And no matter how lost we are, there is always grace. For me it came in the beauty of nature, in the verdant forests and hills of Bavaria, where I found deep consolation. Nature always embraced me when no one else seemed to care. She was the Great Mother to whom I could give myself freely. Her lush beauty and stillness were my saving grace. But when I was six, we moved into the city and these moments of grace became less and less frequent.

Like the tension of the bow needed to shoot an arrow, the difficulties in my youth caused me to set out on the great adventure of a spiritual life. I saw no other solution to my misery than to aim for real and lasting peace, no matter what. It is said in the Bible that "the sins of their fathers" will follow the children for seven generations. I didn't have that much time! Being part of the first generation after the *shoah*, the Hebrew word for "calamity" or "destruction," I had to find freedom now! I lived in an ocean of pain and could have drowned in it but for my desire for liberation. And because my yearning was urgent and genuine, eventually it cracked open the deep well of my heart. What grace! My pain taught me that I had nothing to lose but the pain itself, and so I became willing to gamble everything for love.

LANDSCAPE IN UPPER BAVARIA

I am not alone in this quest to transcend inherited pain. The new generations in Germany have done tremendous work to overcome the poison of fascism. With much honesty, they are discussing the past and have created a new nation that is immensely better than what had come before. This is a great source of joy for me. In a recent international poll that explored how people world-wide see other countries, Germany was voted the most esteemed among nations. Imagine that! And yet many are still burdened by the unconscious fear of that inner imagined monster that better not manifest again. This ancient shame can be resolved through the infinitely greater love that waits in the innermost cave of the Heart in all of us. It is the timeless quest for a true end to suffering, for enlightenment, liberation, the peace that passes all understanding, *Brahman*, Self-realization. I use these words interchangeably. Enlightenment alone is true happiness; everything else is a sham.

And so a powerful yearning for true freedom arose in me. It seemed both so very far away and so very close. In some ways it seemed impossible that I, with my fear-filled neurotic life, could ever gain such release. Yet, at the same time, I knew that it was completely available. We realize enlightenment not by searching for something we must find, but by awakening to our true essence, by realizing *what we already are*, although it has been hidden from us.

We go through cycles. At times we are stuck in a sea of unhappiness that feels as if it will continue forever. Then our sorrow suddenly lifts and our happiness seems so natural that we believe we couldn't ever be sad again. Then pain comes back. Gradually, the cycles become more transparent. We become less attached to the drama of our lives and begin to see that what separates us from our true Self is not substantial. It is merely the clouds of stressful thoughts and emotions that confuse the mind and burden the heart. Suddenly, a ray of pure sunshine breaks through and the darkness is gone. Perhaps it lasts for only a moment, but that moment shows us what we are. It points the way to the Self. It shows us the goal of the journey, the summit of human existence, a state of pure awareness and love.

2

Waking Up In Heaven One Day

B Y THE TIME I WAS A teenager, I was living at the bottom of my personal hell and couldn't find a way out. It seemed there was nothing to look forward to but more of the same anxiety, depression, confusion, and shame. At times I thought about ending my life, but somehow I sensed that would just make matters worse. There seemed to be no escape.

When I was 18, two friends and I went into the country for a weekend. That Saturday evening we took LSD. During the 60's it was common to expand ones consciousness with the help of drugs. I had used psychedelics[1] on a few occasions, hoping they might show me a way out of my depressed state of mind. This was before the ill-fated "war on drugs" created a drug mafia, criminalized millions of people, and blacked out unbiased information about both the benefits and dangers of these substances. In those days this information was available[2] and I was careful about what I put into my body. After some study, it appeared that psychedelic drugs with their consciousness-expanding effect were relatively safe when taken in a pure form, in the right amount, with the right attitude, and in the right circumstances. I carefully stayed away from all other drugs.

Like explorers in an unknown world, the world of spirit, the three of us sat around the kitchen table in the old farmhouse as the LSD kicked in. The mind's habitual degrading activity stopped and we began to move peacefully from one amazing insight to the next. For many hours we were immersed in the sacredness and depth of our being. With the thinking mind still and our hearts wide open, our consciousness linked one to another in a seamless flow of telepathic communion. We moved in a state of oneness, in the inner reality of profound love, in a fundamental merging at the core of our being. These were hours of deeply peaceful spiritual union. But the most remarkable experience was yet to come.

The following day after breakfast I was back in my everyday state of mind. I walked alone to the top of a hill behind the farmhouse and spread out in the tall, unmowed grass, still moist from the dew. It was one of the most gorgeous summer days of that year, but my mind was burdened again by the usual troubled thoughts and emotions that created my world. Then, without warning, I saw—really saw—what a minute before I had only been looking at. The difference was absolutely breathtaking. From one moment to the next, the world around me suddenly shone in an astounding brilliance. A vast cloudless sky embraced the world, the air was fresh and clean, and larks and other birds were singing songs of joy high above me. Right past my outstretched feet the snow-clad peaks of the Alps sparkled in the sun. A second ago I had seen life in dark shades of gray; now, in an instant, my gloomy world had blossomed into full glorious color . . . and from a deep core inside me, I came alive.

The doors of perception had swung wide open, so wide that I was forever changed. It was my first conscious awakening into spirit. I was able to see past my usual stress-riddled thoughts and emotions into the magnificent inner truth of creation. Around me was the same world I knew, but now it was drenched in light. My perception had become luminous, my mind and heart had found peace. I had awakened in paradise.

The impact of this experience was earth-shaking. My mind was one with the vast sky and just as clear. The sun radiated out of my heart. The birds sang my own jubilant song of thanksgiving. The far-away mountains were as intimate as the bones of my body. The tall grass was teeming with the same life that ran through my veins. Everything, Earth herself, was completely alive and conscious and breathtakingly beautiful. I had felt so separate, weak, and afraid, and now nature embraced me as Her most intimate lover. Her stunning beauty left an indelible mark on my mind and my heart. I was embraced in the arms of the Goddess. I had come home.

> This common everyday world is truly the world of God.[3]

Once I gained my bearings, I realized that this world, this common everyday world we take so much for granted, is truly the world of God[3]. This ultimate consciousness, this complete love we call God is not hiding from us in some remote heaven. Without knowing it, we live in a world of bliss. In this refined state of awareness my perception of colors, textures, and space had become incredibly heightened. My mind was crystal clear, my heart open beyond bursting. I found myself in the first moment of creation and realized that every moment is this new, this complete, when seen with an open mind. I looked around me in awe. I existed in this world and this world existed in me. God, nature, and what I had known as myself—it was all one and the same.

I went deeper still. In this oneness with nature and the presence of God in all things, I realized that the primal force, the most basic reality at the core of Creation, is complete unconditional love—the vibrant ever-present force that keeps the world going. It is not a love that wants and rejects. It is a love that knows no bounds and no limits. It is a state of transcendent abundance and utter surrender. I realized that this is my true potential, the core of what I am. I AM that love, and so are you. *So are you!*

Reality is one seamless whole. The divine Father and Mother, the formless Ground of Being and Creation, are one. The expression of this oneness is divine love. It is *in* everything and it *is* everything; it shines in all light and all darkness. It creates the world moment to moment and it maintains and transforms it. Creation exists for pure joy, for the immaculate beauty it is, and for the love it expresses. Creation is love making love to itself. It is absolute happiness. In this love, all dualities are united and all the apparent conflicts resolved. In this love, we are at peace.

> Creation exists for pure joy, for the immaculate beauty it is, and for the love it expresses. Creation is love making love to itself.

This exalted experience of absolute happiness lasted for a long while on that warm sunny day in Bavaria, and then it began to fade. But its radiant memory is an unshakable truth: I can return to this beauty and completeness again and again until the shadow of the separate "I" merges into this brilliance forever. This bright and pristine ray of sunshine came into my darkness like sacred food for my starving heart, and turned around my seemingly senseless existence.

I had been summoned to the path of the heart. And because life is so generous, I already had received three of the four gifts that are necessary to develop the yogic sentiment of devotion. First, I had learned to *let go of attachments*. Fuelled by my pain, my yearning for freedom was so strong that I was able to step outside the boundaries of the kind of life my parents and society had in mind for me. Then, on that sun-drenched hill, came the second gift—*the great revelation that spirit or God is present in all things everywhere.* Along with that awareness arose a sensation of reverence toward the sacredness of all life. The third gift is a *sense of worship*, an ability for adoration and awe that expands and develops the heart. Once I had received these gifts, I had to practice and deepen them so they would replace my unconscious tendency to hold on to old pain.

What was still to come, the fourth gift, was the most important teaching for the heart—the grace of a relationship with a great soul, who provided an example of how to live in the love and presence of the divine right here in this world. This gift came later as a direct transmission, an intuitive understanding beyond words and beyond thoughts, received from a perfect teacher.

The Mandala of My Sanity

As my friends and I drove back to the city, my old state of mind with its pain and flat lifelessness began to grip me again. Previously, I had assumed that the depressing grayness of my life was simply inevitable, that everyone more or less lived in that state. Caught in that mindset, I couldn't aspire to anything higher. Without knowing it, I had surrendered to hopelessness. But now I knew there was a choice. The brilliance I had just experienced beckoned me. The contrast between the encroaching cold darkness of my old state of mind and the dazzling beauty and love I had felt was almost unbearable.

Now I knew that my old limited way of being, which I had taken for granted just a day earlier, was the worst prison I could imagine, but I did not yet have a secure foothold in the world of the spirit. I felt that if I could not sustain at least some of my new-found awareness, I literally would "crack up" like a shattered mirror. I had a visceral sense that my mind would fracture into a thousand pieces if I could not hold on to this new awareness; it was a present and imminent danger.

I sat in the living room with my friends, silent, unable to communicate what I was experiencing, feeling cut off and stressed out. As if they intuitively understood that I needed to be alone, my friends left, one by one. Then even the cat walked away, as if to make a point. I had to face this abyss completely alone. I was confronted by the possible loss of the profound light and love I had just tasted. Would I again plunge into my usual overwhelming hopelessness? It felt as though my mind could not expand far enough to contain these contradicting realities and threatened to melt down. Then something curious happened: from a deeper part of my being I suddenly knew what to do. I drew a basic diagram of the soul, a mandala—a circle, and within the circle a square and a triangle. It arose from an ancient knowing,

> Whether I lived in heaven or in the bowels of hell was a function of my own consciousness.

and it was just what I needed. Using this mandala as an object of contemplation gave me a new basis for sanity and stability.

This simple shape was a structure of balance and spiritual harmony for my mind. It felt like an anchor, a foundation on which thought and perception could reorient and rebuild themselves. Gazing deeply at this mandala gave my mind a measure of stability, order, and strength. And then I suddenly realized with absolute certainty what I had to do with my life: It was clear beyond doubt that whether I lived in heaven or in the bowels of hell was a function of my own consciousness. I had to learn how to elevate my awareness so I could live permanently in the state of consciousness I had tasted on that hill. Nothing, nothing at all, was more important than that!

Only later did I realize that something was missing in my mandala. Within the circle of spirit and the square of the earth there was the male triangle with its firm base of stability and a sense of calm. What was missing was the downward-facing feminine triangle, the empowering *shakti* or power to live and manifest what I had seen. I had to find the balance of the masculine and feminine elements of my being to participate fully in the divine dance.[4]

The same world can be experienced in completely different ways, depending on our awareness. I had been trapped in a nightmare of unhappiness of my own making. I had thought that what hurt me was outside myself. But after my experience on the hill, I knew that external circumstances were not to blame for my misery. What had all my blaming done for me anyway? Like Don Quixote de la Man-cha[5] I had forever attacked windmills, hopelessly fighting against something that was part of me! How futile to try to escape from my own mind, my own dream of pain. Now nothing attracted me more than the idea of living continuously in the clarity and love I knew was possible. I could wake up! Although I had no idea how to go about doing so, from that day on I devoted myself to awakening.

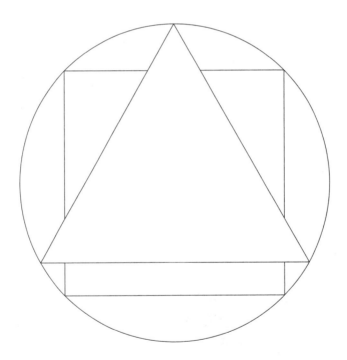

3

Earth School

M Y STORY IS NOT SPECIAL. EVERYONE has a tale to tell of how the pain of the world came to sit in their gut. One way or another we suffer fear, alienation, and confusion and try in countless ways to relieve ourselves of pain. Often we seem to make little progress, but eventually a light breaks through the dark clouds in the mind, the heart opens, and for a moment we taste what life could be like. This is how our higher aspiration calls us. Unfortunately, many cannot heed the call because they don't understand the meaning of their experience. They may be left with a vague sense of yearning for something they cannot define clearly—a greater love, freedom, or peace—but they don't know they can turn this yearning into reality. And so a dissatisfaction remains, a sense of frustration that one has somehow missed the purpose of life. If we don't recognize the call, we cannot awaken until suffering or grace open the door once again.

> A light breaks through the dark clouds in the mind, the heart opens, and for a moment we taste what life could be like.

This is Earth School. Living here on Earth, we have the enormous opportunity to awaken into enlightenment, but at first we don't understand we're in school. We try to escape what we don't like and to fulfill our many desires, but sooner or later we find out that these efforts don't end up making us happy. Then disillusionment can come over us that may feel a lot like depression. Dis-illusionment means we are losing our illusions. It is the dawning of wisdom, of the realization that our purpose here is not necessarily to make as much money or have as many fleeting pleasures as possible, but to experience the immeasurable depth of the heart by disentangling the knots of the mind and dispersing the clouds of stressful emotions.

> Our purpose is to experience the immeasurable depth of the heart by disentangling the knots of the mind.

Life gives us two types of experiences: the love and support we cherish, and the challenges and obstacles that offer precious teachings to us—humility, patience, commitment, strength, knowledge, and how to transcend duality by surrender into our inborn wisdom and love. Both kinds of experiences are equally necessary to take us through the four phases of Earth School. Even times of turmoil and violence are ultimately beneficial because if we are open, they can teach us more than anything that this universe is a place of profound goodness.

Phase One: Seduced by False Freedom

Earth School begins when we fall out of the original Oneness of early childhood and perceive ourselves as separate individuals in a world that is at times hostile or difficult. We become "an ego in a bag of skin," as Alan Watts has said. Our higher potential lies dormant as we struggle with the challenges of survival and the search for pleasure. We have little or no awareness of love as the primal force in our lives; instead we battle with fear and all the difficult emotions that grow out of fear. As our primary tool for survival in this hostile world, we develop the *thinking mind*—and get caught in the endless stream of thoughts, forgetting original wholeness and bliss of the heart.

After my family moved into the city, my childhood paradise in the green rolling hills of Bavaria was gone. As puberty brought its surging hormones and angst, I became lost in materialism and hard dualities— "you versus me" and "every man for himself." I saw clearly how the grown-ups suffered. Work was not joy. For some, it was a chore, an unloved duty, something one had to do to survive. For others, work was an addiction, a hopeless attempt to ward off the unconscious presence of fear by seeking power, wealth, a shallow sense of success and sensual distractions.

I experienced these people mostly as insensitive, angry, or sad. But there was a tiny speck of awareness in me that told me something was wrong, that life wasn't meant to be this way. *Is this all I have to look forward to in life: to become a decent citizen, raise a family, save for retirement, and then die? Am I nothing more than an insignificant cog in the wheel of an uncaring society?* The cultural expectations and norms didn't make sense to me, but if there was an alternative, I couldn't see it.

The ideal of Western culture is the independent and rugged individualist, the self-made billionaire, the Marlboro man—the ego as the pinnacle of evolution. What a travesty! All around me there was proof of Goethe's prophetic words: "None are more hopelessly enslaved than those who falsely believe they are free." Thank God for my neurosis and pain, which would not let me stay trapped in the kind of "ideal" life my culture offered. The sting of my unhappiness forced me to look further and deeper.

I was seeking, yes, but I felt pushed around by unseen powers and random events. At any time, some unexpected disaster could hit and push my life in a completely different direction; I was never safe, never at rest. Wasn't the Holocaust the ultimate proof that we are fundamentally insecure? A whole people ripped out of the middle of life and burnt in the ovens! I could be next. I suffered from existential insecurity. The anxiety choked me. I became closed, resistant, rebellious.

> Universal love is already fully present in each of us.

I could have considered therapy, but it wasn't available to me. Now, after having been a therapist for many years, I realize that may have been a blessing as well. Many therapies don't do much more than redecorate the jail cell in the mind. We invite a therapist, a minister, or a mediocre spiritual teacher to help us out of the dungeon of our stressful thoughts and emotions and immediately we feel better. *Ah, at last I have found someone who understands!* If it is genuine, the heart connection with such a helper is real and precious, but our new friend may turn out to be nothing more than an expert interior decorator. *Why don't we move the couch over there and the table here? How about painting those grey walls a nice sunny yellow? And let's hang some pretty curtains over those ugly bars in the window.* What a relief! We are no longer alone, and now our cell is much prettier and we are much more comfortable.

There is nothing at all wrong with being comfortable. The desire for comfort is built into our human condition. But comfort doesn't serve us when it hides the fact that we are still in jail. Indeed, nothing enslaves us more hopelessly than the false belief we are free. I, however, was not at all comfortable in my jail cell and so I tried to escape many times. A strong enough drug will get you out of jail, at least for a little while. So will an exotic vacation, a new love affair, or getting that red convertible sports car. Inevitably, though, you will find yourself back within the constricting bars of your habitual stressful thoughts and emotions.

The only solution that can lead to true freedom is to *take down the jail.* Dismantle the walls! Dissolve the thoughts and emotions that keep you locked in unhealthy behaviors and fear of a dangerous world. The only true road to the supreme comfort of liberated awareness is a complete paradigm shift.

Phase Two: The First Heart Opening

We enter the middle grades of Earth School when the veil of materialism starts to lift. Perhaps it begins with a heart opening, a sudden moment of peace or joy that triggers a yearning for a more constant experience of unconditional love. This is not an emotional attachment that breeds dependency and fear of loss. It is a diamond-like love with power and clarity, a taste of the universal love that is already fully present in each of us, deep in the core of our hearts. Activating this great love makes life not only worthwhile, but also deeply delightful. This is the path of the heart.

Phase two can also begin with a moment of insight that awakens a desire to clear the mind of confusion and stress. Clarity and inner peace can take us to transcendent heights where all suffering is dispelled. This is the path of the mind. The journeys of heart and mind are not two different paths; both lead to the same goal. They entwine, interact, and sustain each other to form a powerfully integrated spiritual practice that uses the full capacity of our will, knowledge, action, and feeling.

In the mind-dominated technological culture of today, constriction and dryness of the heart is the most common dis-ease. It manifests most strongly in the negative attitudes we have toward ourselves, toward others, and toward life itself. Being cut off from the great love in our hearts makes us incapable of realizing our real potential, and because it is so common, we take our alienation from the heart for granted. Becoming whole means to reconnect with the ever-flowing water of life from the heart and to engage with life fully with a very clear mind.

The first opening of the heart is delightful; it's our honeymoon with the Spirit. Like children playing with exciting new toys, we sample different approaches to spiritual emancipation. Beginning to learn how to nurture ourselves, we window-shop, experiment, and get a sense of what the spiritual landscape has to offer us. It is a time to enjoy and explore. It is not yet the time to go deep, to scrape away what doesn't serve us, to shed light into the shadow. It is a time to learn, not to unlearn. It is a stage of adding, not yet the stage of subtracting.

What we cannot yet see at this stage is that, in so many ways, we are simply busy trying to escape to a more pleasant illusion. By and large we are repeating the same patterns of acquisition we learned in the world of materialism: we collect exciting experiences. We decorate our jail cell with the paraphernalia of spirituality. We collect knowledge, books, crystals and pyramids, prayer beads, incense, angel cards, tribes to belong to, a host of teachers and seminars. We are proud when we can twist our bodies into pretzels, adopt wise ways of talking, and construct a super cool spiritual ego. We have fallen into the trap of *spiritual materialism*.

We try to see everything as good by ignoring that which is bad; we become "light workers" by avoiding the dark. We use spirituality to distract us from our reality. Our sense of self-importance grows rather than shrinks—before we know how to save ourselves, we are the ones who will save the world. Even while we seek the truth, we avoid it. After a while, the drive to spiritual acquisition and grandiosity reveals itself as a trap: we can't shop, think, tantra-party, or pretend our way into heaven.

Heaven knows I tried. I began by reading the accounts of the sages, whose stories provided invaluable maps for the journey. I read about

Christian, Sufi, and Jewish mystics, Chinese sages, Indian saints, Native medicine women and men, whole worlds of higher beings, angels, and deities. I devoured the *Tibetan Book of the Dead*, the *I Ching*, and the *Bhagavad Gita*. I learned of *chakras* and *kundalini*, *karma* and reincarnation. I experienced psychic phenomena. I practiced shamanic rituals, hypnosis, and imagery; took long journeys with power animals and spirits into the infinite worlds of the imagination; I plunged into psychology, explored past lives, and studied anything I could find that gave me access into a greater depth of perception. I had been invited to the feast and wouldn't leave until I had eaten my fill.

Examining Religious Beliefs

For most people, entering the quest for liberation necessitates a re-examination of traditional religious beliefs. I, too, had to question the faith of my childhood. On one hand, I had been taught that "God is Love," which I knew to be true beyond doubt. Despite the pain in my world, even before my experience on that hill, somehow deep in my bones I understood that absolute love had to exist. It was what sustained me. But then this intuitive understanding of love, of "original goodness," collided head on with the teachings of "original sin" and "eternal damnation." If God is indeed love, that God would not threaten me with eternal damnation. It just didn't fit. Was God love, or a tyrant, displeased and condemning when His laws were disobeyed? This intolerable conflict threw me into an existential predicament, a crisis of faith. What was I, a mere kid, to do? Could I stand up against the authority of religious teachings that were thousands of years old?

Slowly I came to understand that the same God that made me the way I am also gave me the ability to reason logically, and logic told me that Universal Love and an "eternal hell" could not coexist. Despite the immaculate example of Christ, the image of God presented to me by the church was that of a disembodied remote authoritarian being in heaven above, or 2,000 years ago—but certainly not here, not now. I realized that if I kept these beliefs, they would turn me into a perpetually immature child who had to believe and do as I was told, unable to seek the truth for myself. It seemed to me that this was the motivation behind the creation of fear-based religions.

Clearly, in order to know the God of Love, I had to choose love over fear.

———————————————————

How small is a God who is not the God of All?

———————————————————

The teachings also said that there was only one true religion—ours. That confused me. According to this belief, most of humanity was damned and would end up in eternal hell. This was not compassion and could not be truth; it was a ploy for market share and power, not love. How small is a God who is not the God of All?

To divide the world into believers and non-believers is an archaic belief that should have long gone the way of the dinosaurs. Since so many people around me carried such cruel beliefs, belief itself became suspect to me. Beliefs like this are the outcome of generations believing what they've been told without examination and without introspection—the time-honored tradition of the blind leading the blind.

The people in my church were good people. They meant well. The measure of devotion they had was real, and their faith kept them comfortable to a degree, but they could not transmit to me the deeply thrilling essence of the living spirit of Christ. They were administrators of an old way of thinking, not practicing mystics who derive their knowledge and passion directly from Source. My burning questions bewildered them. They could not feed my hunger to know the God of true love. Later I came to know that true mystics can be found inside and outside all organized religions, but by that time I had already left the fold. To this day I treasure very highly the genuine faith, the richness of devotion, and the great variety of devotional practices in all religions. I believe we can keep what is excellent in religion and let go of what doesn't work for us.

I had indeed a great hunger for "higher states of consciousness," as I called it at the time. Instead of looking for solutions outward in the material world, as science would have me do, or "up above" as religion taught, I was drawn to look inward for insight and inspiration. I experienced different states of awareness through the means that were available to me: by spending time in nature and with like-minded friends, in meditation, through painting and sculpting, the occasional use of hashish and, a few times, LSD. I discovered dazzling dimensions of reality that quickly changed my perceptions of life. During my experience on the hill, "out there," "up above," and "right here" all came together in the brilliance of the Now, which led to the unshakable realization that real freedom exists because *it is what we already are.* To realize our true identity as this freedom, this boundless love, we have to peel away the layers of confusion of what we have come to believe.

Phase Three: Working on the Shadow

Sooner or later we learn that our task is not to recapture the fleeting bliss states of our early awakening, nor to make our lives perfect according to our ego desires or someone else's venerable old rules, but to *enter a new state of being.* Rather than merely redecorating the jail cell of our conditioning, we start in earnest to disassemble the jail. This is done by releasing the emotional constrictions around the heart, by realizing a truth beyond our stressful beliefs, and by surrendering to the depth of the heart. This is the deep inner work of becoming free.

As we outgrow the playground mentality of spiritual wonderland, the formerly hidden shadow elements of the psyche begin to demand our attention. No amount of feel-good spirituality will be able to keep them at bay. It may appear then that we have fallen from grace because darkness threatens to swallow us up. But in truth, it is that the honeymoon phase is simply giving way to a more mature relationship with spirit and with ourselves. Now the darkness we face calls for the light, and that light is in us. What looks at first like failure or regression is actually progress. We are called by our own commitment to become serious in our practice. If we want to realize more than momentary states of rapture, if we want true enlightenment with its enduring freedom and bliss, our effort must not only reach up to the heights, but also down into the morass of darkness and pain.

When I entered this stage of Earth School, I continued my efforts to get high in any way I could, which granted me short excursions out of my usual wallowing in angst and dejection. I enjoyed deep insights, occasional unearthly luminosity, and moments of brilliant love, but invariably I would crash again into my old misery. I couldn't get airborne for long, and so I was finally forced to attend to my problems. I realized that in order to know my divinity, I had to embrace my humanity—definitely the last thing I wanted to do! I wanted to fly away from my problems into a world filled with light. But weighed down by fear, anger, self-rejection, and shame, I could not find my wings. Begrudgingly, I had to admit that if I wanted to be sincere about loving God, I had to learn to love *all* of life.

There were a lot of things I rejected, starting with not wanting to live in this world. I had cultivated rejection into a high art, one of my most delightful personality traits. How could you not love someone like me who wanted nothing more than to be left alone while feeling bitter and complaining about life! Eventually I realized that I had to come to peace with the fact I was here. I had to welcome life with all its beauty, violence, and pain. Only by embracing my very ordinary, messy, smelly humanity could I gain stability in my spiritual Self. In order to grow into the sky, I had to sink roots down into the ground, into the earth.

Embracing what has been rejected and repressed for so long is no easy task. It takes either desperation or courage. I had both, especially despair. Dealing openly with my darkness and terror wasn't fun, but it was far better than living in unconscious slavery to repressed inner pain. Through the grace of my teachers and with the help of the skills I gradually picked up on the way, I experienced in a very concrete way a growing freedom from what had felt like a permanent curse on my life.

Over time this freedom was undeniable. I could feel it in me and over and over I could see it emerging in others. One of my students, Gabrielle, was a spiritual woman in her mid-forties, fresh out of a divorce and struggling with the aftermath of cancer; she took high daily doses of antidepressants and sleeping pills. Her intense insecurity and fear of financial instability, illness, and loneliness manifested as an obsession that *something terrible is going to happen to me.* Her extreme emotions manifested as a great pain and emptiness in her chest. She was deep in the dark night of the soul.

Gabrielle had to get to the root of her problem because nothing she had tried was working. We began to use the skills that will be explored in this book. At first she addressed her emotional pain—that great ache in her chest—and connected it to the nurturing energy of the spiritual heart, which gradually filled the empty space inside her. Then she investigated her most paralyzing thought—*something terrible is going to happen to me*—and found that it was simply not true. When she looked deeply, she realized that whatever she had faced in life—cancer, divorce, financial hardship, depression, and fear—had made her stronger, more resourceful, and caring.

This was more than an intellectual insight. It was a gut-level realization, which changed her view of the past, and showed her that she could only grow from whatever the future held. As that insight took hold, she found relief from her fear and a deep sense of peace arose. Security, she realized, is not about avoiding life, but about standing firmly in it, with your face in the wind. This brought her increasing strength to deal with the demands of the world. She became happy, and this happiness had a firm source in the heart. Since happiness is as good for the body as it is for the mind, her health also improved. Such a journey into darkness and back to the light is a profound spiritual transformation.

> Our problems are the very path to their resolution. They are gifts in disguise.

If you change your mind, you change your world. You won't always get such quick results, but before long the effects will be undeniable: you will be able to make peace with what you previously rejected or feared. What you dread turns out to be the very source of your healing. What life brings is exactly what you need in order to grow the seeds of light that are nourished in your rich inner darkness.

Identifying your Lessons

The lessons of Earth School aren't "head lessons" that can be solved through better thinking. They are "life lessons"—challenges we must master with our entire being, and most of all with the wisdom of the heart. What then are your particular lessons? You can find them by first identifying your most difficult and repetitive challenges. What are your patterns of pain? Do you repeatedly change partners, jobs, doctors, or diets, only to find that the problems persist? Do you struggle with fear, anger, resentment, insecurities, relationship conflicts, jealousy, or stress around money? Are there certain things you have complained about for a long time? Are you in the grip of an addiction or old grief? What are you most ashamed of?

Identify the predominant thoughts, feelings, and behaviors you experience during difficult times. Write down a list of your primary problems. Then identify the *opposite* of each issue. This opposite is what you are destined to learn. For example, early in life I suffered from a deep sense of insecurity, covered up with arrogance. I could flip in a heartbeat from feeling like insignificant rubbish to pretending I was better than everyone else. Of course, the only one I was fooling was me. It was no surprise that my interactions with people didn't go well. Adults seemed harsh and aloof, the neigh-

Awakening is a revelation.

borhood bullies beat me up, and I developed few lasting friendships. I was a recluse, a loner, afraid to be around people. What were the lessons in all that?

I can't tell you how well my insecurity served me! It inspired me to apprentice myself to the remarkable spiritual masters who offered me their hearts and their wisdom, and it made me a very committed student. It moved me to complete a long course of university study. The harshness and arrogance I experienced in people made me aware that these were qualities I had as well. It made me more humble and helped me develop a deep appreciation of kindness. Being a loner forced me to learn, and later share, the fundamental steps of how to genuinely love people. Out of that came wonderful, lifelong friends, and the discovery that the Source of the eternal love I was trying to find was in me, and in everyone else. Over time it led to a deep sense of security that allows me now to share with you the gifts I have received.

- If you are prone to anger and rage, you can learn to find consistent inner peace and genuine kindness.
- If you are your own worst critic, you are meant to develop self-acceptance and self-love.
- If you suffer from shame, you have signed up to realize

your true worth, and to learn that there is nothing ever to be ashamed of.

Come to think of it, all those lessons were mine too. Look for your primary patterns of pain and find their opposite. Suffering always shows us the way to its own resolution.

Our problems are the very path to their resolution. They are gifts in disguise. This understanding makes the cycles of remembering and forgetting, of happiness and pain, more manageable and transparent. We will go through them as long as we have more to learn, and the pain is still real, but we know that the greater purpose behind of suffering is our freedom. And so we will not fight against our darkness as much, but instead shine the light of awareness into the shadow so it can dissolve.

Phase Four: The Exquisite State of Enlightenment

Awakening is a magnificent process. Yes, it takes courage to shed light into the darkness, but the prize is the bliss of eternal life. The lessons of Earth School aren't easy. One day you can have a deeply enlightening experience, the next you may struggle with boredom or survival fears. One day you are captivated by new exciting abilities or spiritual insights, the next it seems you have learned nothing at all. Periods of upheaval are followed by times of apparent stagnation. It can be quite confusing. However, as we love ourselves more and more and shine the light of awareness into our darkness, the source of our suffering diminishes and we increasingly taste freedom.

Some people think that in order to become enlightened you have to be always loving, never angry or sad, completely fearless, and so on. This is a common misconception that can make us feel even more self-critical, self-condemning, or hopeless. If a perfect personality were a precondition to awakening, let's be frank, none of us would stand a chance. Trying to be a spiritual superman does not get anyone enlightened. Awakening is about *seeing through* our delusions and personality foibles, and no longer being at their mercy.

Awakening is a revelation, as though our head comes up from under water, from the limited consciousness where we have lived for so long; and in awestruck wonder we look around in this new dimension of enlightened awareness, this loving new way of Being. And in this moment of awe and rapture we may notice that it feels completely natural and effortless, because we have awakened to our true nature.

And we wonder, "How could I ever have forgotten?"

Bring your mind to one point and wait for grace.
                                                    –Neem Karoli Baba

Ever since we've learned to think, we have been involved in "the drama of me." We've had an ironclad commitment to it. It is deeply conditioned into our mind, our emotions and our behavior, and makes us forever chase unfulfilling desires and escape broken dreams, vacillate between desire, aversion and confusion. And we have believed it to be real, again and again. It has imprisoned us in its nightmare of emotional suffering, dashed hopes and unbalanced behaviors. But we are not this unhappy story we tell; we are the consciousness in which the telling occurs. This insight alone can awaken us! It is the pristine clarity of the observer, the witness mind. It is neutral, discerning, and always present. It is the real "I." It alone knows the reality of true love and it can awaken us from the hypnosis of a world of false mental constructs. And as we stop believing the story of the unhappy me, then this fabricated, suffering self dissolves into the eternal bliss and the absolute fulfillment of our true being.

There are extraordinary people who can maintain the awareness of their freedom from their first awakening on. Eckhart Tolle and Byron Katie are two such remarkable beings. But this is very rare. Instant enlightenment has matured over 10,000 lifetimes. For most of us, the initial awakening is followed by falling asleep again—though not quite as deeply—and then going through a lengthy sequence of remembering and forgetting our awakened state, remembering more and forgetting less each time.

> Enlightenment is the most obvious of all truths.

Gradually, through many cycles of remembering and forgetting, we learn to maintain a clearer, more heart-centered state. We learn to keep our attention in the here and now and to live out of the heart more often. Slowly, our freedom becomes more tangible, more real. And every time we fall into forgetfulness, it is a blessing that allows us to overcome a bit more of our pain, for we cannot awaken from what we cannot yet see. Eventually we tire of our desires and aversions, of the confusion and drama of the unhappy "me." We see through the ego's insistence to maintain itself and we recognize that it has no substantial reality at all. We cease to believe our judgments and become more kind. By accepting the way things are, we learn to follow a deeper truth; by cultivating the power of our hearts, we become agents of change—"becoming the change we seek," as Gandhi said. In short, we learn to live with an open heart here and now.

Freedom arrives like a ray of sunshine that breaks through the clouds and we see the world in a new light. Enlightenment is a state of *Oneness*, of absolute simplicity. Once we awaken to it, it is the most obvious of all truths. It is at the same time extraordinary, sacred, and not special at all. It is the realization of what we are. We are not the body, mind, and emotions we call "I," but pure awareness, timeless, unlimited, profoundly blissful. With that comes a fundamental shift of our point of view. Now we experience the world inside this boundless consciousness that we are. Where we previously identified with a small individual wave, now we realize that we are the cosmic ocean itself. This vastness is known as Brahman, the eternal, unchanging, infinite reality of the Self. This is the end of fear.

The experience of Self-realization is our graduation from Earth School. With no confusion or obstacle left, we realize we are the manifestation of grace, wisdom, and love in this world. After many times of awakening and forgetting again, we have come to know that we are what we have been seeking. We are free.

We have awakened to the Self. We live in Oneness with everything. Our heart radiates joy into the world. We are fully awake to this moment just as it is. This alone is true happiness, unshakable and unending. We are no longer identified with a separate and limited ego housed in a bag of skin. We are the boundless field of awareness in which all creation, including the body, arises and disappears. As it has been said: *You are the endless sea in whom all the worlds like waves naturally rise and fall.*[1] Nothing can harm us. We remain in this world by choice out of compassionate love for all beings. Only a transparent ego remains to act for a while as a teacher in Earth School.

THE FIRST SKILL:
STILLNESS

4

Gold Is Found In The Valleys

W E LIVE IN A GREAT TIME, full of promise and difficulties, when darkness is giving way to new light,
a time of turmoil, when a part of humanity is transcending
the stage of materialism to reach a higher awareness. We are
witnessing the birth of a greater abil-
ity to use our inborn compassion and
wisdom. Our world will not change
overnight. Much of the change will
be difficult, but inevitably a new consciousness is emerging. We can see
this in the appearance of new teachers, teachings, and skills, and it is an
intuitive knowing inside our hearts.
We are creating spiritual community
in countless forms. While we may tend

When we slip back
into fear-based old
mind-sets, it helps to
remember that the
peace we seek is
already fully present in
us; it is our natural state.

to get overwhelmed at times by the troubles and cares of this
world, we can remember the prophetic words of the great sage
Ramana Maharshi: *"Let Him who created this world see to its
maintenance. Meanwhile, find out who you are."* This is the op-

posite of being selfish; it is the most compassionate thing we can do.

Layers of the old fear-dominated consciousness are being shed like the worn-out skin of a snake. For humanity as a whole it will be an immense birthing process with fierce contractions, as the most unpleasant contents of our collective shadow emerge in a last big fury before they dissolve. But if we open to our own transformation, we point the way for many and make it much easier. And when we fall back into the fears and terrors of our ancient conditioning, we do so only to awaken again each time as the phoenix of consciousness rises from its own ashes. This process of forgetting and remembering, of death, rebirth and renewal, can be dramatic, but it is unfailingly guided from a higher source and completely safe.

> If we listen to our heart, we're on our way, even though it would be much easier to stay comfortably asleep.

When we slip back into fear-based old mind-sets, it helps to remember that the peace we seek is already fully present in us; it is our natural state. Knowing this, we can embrace the astounding reality of what is being born—the brilliant consciousness we are, in freedom and love.

So here we are—on the first peak experience of our journey, our first hilltop. We rub our eyes and get used to the altitude. We notice that our mind is clear, our heart open, and our attention in the Here and Now. We can look back to where we came from—the flatlands: hot, vast, and dusty, filled with millions of people who are busy with their all-important pursuits and distractions. We know it well, this two-dimensional materialism and suffering, but when we look forward to what is possible, we can see in the distance the awe-inspiring high mountain summits. It seems as if we can taste that cool, invigorating mountain air, and we yearn to be up there on the top of the world. These majestic mountaintops stand for the state of mind when *we no longer get lost* in thoughts of past or future, when the heart is no longer burdened, but radiates its immortal essence freely into the world. It's no wonder that the gods are said to have their abode in these lofty heights.

Between where we stand and those distant peaks, lies an expanse of valleys and hills, the slowly rising foothills that cover the distance to the great mountains. Something is calling us to travel that distance, to reach those high altitudes, to explore those breathtaking sights. An immense yearning arises, an irresistible desire for the fulfillment those peaks symbolize. If we listen to our heart, we're on our way, even though it would be much easier to stay comfortably asleep. But that nagging inner voice asks, "Won't you always long for a higher realization, a deeper fulfillment?" We have no choice. Our life has changed; we're on the way.

> As long as there is even a trace of fear or confusion, there is a path.

This greatest of all journeys will challenge every part of us, will demand of us to overcome all our negative tendencies, everything that stands in the way of the realization of our inborn perfection. Are we up to that challenge? Are we willing to climb a mountain higher than we have ever dreamt possible?

But something seems to be wrong: isn't the concept of a journey to a goal an obstacle that prevents us from being in the present moment? Liberation is about living in the Now, the ultimate place of refuge. In the Now there is no path. When attention rests in the Now there is no past, no future and no journey through valleys and hills. If we live in the present always, we are free. But we also travel a path in time. So which is it then? Is there a path or no path?

For the masses, enlightenment appears too distant and so they do not attempt to reach it. An aspirant knows that the Self is not a distant goal; it is already and always our natural state, and therefore even the want for enlightenment creates a duality we must transcend. But this aspiration for Self-realization has a higher degree of reality than the desire for the objects of the world. Higher forms of imagination replace lower forms of imagination. The more powerful the aspiration for enlightenment is, the more quickly it overcomes distractions and emotional attachments. Therefore there is a path and there is no path—we walk on the path until the confusion of the one who walks disappears.

> Our quest leads not only to the end of time, the NOW of the mind, but also to the end of space, the HERE of the heart. To be present in both is the gift of all gifts.

A journey to a goal exists during the process of *sadhana*. As long as there is even a trace of fear or confusion, there is a path. It is the path out of the delusion that we are not yet enlightened, or that we are. Too easily the ego tries to escape the purification process and uses the belief that perfection is already attained for its escape. Immature claims of enlightenment are a common trap. As long as any illusion holds sway, as long as there is still remembering and forgetting, valleys and hills, there is a path. There is a saying in yoga literature, "Liberation is the maid-servant of devotion." The mind creates an abyss and the heart playfully jumps over it.

The apparent conflict between these two ways of thinking is simply mind-created. The mind loves to generate conflict where there is none—and we fall for it. By the same token so many fall for strategies for fulfilling the ego's ambitions that are sold to us promising spiritual liberation. From meditations to enhance 'the wonderful you' to the current craze of 'manifesting your desires,' such approaches are deceptive, preposterous and wildly popular. Any such efforts tend to imprison us in more ego while pretending to free us. All truly liberating spiritual practice dissolves the compulsive, veiling nature of mind and brings us closer to the natural state of no effort. To relax completely into our original nature we use the effort of sadhana like

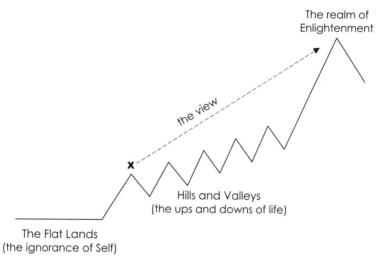

The Path to the Mountains

a thorn that removes another thorn in our foot. Only one of them hurts. When ego-driven thoughts and emotions have become subtle enough, effortful practice effortlessly merges into vast peace.

Our quest leads not only to the end of time, the NOW of the mind, but also to the end of space, the HERE of the heart. To be present in both is the gift of all gifts. It is possible for us to open our heart in the Now so completely that we are in love with all things. It

Once we have the goal of spiritual liberation, our obstacles become the pathway to our freedom.

is possible for us to see the divine presence everywhere, even in darkness and intense pain, our own and that of others. Then—and not before—our journey is done. There is a path to that place.

How do we reach this great goal of enlightenment—of living in the Now and in unconditional love? It is simple and inevitable. Time reasserts itself in the timelessness of the first hilltop and we take the first step.

And down we go into the valley ahead. *Oh no!* We want to stay high; we love it up here in the pristine air of the hills, in the pure Here and Now, in clear view of the goal, not bothered by the inconveniences and problems of life. But to overcome our troubles for good, we must meet them with skill so they clear the way for us to proceed. Many have tried to steer clear of the dark valleys, but we cannot avoid ourselves for very long. Once we have the goal of spiritual liberation, our obstacles become the pathway to our freedom.

> We cannot change the world, but we can change the way we react to the world.

The first purpose of *sadhana*, spiritual practice, is to cultivate the ability to live in the present moment. We experience the Now countless times; gradually these experiences become deeper and more lasting. The second goal, which is not separate from the first, is to love. This is how we build *sadhana shakti*, the power generated by spiritual practice, which culminates when the *soul force* fully realizes its identity with the Absolute Self and no longer falls into confusion. But until we live in this absolute oneness, we are still in training. As long as our heart still closes, there is a path.

On this path it is not life itself, but our *stressful reactions to life* that disrupt the pristine quality of the Now and plunge us into a valley. External things are what we get upset about, but what upsets us are our stressful thoughts and the way we become entangled in negative emotional habits. People and situations do not have the power to make us suffer, no matter how challenging they may be. All suffering arises within us. We cannot change the world, but we can change the way we react to the world. This is the key to freedom.

Crossing the Swamp of Depression

We desperately try to avoid the valleys, but when our time comes, down we go. When I came back to the city of Munich after the light and the love had flooded through me on that Bavarian hill, it was clear to me that I had to become free, but I had no clue how to do it. Beyond any doubt I knew that if I continued to live the way I had in the past, I would rot in the nightmarish world I had known.

Good skills and personal guidance are a lubricant for rebirth.

My desire for freedom was born, but who knew how to do this? I had no teacher, no guidance. Who could show me how to navigate the dark tides of my mind?

I turned to the leaders of my church, but the urgency of my longing bewildered them. They didn't seem to know a God who was as intimate and present as what I had experienced. I was lucky they didn't send me to a psychiatrist. The God I had experienced could be known if—and this was the big question—if I could be present and open enough. But religion offered me beliefs rather than direct experience, hope of future salvation instead of a viable practice. I realized I had to look somewhere else, but I did not know exactly what I was looking for.

Nothing in my life was more urgent than this longing. I became disinterested in almost everything else. A normal life and career seemed like prison to me, and so, to the great dismay of my parents, I dropped out of school and began to travel around Europe. I was a spiritual vagabond seeking only one thing: to discover a way to become free, to find this happiness I knew was waiting for me, somewhere, somehow.

I traveled to the south of France, to Italy, Switzerland, Holland. It was the late Sixties and the consciousness revolution was in full swing. Eastern spirituality had just begun to pour into the West in response to the authentic hunger of souls like my own. Everywhere I came across like-minded people who were living simply, helping each other get by. Intuitively, we recognized each other as brothers and sisters on a journey into the world of the spirit. We were explorers, adventurers into the unknown, on a quest into the mystery. My new friends gave me a crucial sense of support. We formed instant communities that dissolved again as we moved on, leaving memories of shared understanding and love I treasure to this day.

> Every time I felt near the breaking point, I realized that I was stronger than I had thought.

After searching all over Europe to find teachers, I settled down in Amsterdam, where I was able to study meditation, yoga, tai chi, Eastern philosophy, and healthier ways to eat. I adopted a more balanced lifestyle focused on my higher goal. But most of the time the light seemed very much hidden from me and my resolve to find it was tested again and again.

I was still trapped in a cage of internal pain that sat inside my body like a solid block of steel and would not move. I could not distinguish its features and had no idea how to dissolve it. When I attempted to meditate, the internal torment only intensified and my confusion, anxiety, and depression came in continuous waves. I was caught in my "dark night of the soul," but deep inside I knew this process was bringing the obstructing elements in my psyche to my awareness so they could be released. What sustained me was the insight that the fire of purification, sparked by my yearning, by my own decision for freedom, had begun to incinerate everything that separated me from to my goal.

This terrible valley seemed like an endless swamp of fear and despair where my feet got sucked into the muck at every step and I appeared to make no progress at all. Often it felt as though I was being tested beyond endurance. My mind, with its insistent habit of dramatizing my situation, was telling me that it was too much, that I needed relief. I did not know then that I could question these thoughts, and so I was unable to stop their insistent barrage. I simply kept going the best I could and hoped that someday this torture would end.

Somewhere along the line I heard the expression: *The only way out is through.* How true that is, and how necessary it is to develop strong resolve and perseverance, especially when, on the way of giving birth to yourself, you're trying to get through the birth canal without many skills. Good skills and personal guidance are a lubricant for rebirth.

I vividly remember walking along the canals in Amsterdam, looking at the dark waters, longing for the end of my pain, but I knew too well that suicide was not a smart option. I would have to walk this path again in another body, and another, and deal with always the same inner problems, until I found a way out of my darkness into the light. Killing my body would make everything even harder for my consciousness. On the other hand, I felt a vague sense of guidance.

> Over time, everything that is based on fear dissolves. What awakens? Wholeness and love. Once we let go of the old, our inevitable awakening occurs because the most fundamental force in creation is love, and we are destined to awaken in love.

All I could do was to hold on to my aspiration to reach liberation and give myself to this process, this internal churning and burning that seemed to be far more powerful than I was, and trust that it would somehow take me where I was longing to go. Gradually I realized that every day was another step that increased my strength and my ability to persevere through confusion and turmoil.

One day I read, *It's always darkest before the dawn.* That encouraged me to go on when all hope seemed to be lost. Yet the sun was taking its sweet time coming up! The darkness and confusion in my mind pushed me right to the brink many times. And every time I felt near the breaking point, I realized that I was stronger than I had thought.

The Cycle of Transformation

The descent into darkness followed by the emergence into the light is an archetypal initiation into truth, into wholeness. The death of the old leads to rebirth into a new stage of realization. It is as natural as the disappearance of the sun every evening and its reappearance at the dawn of the next day.

One of the oldest written stories of humanity, perhaps 6,000 years old, is the Sumerian tale of the descent of Inanna, the Queen of Heaven/Goddess of Light. One day she begins to descend into the underworld. On the way, she crosses through seven gates, and at each gate another piece of her divine regalia is stripped away—a golden ring, her lapis lazuli necklace, the beads upon her breast, her turban, her garments, her scepter, her crown—until she arrives in the netherworld stripped bare, vulnerable, and bereft of her powers. There she is killed and her lifeless body is hung on a meat hook for three days, until she is revived and once more ascends into the light. With this journey she has achieved union—she has become the Goddess of Light *and* of Darkness, Queen of the Above and Below, of heaven and earth, a Being of Wholeness.

We see the same cycle of transformation in the crucifixion of Jesus and his descent into the grave for three days, followed by his resurrection and rise into the undying divine light. We see this process of death and rebirth everywhere around us: it is the fruit that falls to the ground, rots, and dissolves so new life can sprout from its seed. It is the cloud in the sky that dissolves in rain so the land can bloom. For humans, it is the universal process of initiation into the recognition of the changeless presence of God in us and into the immortal oneness of the soul with God. With each rebirth this awareness becomes a little more alive in us.

When you look back into your life and examine past crises in this light, you can probably detect the same pattern. What dies? The old ways and habits we no longer need. Over time, everything that is based on fear dissolves. What awakens? Wholeness and love. Once we let go of the old, our inevitable awakening occurs because the most fundamental force in creation is love, and we are destined to awaken in love.

Certainly we can obstruct our awakening by resistance and fear. We can complain, anesthetize ourselves as much as possible, fight, attempt to escape—none of which works in the long run. As a Hebrew proverb says: Change takes but an instant. Resistance to change can last a lifetime. What we can do is to enter our darkness consciously, armed with purpose, skill, and support—and always in the awareness that what we fear is ultimately an illusion. Deliberately choosing transformation over despair, we can overcome whatever obstructs the light. Darkness can never annihilate what we really are. When we turn skillfully toward the darker aspects of life, we accomplish three fundamental tasks:

1. We reduce and eventually become free of the compulsive noise, confusion, and negativity of the mind. Lasting clarity and inner peace come when we are still and no longer believe the stressful thoughts that arise.
2. We remove the burdens of emotional conflict, trauma, and stress. Stable emotional balance and harmony come as the unconscious compulsion to seek pain dissolves.
3. We allow the heart to radiate unconditional love, its true nature. Immeasurable love lives in the boundless depth of the heart. From there it can permeate every

aspect of our being and world. This is the manifestation of aliveness and fullness.

Clarity and stillness, fullness and emptiness, balance and harmony, aliveness and peace are qualities of our already enlightened Self.

> *Love says "I am everything." Wisdom says "I am nothing."*
> *Between the two, my life flows.*
>
> —Nisargadatta Maharaj

The Birth of Stillness

The way to love leads through darkness into the light, but usually we do our best to avoid facing the dark and murky contents of our unconscious. We sense danger there and shut down in fear, but we cannot find inner peace as long as we remain locked into escape-and-repress mode. After all, at first sight the prospect of facing our inner demons appears to be as insane as going unprotected into the cave of a tiger. Who in their right mind would face the monsters we imagine there? But the place where our repressed terrors, addictions, hatred, or shame are hiding is not a dark, threatening cave, not a dead-end that could swallow us up. It is a passageway, a birth canal that leads through the darkness into the light. Passing through here we give birth to us. And the monsters we imagine there do not have any teeth; in reality they have no substance at all. They are nothing but our projections. We created our monsters and we can un-create them. Once we examine

> Resistance brings pain. There is no way to stop the inevitable process of labor once the true Self is ready to be born.

them, they will vanish like the threat of the snake disappears instantly as soon as we see the rope.

In those days in Amsterdam, I faced this essential choice: I could reject the effort my awakening demanded and numb myself back into oblivion, or open to this process of giving birth to myself and make the effort to move inch by inch through the birth canal. Then I realized that I had already made my choice as I came down from that hill in Bavaria: I had set the wheels in motion and they were carrying me inescapably forward. Realizing this brought a small measure of stillness and joy. My awakening was unfolding despite the uncounted attempts of my ego to sabotage it and escape back into sleep.

Resistance brings pain. There is no way to stop the inevitable process of labor once the true Self is ready to be born. One way or the other I was going to get through whatever valleys I had to traverse. Here and there I tasted moments of peace that gave me the determination to continue my practice of meditation. And as that stillness slowly grew within me, the capacity to understand myself grew as well. Gradually I discovered the gold in the valleys.

5

Meditation

Under the guidance of my first teacher, Maarten, I tried to calm my unruly, turbulent mind. I signed up for a meditation retreat where I was going to practice all day long for two weeks. Finally I had some proper instructions. I crossed my legs and immediately ran into big trouble! All my inner "demons" seemed to rise up at once. They didn't like this interference with their dominance and put up a hell of a fight. They tried every trick in the book to have me give up this ridiculous practice of sitting still and watching my thoughts and my breath. They knew that the practice of meditation would eventually lead to their demise. Negative thoughts and emotions had ruled me for many years and they did what all old habits do—they tried to maintain control. As I sat still to become aware of the movement of mind, they became fiercer than ever.

I had been instructed to watch what was going on and not to fight the inner turmoil, which would simply empower the negative energies. That was easier said than done. Emotional upheaval arose in relentless waves, causing great anguish and strong body pains. There was no physical cause of this pain; it would start a minute into meditation and stop as soon as I would get up; it was the raw expression of expelling confusion, resistance, turmoil, and fear.

It is very helpful to have a capable guide when descending into the deeper layers of mind. Books can be helpful, but personal guidance is priceless. After searching all over Europe, I now had found someone who knew how to lead me into meditation. And on a deeper level—of which I was not yet aware—I also had the guidance of one of the greatest masters of our time.

My first two-week retreat was pure torture. But was it really so much worse than my daily life? No, as I faced the turmoil it was just more concentrated and obvious. I had no choice but to sit through it. I had been summoned to this work of purification and I had to answer the call. At the end of the two weeks I had found some measure of relief, which showed me I was on the right path. True peace was still quite a way off, but sitting still was a great victory won against great resistance.

I was in the beginning stages of the journey. Tibetan teachings[1] describe the type of meditation I was doing "like a waterfall pouring down a cliff." One thought followed another endlessly and for a while my state of mind seemed to get more turbulent than before. But meditation was the right medicine; it tastes bitter at first and becomes more and more sweet over time. This first stage is followed by four others that are increasingly peaceful. In the second stage, meditation becomes like a river rushing through mountain gorges as the mind alternates between periods of calm and great turbulence. Then it becomes like a wide river flowing easily. Circumstances still disturb the mind, but otherwise it moves peacefully. In the fourth stage, meditation becomes like a lake with slight ripples along its surface while the mind remains calm and present in its depth. And finally meditation becomes like a vast ocean of unshakable and ef-fortless stillness and peace.

Step by step, the practice of meditation gave me access to the still-ness within, where my pain and confusion were less dominant, where I could begin to drink from a deep source of peace. And while the battle was far from over, I kept surrendering to the process. When-ever I got a reprieve from the inner onslaught, whenever I made it up onto another small hilltop from where I could see my progress, the new view of the goal was so thrilling, so promising, so irresistible, that I asked for more of my "stuff" to come up so I could get free.

An unknown source of strength, a wonderful grace kept me glued to that pillow every day. My mind screamed at me to do something else—anything else—rather than sit still and observe this internal battle. But instinctively I knew that freedom lay on the other side of my turmoil and that liberation was indeed possible. I knew that passing through the valley was the only way I could get to the next peak and eventually to the great mountains of unending joy.

For more detailed meditation instructions, please see Appendix I

6

The Ego

THERE ARE TWO FORCES IN US that are in conflict. One is our yearning for truth, completion and peace, our devotion to God, our motivation to achieve enlightenment for the benefit of all beings. This inner-directed movement is based on love.

The other force comes from the way we are attached to the duality of craving and aversion. We are caught in the drive not only to satisfy our needs, but to want incessantly more, and on the other hand to want to get rid of everything we hate and reject. Our attachment to these twin forces of craving and aversion creates the fundamentally conflicted nature of the ego and keeps us in ignorance of the blissful, always whole, divine Self. As long as we want something we don't have, or reject what the moment brings, we are unable to keep our attention in the now. This attachment to wanting and rejecting restricts us to a life where fear is predominant.

> Everything we experience as stressful is so, because it is not true to who we are.

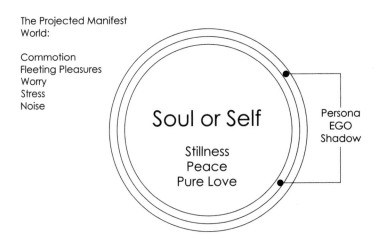

The Projected Manifest World:

Commotion
Fleeting Pleasures
Worry
Stress
Noise

Soul or Self

Stillness
Peace
Pure Love

Persona
EGO
Shadow

THE HUMAN STRUCTURE AND STILLNESS

In its unrefined state, the ego lives primarily in thoughts, beliefs and emotions that are based on judgments and are out of harmony with the truth of our Being. We can identify these movements of mind simply: they are stressful. Who we are, the Self, is peace, truth, and unconditional love. Everything we experience as stressful is so, because it is not true to who we are.

We cannot perceive our true identity as long as our consciousness is ruled by the ego. The ego makes a great servant but a lousy master. As long as it rules, it does *not at all* have our best interest in mind. It simply wants to maintain its mistaken identity—what we *think* we are. Ironically there is nothing special or distinctive about who we think we are. We have this ego in common with everyone; it is all conditioned and entirely unoriginal, especially the thought that we are so unique. To free ourselves of ego conditioning and the suffering it brings is the most important accomplishment. Everything else pales next to it. To be who we actually are, means to be one with all things.

We discover the true Self in the wonderful stillness that is present beneath the surface layers of the psyche "like a precious jewel buried under a poor man's house." But the afflictions of the immature ego pull our attention outward and separate us from the great peace within. We can picture the basic structure of our being in this very simplified way:

The ego's outermost layer is the *persona*, a word that comes from the Greek term meaning "mask." It is the way we present ourselves to the world, our "official" face, our façade or public image. Most people live almost exclusively in this outermost layer of

> Dealing with the shadow is the key to our liberation. It opens us to freedom and joy

the personality and mistake the mask they wear and the roles they play for who they are. A good persona is necessary and useful in many ways, especially when it is transparent to the Self, but believing we are the masks we wear is stifling self-deceit. We are the majestic Self, not the thin façade of the ego.

The persona is connected with the subconscious layer of the *shadow*, which is filled with mental noise and emotional turmoil. Here live our repressed experiences, unresolved painful memories of the past, and fear of the future. Terror and anxiety, aversion and anger, hatred and aggression, desire, greed, attachment, pride, arrogance, and prejudice all have their roots here. Who isn't aware of some of their unresolved emotional issues, our trigger points? They are clear enough to see when someone or something "pushes our buttons." But other parts of the shadow remain completely buried and unconscious until we are ready to deal with them. As long as we have not freed the contents of our shadow, we have no choice but to live with the toxic effects our hidden inner conflicts have on our lives.

As we've discussed before, most people are determined to keep the shadow buried, because it can appear very threatening. But we need not fear its contents. We need to respect them and treat them with care, yes, but they are not enemies we must battle, no matter how scary or difficult they appear to be. In the shadow we find the hurt and shunned parts of us that yearn to be set free. *Dealing with the shadow is the key to our liberation. It opens us to freedom and joy.* But as long as we shy away and try to avoid it, we remain caught. What we resist will persist. We pay a tremendous price for that continued repression: the continuation of our suffering.

When the internal pain rises to the surface, it is our opportunity to become free. We have a choice: we can reject it, repress it again, and continue to live with its toxic effects inside us. Or we can open to it so the light of consciousness can enter the darkness within and dissolve it. This is extremely important work, but the ego stands in the way. It clings to the story of who it has been.

> *This existence of ours is as transient as autumn clouds.*
> *To watch the birth and death of beings is like looking at*
> *the movements of a dance.*
> *A lifetime is like a flash of lightning in the sky,*
> *Rushing by, like a torrent down a steep mountain.*
>
> —The Buddha

The Three Aspects of the Ego

As long as we are alive, we need an ego to function in this world. Therefore the ego has three aspects; the first is the root of suffering and must be destroyed; the second is beneficial; the third is supreme.

The first kind is *the ego of ignorance*, the cause of all suffering. It maintains illusions such as, "I am this body and finite personality. I can experience fulfillment by gaining the objects of my desires." This illusory sense of self is our "mistaken identity." It is committed to maintain the negative mental/emotional complexes, which it takes to be an indispensable part of itself. Therefore it suffers. It experiences the potential loss of its false sense of identity to be a mortal threat; it will do anything to maintain itself and to sabotage any efforts to bring its rule to an end. This illusion must be defeated by a ruthless commitment to freedom from its rule.

> Every thought gives us the sense of being an "I" that thinks, but the truth is that thoughts simply arise.

The ego of aspiration is positive and precious. It begins with the desire for spiritual awakening and in the course of *sadhana*, spiritual practice; it strengthens and becomes increasingly transparent. It might express itself in this way: "I know the essence of truth and bliss lies in me and I am completely committed to removing all obstructions to this realization. In my heart lies the Presence and Love of God and to realize this fully is the purpose of my existence. I am detached from desires for the objects of the world and attached to the presence of God in the cave of the Heart." This form of ego enables us to dissolve our confusion and attain Self-Realization.

Most auspicious is *the ego of the sage*. It is completely transparent to the view of the Self. If we give it words, it might express itself in the following ways: "I am one with all there is. I am the Non-Dual Reality behind all illusory names and forms, I am one with the immortal and ever-present Ground of Being." Or, in the words of Jesus, "I and the Father are one." This is only a semblance of an ego. It appears to be an ego, but is in fact egolessness. This is the way a realized being operates.

I Think – I Feel – I Do – I Am.

When we become still we notice that in the waking state an unceasing stream of thoughts arises whether we invite it or not. These thoughts arise along with a subtle sense of "I" – "*I* am thinking this and it means this or that about *me.*" This is the effect of *ahamkara*, the "I-making tendency" of the mind, a more precise description of ego. Every thought gives us the sense of being an "I" that thinks, but the truth is that thoughts simply arise. They are not personal, but we take them to be personal. They may be true or false, correct or mistaken, but we identify with them. "This is my opinion!" "I am right." "This is true about me." We are unconsciously attached to what we think and defend it vigorously, even though it is the source of all pain.

And it doesn't stop there. After we identify with a thought, a chain of events begins that is easy to observe.

1. ***Thoughts*** arise on the foundation of ego (*ahamkara*).
2. These thoughts create ***emotions***.
3. The emotions drive ***actions and behavior***.
4. Actions produce ***physical manifestations***.

The short version of this sequence is: I think – I feel – I do – I am. The entire progression begins in the mind and leads us to identify with our thoughts, feelings, actions and body, possessions, relationships and so on—in other words, with everything that passes away, everything that is temporary, *everything we are not.* This is blindness. To find out what we are, we have to carefully examine this process. We have to become Self-aware.

A stressful thought arises, *"John hurt me."* If we simply let it pass, no harm is done. If we believe it, the thought becomes more solid and turns into a negative emotion, like pain, stress or anger. Emotions in turn drive behavior, and behavior that is compelled by stress tends to be unskilled and harmful. Our actions will therefore create negative physical manifestations—conflicts, losses, illness, accidents, addictions, or chemical imbalances in the brain due to depression, anger, or fear.

We get attached so easily to our unexamined stressful reactions. A constant stream of judgments runs our lives. We cling to beliefs like *it's hard to succeed, life is difficult, people are out for their own good, my partner doesn't care about me, I'm too fat, too lazy, not good enough*, and so on. Then we see the world through the lens of our beliefs. The mind finds (or fabricates) plenty of evidence to support its opinion, no matter how painful it may be, and it ignores what does not match its negative view. The result is that we live in a stressful, uncaring world of our own making.

> The true causes of pain, conflict and stress are our ego-motivated reactions

On the other hand, a clear and peaceful mind brings with it precision of thought, balanced and harmonious emotions, clear, decisive, and skillful behavior, and caring and supportive relationships. It supports physical health, financial abundance, a sense of personal mastery, joy, and wisdom. It helps us realize the truth in the words of Lao Tsu: *Compassionate toward yourself you reconcile all beings in the world.*[1]

Later we will see how we can free ourselves of stressful thoughts and emotions so the negative behaviors, relationship conflicts, and physical manifestations will stop, but first we must take a look at how we so easily sabotage ourselves.

Overcoming the Sabotage of the Pain Body[2]

When we undertake any type of transformative spiritual practice like meditation or the other skills described in this book, there is a part of the mind that will do its best to sabotage what we're try-ing to do. This internal saboteur is the mind's unconscious addiction to distractions, com-motion, impatience, and pain. Eckhart Tolle called it the pain body. It's the part of us that doesn't want to wake up; it wants to keep its old ways going and those are the ways of pain. This part of the ego-mind indeed does not have our best inter-ests in mind!

> All suffering arises in the mind.

In its effort to maintain itself, the ego partners with unhappiness, pain, and stress to keep up the drama of "I." *I am used to a certain kind and amount of pain—that is who I am.* Although consciously we don't like to suffer, unconsciously we are attached to our familiar patterns, so the mind maintains *an unconscious addiction to pain.* The ego can-not tolerate anything that questions its rule, so it has become very good at using every trick in the book to distract us from waking up. *I meditated enough yesterday. I need to complain about this. I'm bored. I'm tired. I am wasting my time. I have more important things to do.* It tries to convince us that awakening from the trance of "I" is really the last thing we should do. If we want to find peace, we need to see through all the ego's ploys and disguises.

To overcome the ego's interference, it is best to develop a "thought-less" attitude to daily spiritual practice. We don't argue with ourselves whether or not we should brush our teeth? No, we just do it. Once our commitment to practice becomes that habitual, the ego will have much less chance to interfere.

The True Cause of Suffering

Where is our unhappiness or pain located? It arises *in us*, is that not so? It does not arise out there in the people and circumstances we blame. *The true causes of pain, conflict and stress are our ego-motivated reactions* to the people and situations we encounter, including our judgments against us. The true cause of suffering is clinging to the ego. A great Buddhist sage put it this way:

> *All the harm with which this world is rife,*
> *All the fear and suffering that there is:*
> *Clinging to the "I" has caused it!*
> *What am I to do with this great demon?*
>
> *O you, my mind, for countless ages past*
> *Have sought the welfare of yourself;*
> *Oh, the weariness it brought upon you!*
> *And all you got was sorrow in return.*
>
> *A hundred harms you've done me;*
> *Wandering in cycles of existence;*
> *Now your malice I remember*
> *And I will crush your selfish schemes!*
>
> *That time when you could beat me down*
> *Is in the past; it's no more here.*
> *Now I see you! Where will you escape?*
> *I will crush your haughty insolence!*
> —Shantideva, *Bodhicharyavatara*

Instead of recognizing and eliminating the true source of our suffering, what do we do? We try our very best to enhance the ego. We make it stronger and richer, decorate and pamper it, defend, indulge, and improve it. This is the opposite of self-love; it is ego-clinging. Instead of freeing ourselves from jail, we work very hard to make it ever more homey in our cell. This will never be successful. If the Eastern wisdom is to be believed, we have done it for uncounted lifetimes. No wonder some of us are becoming weary. We get what we want for a little while and then we lose it again and suffer. Even when we help others, we become prideful about it. The *kleshas* are the poisons that rule our minds: ignorance, egoism, attachment, aversion and fear, which produce anger and aggression, desire, pride, arrogance, and depression. They make us blind to the great miracle of what we are, to our immortality, our great freedom. But there is hope as soon as we recognize our true enemies—the ones that resides right inside the mind.

> Maintaining an awareness of stillness is an act of devotion in which everything we do becomes sacred.

All suffering arises in the mind. For thousands of years we have tried to change our outer circumstances, to what effect? Has it made the world a better place, a happier place? We get rid of one offending person or situation and another takes its place. We fulfill one desire and another arises. Now we can see the hopelessness of the situation and apply the true antidote to the ego's poison.

Freedom beckons right beyond our addiction to ego. Peace and a great love are always within us; we simply need to remove what covers them up. When, through practice, the ego ceases to be an obstruction and a cause of suffering, it becomes a good friend, an amazing servant. When its consciousness-limiting properties dissolve, we can move through the world as a free being. Then we will have the ego of a sage, a pure channel through which love and compassion can enter the world, a flute on which the Absolute can play its divine melody. This realization affects society beyond measure.

Stillness in Action

There is formal meditation and stillness in action. Meditation is a core skill; if we make it a daily habit, it will soon be a constant source of rejuvenation and peace. Before long we won't want to miss even a single day of your practice. But to practice stillness, one doesn't necessarily have to sit still. Stillness comes from clear and peaceful awareness, not simply from lack of movement. Most people experience moments of stillness in action when they are doing some activity they love. When our actions come from the heart, everything we do is part of our spiritual practice.

One of my favorite ways to experience stillness in action is through sculpting. As my fingers work with the clay, my thoughts take a vacation. In this type of activity, the thinking mind would merely get in the way. There is a deeper intelligence that runs the show very well.

I see and feel in my sculptures what is being birthed in myself—a sense of order, beauty, warmth, and insight, reality experienced with a clear and untroubled mind. When I sculpt images of Indian deities—the elephant-headed Ganesha, the majestic grandeur of Shiva, the warm presence of the Divine Mother—these deities come alive for me. They are symbols of the enlightened mind, of deep wisdom, of the ways the human soul has expressed the mystery of divine love. As the sculptures come to life in my hands, I feel blessed by the life they are giving me.

> When our actions come from the heart, everything we do is part of our spiritual practice.

All action can be like this. Making a sculpture is not different from doing the dishes, driving a car, sorting through papers, discussing a project, or turning a screwdriver. We are always creative. To the extent we are present in the here and now, we live in the great peace that gives birth to all action, even while performing everyday chores. Stillness helps us to be aware.

When we attune ourselves to stillness, we can get in touch with the heart.

> Stillness is everywhere; we can sense it if we take the time to tune in. It makes our old negative habits transparent and they will cease to control us as much.

Once we can sense stillness in what we love, we can learn to love whatever we do. We can find stillness while jogging, working, cooking, or cleaning. We can remember to enjoy stillness in the middle of a conversation, when waiting in line, or while paying our bills. Just like space, stillness is always present. It means to stay centered in that silent space in the heart. Maintaining an awareness of stillness is an act of devotion in which everything we do becomes sacred.

As we cultivate an awareness of stillness, the old unconscious ties to our suffering loosen and the pain body dissolves. Stillness means to become more self-aware. Stillness is peace.

What would happen to our habitual dramas if stillness permeated our mind? Who would we be if we were internally peaceful and present during our normal activities? Do we really function better when we are driven by worries and wants, deadlines and commitments, or when we act out of the clarity that comes from inner peace? The answers are obvious, but to overcome the mind's unconscious addiction to turmoil, intellectual insight alone is not enough. It has to become gut-level realization. Practicing stillness can take us there.

Stillness is everywhere; we can sense it if we take the time to tune in. It makes our old negative habits transparent and they will cease to control us as much. As we pass through a valley, moments of stillness can remind us of the peace and harmony of past peak experiences. They will be more than a memory; we will feel them again as they encourage and strengthen us and put us back in touch with who we really are.

SHIVA, THE LORD OF YOGIS
(SCULPTURE BY RAMGIRI)

Lovers don't finally meet somewhere.
They're in each other all along.

--Rumi

7

The Messenger Appears

N O MATTER HOW LONG WE HAVE been trapped in our personal hell, eventually the path will open up again, and often in an entirely unexpected way. After I had spent several months meditating in Holland, the inner pressure I felt subsided a bit. I had a little more breathing space and felt a little happier. I was ready for an adventure. Saving up a little money I made plans to travel to Scotland, where Trungpa Rinpoche, the great Tibetan teacher lived. I thought I might visit him and roaming around the far North sounded rough and romantic. I was looking forward to traveling into the unknown. Little did I know just how unknown it was going to get.

On the evening before my departure, I was at a friend's apartment and found a book with a curious title, *Be Here Now*. It told the story of Dr. Richard Alpert, a psychologist who had been Timothy Leary's sidekick at Harvard. They were icons of the psychedelic drug culture of the 60s, and their call to "turn on, tune in, and drop out" was heard by a youthful generation that rejected the old ways and sought to explore new dimensions of consciousness. Alpert wrote that he had taken so much LSD that he ended up feeling like a yo-yo, one moment up in the presence of God and down into outer darkness the next. Although he had had many transcendental experiences, he still hadn't found the answers he was seeking, so he went to India in the hope of finding someone who could show him what this consciousness thing was all about. Eventually he was led to an "old man in a blanket" who blew his mind far more than LSD ever had—Neem Karoli Baba, known affectionately as *Maharajji*.[1] He was one of the rarest of realized beings, known as an *avadhut* or *mahasiddha* in India.

At their first meeting, Maharajji playfully let Alpert know that he knew every private thought in his mind. It was unknown in the West that a human being could have this ability, and yet the proof was unmistakable. The realization that all his deep dark secrets lay completely revealed plunged Alpert into a moment of intense paranoia and fear. His mind raced faster and faster, but he couldn't get a handle on Maharajji. With its obsessive grasping for control facing complete defeat, the ego gave up. The very instant his mind surrendered, his heart burst open into a love so pure and powerful that it changed him forever. For the first time in his life, he felt completely and unconditionally loved. He had come home.

It was astounding to read that there was someone who knew everything in the mind of another, but this was only the first revelation in the book. Apparently, a constant stream of miracles occurred around this remarkable man, but I was touched most intensely by the accounts of his profound unconditional love. On the hill in Bavaria, I had been granted a glimpse of the absolute love that lies at the core of creation, and now here was someone who not only *knew* this love, but was able to *live* it. Imagine a state of mind so clear that all things could be known and a state of heart so exalted that it could love everything and everyone! This realization significantly changed my understanding about our human potential. Clearly, if one person can live in such an enlightened state, it means we all can aspire to it.

I read about half the book before I had to get on my way. Alpert, whom Maharajji had named Baba Ram Dass, made it very clear that his guru was not the least bit interested in collecting followers, and Ram Dass was under strict instructions not to disclose his whereabouts. The idea of meeting him never occurred to me. I read the book as a very impressive and heartwarming story of someone else's spiritual adventure. I didn't realize until many years later that while I was reading *Be Here Now* and looking at pictures of Maharajji, I received a powerful transmission—a direct impression on my mind and heart of the extraordinary space of love the book spoke about— but my mind was still too coarse to be aware of this. It registered unconsciously and prepared me for what was to happen next.

The following night was rainy and cold. On my way to Scotland— I thought—I had just found the only health food restaurant in all of London at the time, a little "hole in the wall" with about five tables. I had hardly sat down as the door opened and Ram Dass stood in the doorway, radiating a breathtaking light. I had never seen anything like it. He was glowing with a powerful luminescence that radiated outward. He came in with a group of his friends, all dressed in flowing white Indian robes. They too carried the same light. I felt a deep love emanating from them all.

As Ram Dass walked past my table, I caught his attention and said, "Thank you for your book." He stopped, sat down across from me, and we talked. It turned out that they had arrived in London from India the same hour I had come from Amsterdam. When I told him that I was planning to go to India in a year, something curious happened. His right eye opened up inwardly, like extending a telescope deep into a bottomless well. I fell into that well and lost myself in it completely.

To this day I don't know what happened. For just an instant, "I" ceased to exist. When I returned to myself, Ram Dass gave me a curious look and said, "Oh, this is going to be good." He took out a little scrap of paper and wrote down "Evelyn Hotel, Nainital, U.P." He said, "These are some friends of mine. You should go see them when you're in India." I didn't think much of it and put the note into my pocket. A few minutes later they all left because the restaurant was too small for their large group. I was aware that the light they carried, this refined and tangible essence of love, nourished me more than any food ever could.

As I walked outside into the dark night and the drizzling rain, I knew that something very important had happened. When I had asked Ram Dass, "What are you going to do now, back here in the West?" he said, "I don't know. I'll just follow the voice of my heart." *Follow the voice of my heart.* The implication was that this voice would guide him. I asked myself, "What is the voice of my heart telling me to do now?" I became still and listened. To my dismay, the voice of my heart said nothing whatsoever about Scotland. It said, "Go back to Amsterdam." Damn, I had just come from there! But something in me knew to obey this inner guidance. At two o'clock in the morning, I hitchhiked back down to the coast, caught the first boat to France, and by evening had made my way back to Amsterdam.

I didn't know what to do next. I stopped in a square filled with people. A dark-skinned stranger approached me and asked if I wanted to buy a cheap kilo of hashish. I assumed the police were after him. I declined, but told him that I would check with a friend, who had done some deals in the past, if he was interested. As I came to his apartment, my friend was just heading out for the evening. No, he said, he wasn't dealing drugs any longer, but he invited me to come in and stay for the night. I gladly accepted, for I had no place to go.

After my friend left for the evening, I sat down on the couch and there, right next to me, was that book again, *Be Here Now*. I continued to read where I had stopped. After a while I came to a part in the book with instructions for a visualization of the great Tibetan guru Padmasambhava. It said to imagine him floating in the air several feet in front of you, then to visualize a red beam of light connecting the guru's forehead chakra with your own. Next, connect a white beam of light from the guru's throat chakra to yours. And finally, picture a beam of blue light between Padmasambhava's heart chakra and your own. Then you were to visualize the beam of blue light expanding as wide as a road, and to imagine the guru floating down on that beam of light into your heart.

I had never done anything like this before, but it sounded interesting and exotic, so I put the book down to try it. Before I knew it, there was the image of Padmasambhava floating in the air a few feet in front of me; there were the beams of light, especially the blue one that became wide like a road, and then he floated down on that beam of light into my heart. As he merged with my heart, everything stopped. My breath stopped completely. There wasn't a single thought in my mind. My body was completely motionless, absolutely still. There was no time. And in that timeless stillness, my heart exploded in love for all beings.

What a strikingly powerful moment! It happened quickly, but took a while to sink in. This was a very long way off from my fear-filled existence It was another call to travel the path of my deepest yearning, to realize that the essence of my heart—of every heart—is this absolute love. If I hadn't known it before, I knew now that something was going on with this strange book, and especially with this old man wrapped in a blanket, Maharajji. I didn't know what it was, but I knew it had to do with my heart, and I knew it was big.

About six months later I was in Copenhagen with friends who had been to India. I told them about the address Ram Dass had scribbled on a piece of paper for me, and they said that this was the way to find Maharajji. They hadn't met him, but word of his whereabouts had leaked out. As I heard that, a bolt of energy rushed up my spine. I realized that Ram Dass had actually given me the master clue in my spiritual treasure hunt. Now I knew exactly where I was going. Three months later, I was in India.

THE SECOND SKILL:
LOVE AND DEVOTION

8

Opening The Devotional Heart

I WAS LIVING IN AN OLD RICKETY ashram on the banks of the Yamuna River in the ancient holy town of Brindavan in North India. This little town, only a two-hour train ride south of bustling New Delhi, might as well have been on a different planet, a planet of deep devotion and peace. Imagine a community of just a few thousand people who are living for nothing other than their passionate love for God, century after century. Brindavan was suffused with the tangible presence of Krishna, "the dark one," who spent his childhood and early youth here. There was a tangible gentleness and softness in the air, as though Krishna, the divine lover, permeated every part of this world. Even the stones on the street seemed to radiate the presence of love.

Living in Brindavan was tender and sweet beyond anything I had ever known. I walked through fragrant fields on the sun-drenched footpath that circled the town, past an endless array of shrines and temples, under ancient banyan trees with peacocks trailing their shimmering tails through the branches. Swarms of parrots shot from tree to tree like brilliant streaks of colored light, and the enchanting concert of birds and insects soothed my every step. I shared the path with pilgrims and cows, wild pigs, an occasional coyote, and many squirrels. Animals and people lived in great harmony with each other, reflecting the spirit of Krishna in a joyful celebration of life. The mesmerizing sound of Krishna's flute still floats among the trees to this day, lifting all hearts into a vast and wonderful peace.

> A good story about love is food for the heart.

I was at ease because the satsang, the community of spiritual seekers, had embraced me with open arms. The small group of Maharajji's western devotees that had gathered in Brindavan was an eclectic mix of young people from around the world, all basking in Maharajji's powerful love. His presence was unmistakable among us: we loved him so deeply that we naturally loved each other. And I noticed how my love for Maharajji was growing every day, even though I had not yet met him! The great warmth of this loving family embraced me, carried me, and helped me to learn about the path of love and devotion.

One of our most important pastimes was sharing stories of Maharajji. As we sat together, sipping *chai* and "gossiping" about him, I noticed how the stories deepened my understanding. A good story about love is food for the heart. We are still telling these stories decades later, and they never cease to have the same thrilling effect.

Day after day, I left the ashram by the river and followed the footpath through the fields to Maharajji's temple, the powdery warm sand squishing softly around my bare toes. Day after day, I was told that Maharajji was not seeing anyone. It didn't bother me. My daily walk on this path had become a ritual of its own, an exercise of devotion, as much a pilgrimage to my own heart as to him. Walking through this pastoral landscape was a gift to my soul. There was nothing else I could possibly want.

On the day of my 22nd birthday, I again walked to the ashram and

NEEM KAROLI BABA, MAHARAJJI

asked the caretaker my usual question: "Is Maharajji seeing anyone today?" expecting the usual answer. To my great shock I was told, "Oh yes, he just walked out to the street. He must be at one of the neighboring temples. You can go see him there." I was stunned. For more than a year every step, every breath I had taken, had led me to this moment. Ever since I had first seen Maharajji's picture, back in that apartment in Amsterdam, the attraction had been growing stronger and stronger. Was I actually going to see him today?

As if in a daze, I walked out to the roadway, turned right, walked a few steps, and there he was, wrapped in his blanket, sitting about fifteen yards back from the road in front of a small temple. He was talking to two young *sadhus*, wandering monks. My feet stopped. Automatically, my hands moved together in front of my heart in the ancient Indian gesture of *Namaste*, which means, "The light in me greets the light in you." I had the distinct feeling that a powerful force was pulling me up by the top of the head, like a puppet on a string. There I stood, completely mesmerized by the first sight of my guru. To this day I remember the smallest details of the moment—the expression on his face, his movements, the short stubble of beard, every single color of that plaid blanket.

Maharajji sat there in a halo of dazzling light—the same light I had seen on the hill in Bavaria and again when Ram Dass was standing in the doorway of the restaurant on that rainy night in London. Here was that light in its most concentrated form, and it stopped the world for me. I couldn't move, nor did I want to. My body and mind were completely still, my entire attention absorbed in what I saw before me. *Let me just stand here and gaze at him without end! Let me bathe in this essence forever!* I was having *darshan*—the gift of being in the presence of a holy being, a great teacher. Darshan also means to absorb the divine through the eyes. When we are capable of perceiving the sacred, its essence can enter us through the pathways of the senses. This is recognition, a remembering, our own essence awakening to itself. Our eyes are opened in the moment of grace.

After a timeless moment, he motioned his head that I should walk on. I did not comprehend. I was too awestruck to have a single thought in my mind. The sadhus were laughing; I must have been quite a sight, standing there stiff as a stick. Maharajji brought his hand out from under his blanket and waved me on. Finally I understood. I *pranamed* (bowed), and my feet began moving again. After rounding a turn in the road, Maharajji was gone from view. My feet kept moving while my heart burst its bounds and a wonderful warmth radiated throughout me. I realized there was no way my mind could explain what had just happened, but the heart knew. The heart *knew*.

The next day Maharajji closed the doors of the ashram again and was not giving darshan. There was no telling when I would see him again. But meanwhile I had to get my visa renewed, not an easy matter in India in those days. Rumors circulated among the westerners about which visa offices were a little easier to deal with or accepted bribes. Luckily, my best chance for a visa extension was in an immigration office close to Bodh Gaya—the place where the Buddha awakened under the ancient banyan tree, 25 centuries ago, vowing not to get up from his meditation until he had reached the supreme goal. I was going to sit in that same place.

> Free of illusion, the satguru IS the way.

Two nights later a rickshaw carried me along a dry riverbed to the place of Buddha's enlightenment. It was the full moon in May—Buddha's birthday—and the shining orb lit the road and the sandy expanse behind the huge trees where people and buffalos roamed in deep peace. The balmy soft air and the muffled sounds of people and animals caressed me with a tenderness that stirred me to tears. Even though he had lived 2500 years ago, this great man's presence was still so tangible in the landscape.

Bodh Gaya was a small dusty village in those days. Surrounding the great Mahabodhi Temple there were a few scattered temples, two or three small retreat centers, and a few huts around an unpaved street. Run down as it was, there was a remarkable depth of peace in this place—not surprising given its history. Soon after my arrival, word reached me that Maharajji had left Brindavan and was traveling in South India. There was now no reason to return to the ashram in Brindavan, so I settled in to study Insight Meditation with a pristine teacher, Anagarika Munindra. Under his expert guidance, I began to understand the true power of meditation to dissolve suffering and delusion. In the stillness of my practice, I also came to comprehend more clearly the depth of my connection with Maharajji. It was a growing inner realization that went deep into my bones.

Without having to be told, I knew that he was my satguru—a bond that goes far deeper than any other relationship.

There are two types of gurus. *Upagurus* are teachers who point the way, specialists of a knowledge or art, they teach yoga, music, or other skills. Today we have secular adaptations (or distortions) of the term, like Wall Street gurus, exercise gurus, marketing gurus, etc. While an upaguru as a spiritual teacher points the way, the satguru functions on a completely different level of existence. As a Self-realized being the satguru has erased his attachment to individuality and merged his mind in the Absolute. Free of illusion, the satguru IS the way. On the personal level the satguru may or may not teach you something, but his primary function lies on a much deeper level.

> "God, guru, and Self are one."

In the true—and formless—identity of his divine freedom, the satguru is the consciousness and love in our heart. He is the light at the end of the tunnel. He is the living embodiment of our enlightenment. When we look through the eye of the deepest wisdom, we are one with the guru. As long as we still live in duality, the guru is the goal in which we can experience our Oneness. Since his consciousness has merged with the light, he IS the light and shines it into this world. Through bhakti yoga, devotion, we practice letting go of ego into divine love. This process culminates in our awakening to the Oneness of being—and that Oneness is the formless essence of the satguru, present everywhere.

The relationship with the satguru continues through lifetimes. We do not choose it. It is simply a fact that some of us one day discover. Just as our mother gives birth to our body, the satguru gives birth to our spiritual awakening. Through his form he is the gate through which we enter into Oneness. In his formless essence, in his enlightenment, he is Oneness. That is why it is said, "God, guru, and Self are one."

And when he sees me in all
and sees all in me,
then I never leave him
and he never leaves me.

And he, who in this oneness of love
loves me in whatever he sees,
wherever this man may live
in truth he lives in me.

--Bhagavad Gita

Maharajji knew me much more deeply and fully than I knew myself. That in itself was a miracle. To be seen fully for who I am established an unbreakable bond between us, but, more importantly, I felt completely and unconditionally loved. I felt loved down to the last fiber of my being, including all the parts of me that were lost in fear and self-rejection. It was a love that transformed me. With intuitive clarity I knew I could trust him completely. And I began to realize that his love would never leave me.

> I felt loved down to the last fiber of my being, including all the parts of me that were lost in fear and self-rejection.

This great love Maharajji showered on us so freely (and continues to do so) was not dependent on what we did—whether we were good or bad, rich or poor, intelligent or not—and it did not depend on being in his presence. It was much deeper, a communion beyond time and space that occurs in the innermost place of the heart for no other reason than because *we are love.*

Form is Emptiness and Emptiness is Form

By March it became too hot to stay in Bodh Gaya. Maharajji was still traveling and unavailable. I decided to go to Nepal, trekking high up into the Himalayas toward Tibet. An ancient pilgrimage trail runs through the deepest gorge in the world, the valley of the Kali Kandaki River, which cut its path between two of the highest mountains on earth, the Annapurna and Dalaugiri massifs. Every day I hiked eight or nine hours into these breathtaking mountains, barefoot, which kept my mind present and focused on every step—the perfect practice of stillness in action. As soon as my attention strayed and I got lost in a thought, I would get a bloody toe. There was no way for the mind to engage in its usual chatter. With every step I became more focused and still. Every so often I would stop to look up at the icy summits glistening under a sky of the most saturated blue I had ever seen. The air was crystal clear and the light became more brilliant the higher I climbed. The images of this spectacular beauty are etched into my mind forever.

The voice of the heart needs no translation.

When night approached, I would knock on the nearest door. The warm Nepalese people always took me in, fed me, and gave me a place on the floor to sleep. Most houses were one-room shacks, some little more than a collection of sticks with something resembling a roof. The poorer the people were, the more genuine and sincere was their hospitality. In my view they were dirt poor, and they gave of the little they had without a thought of tomorrow. This is how I learned about true wealth. It didn't matter that we didn't speak the same language. The voice of the heart needs no translation.

One evening, an old sadhu with flowing white hair and beard came to the house where I was staying. I sat outside on the porch at a respectful distance from him. I noticed he had nothing to eat, so I gestured that I would like to buy him some food. He declined my offer with a kind smile. I sat back down, watching him. He was very still, gazing at the mountains across from us. Soon I fell into a meditative mood. All of a sudden I saw what he saw: the mountains appeared completely insubstantial, empty of substance. It was as if I were looking at a hologram, a projected three-dimensional image, a stage set in a dream, something that appeared real but could never be. In that moment I realized that physical matter is nothing other than a projection of consciousness.

> Physical matter is nothing other than a projection of consciousness.

When we hear the words *empty* or *void*, we think of "nothingness," like a great gaping hole, a limitless abyss that threatens to swallow us up, or of meaninglessness, a barrenness of the heart and the mind, or that life is uncertain and we never know what may happen next. These ideas are scary. But the kind of emptiness I experienced was exactly the opposite of a dark void; it was a penetrating lucidity, a great and surprising freedom. I could perceive the light of God shining in everything. *Oh, that's how it is!* A wave of relief washed through me.

Recognizing the insubstantiality of all appearances, even of great, solid mountains, I felt an enormous release. *I don't have to be afraid!* Imagine you're dreaming, and suddenly you become aware that everything around you is only a dream, a projection of your own mind. Instead of fearing the world of this dream and stressing myself over it, I could look at it and admire and love the magnificence of the projection, the dark-and-light splendor and majesty of this spectacular creation.

It is not only the physical world that is empty, but also our thoughts, our emotions, our personality, habits, pain, and anything else we endow with solidity and importance. Knowing that creation is empty and fundamentally groundless is the root of spiritual insight. In the past I had read the famous line from the Buddhist Heart Sutra, "Form is emptiness and emptiness is form," without real understanding. Back then it sounded mystical and cool; now it explained what I saw. I understood that physical matter is nothing other than consciousness in a solid form. Consciousness, not matter, is the primary reality of creation. The world appears in a vast field of awareness. In that limitless space of consciousness, the Cosmic Mind projects the universe as a play, a *lila*, a dance of the divine in its countless forms and manifestations, from the most subtle all the way down to gross physical matter. This world is a dream we all dream together.

> This world is a dream we all dream together.

The granite of the mountains appeared so completely insubstantial to me at that moment that I had to carefully remind myself that if I were to stub my toe on a rock, it would still bleed. Clearly I would have to treat the physical world with great care, but now I could take it more lightly. The world wasn't as oppressively real as I had thought it to be, although quite real enough to demand my respect. As the sage Ashtavakra said, *"The world with all its wonders is nothing. When you notice, desire melts away. For you are awareness itself. When you know in your heart that there is nothing, you are still."*[1]

As I walked deeper into the mountains toward Tibet, I came into a landscape that lacked any human dimension—no trees, no houses, no people or animals, not even a bush. There was nothing that could give me a sense of scale, only vast expanses of rock, wind, and sky. In this immense scenery I couldn't tell if the next mountain was half an hour or a day's walk away. I felt completely insignificant, smaller then an ant, almost disappearing completely in the majestic scale of the land. My mind took part in that emptiness; it was humbling and magnificent at the same time. In these awe-inspiring surroundings I simply fell silent. I was free and unburdened, gazing in wonderment at the world like a child.

Then, in this inner emptiness and outer vastness, I heard Maharajji calling. I turned around and hiked out of the mountains back into India. Spontaneously the words and melodies of *kirtan* arose in my mind, the ecstatic devotional chanting of the names of God, and these sacred mantras accompanied me all the way to Kainchi, Maharajji's ashram in the foothills of the Himalayas.

Darshan

As I crossed the bridge over the mountain stream and walked through the gate of the ashram, I could hardly breathe. I felt an intense sensation, an exhilarating, expansive feeling in my chest, a great sense of expectation, as though something momentous was about to happen. I saw the steep, pine-covered hills that surround the small valley, took in the fresh mountain air and the ambiance of ringing temple bells, and the deep feeling of peace that permeated the place. Then I joined about two dozen westerners on a small outside porch covered by a few thin straw mats. They were singing a powerful kirtan while waiting for Maharajji. The singing came from a place deep in the heart, clearly much deeper than where my mind was able to go. I joined in. My voice merged so completely with the others around me that all sense of separateness slipped away. My heart opened far past its usual bounds, and I joyfully drowned in the sea of devotion.

Then Maharajji burst through the door on my right and sat down on a low wooden platform, like a small bed, called a *takhat*. It was covered by a firm pad wrapped in coarse brown woolen fabric. There he was, the man I had first met in the pages of *Be Here Now*, the man who by now had taken on mythological status for so many in the West who had been touched by this book, the man who did not want to be found. He began to talk and joke, carrying on half a dozen conversations at the same time in a high, animated voice. It was fascinating to watch him, riveting to my mind, which became absolutely still in his presence, and completely absorbed in the heart. There was a depth and intensity, an immense amount of *shakti*[2] to Maharajji's presence. He radiated an enormous vitality mixed with kindheartedness in complete inner stillness. Within that stillness, his body was in almost continuous motion. I became absorbed in watching his hand and body movements. It was a continuous flow of *mudras*, completely natural sacred gestures, that his long-time devotees were quite adept at reading.

MASTER OF MUDRAS

Sitting in his presence was exhilarating because he was tremendously engaging and aware of countless levels of communication. Life-changing experiences would occur as though there was nothing special to them. And in the inspiring internal stillness you could receive wordless answers to questions, entire teachings, and always profound nurturing.

Just as the power of his love had reached out and brought me from the other side of the world to his feet, now his presence reached ever more deeply inside me. I felt an all-absorbing softness, an absolute kindness, a complete acceptance, and an immense sense of wonder—all of which opened me to increasingly deeper dimensions of my heart. It was irresistible, compelling. I had yearned for it all my life without knowing what I was seeking. Now I knew that I had finally arrived home.

> *The relationship between a pure Master and a* chela *(disciple)*
> *is a matter that has nothing to do with the intellect whatsoever.*
> *There's no choice involved in it at all. There is such deep karma*
> *unfolding that you are drawn to the Master when the moment*
> *is right. The unfolding happens totally at a level where, when it's*
> *right, you just "aaah, aaah, aaah."*
>
> --Ram Dass

Two hours later, on the way to my quarters on the other side of the small valley, I stopped at a bend of the road and gazed down at the small collection of temples and buildings where I had just sat with Maharajji. Two things were clear to me beyond any doubt: Maharajji knew me inside and out, and he loved me completely. He wanted absolutely nothing from me; he loved me for one reason only: *he was love.* And because I could trust his love, I knew that he would guide me unfailingly along my path to the highest realization I would be able to reach. Here, at the feet of the Master, I could find release from my pain, fear, and alienation, and satisfy the burning hunger of my heart. In him I had met the core of me I had somehow forgotten. I could sense a mystical union between us, the sensation of what I really am. And I was utterly free.

Could I empty myself enough to take these gifts into me? Could I, by my own effort, come up with the courage to dissolve myself in that love? I was a confused, unhappy, conflicted kid with no clue of how I could use my precious life in the best possible way. All I knew was that I wanted to be free of my burdens and be free to love, and here before me was the answer to my prayers. Here was the solution.

He was the love I had glimpsed in my best moments. It was solid and unwavering. His very being showed me that absolute, unconditional love was possible in this world. This was the door to freedom, an incredible opportunity to reach completely beyond my small isolated existence into the realization of my highest potential.

Surrendering to the Self

What could I give him in return for showing me the way to myself? On one hand the question was irrelevant because he asked for nothing. On the other hand, it was crucial because giving enables us to receive. The burning question was this: how could I open myself to receive the gift he offered me? And so I did something I never imagined to do: I surrendered my life to Maharajji. I gave myself to love and wisdom in the form of this old man in a blanket. From the deepest place in my heart, I silently and fervently asked him to accept my life as my gift. I laid at his feet the only gift I had, the only thing I had to give him. *I asked that he make me an instrument of his love.* It was a silent prayer. As was the case with him most of the time, no words had to be spoken. Over time I have found that he has accepted my offering.

> True surrender is always surrender to the essence of Truth and Oneness in us

Surrendering my life to another human being was something I would never do. After all, I had experienced firsthand what blind adulation can do. Hitler had been greatly adored by his followers. In their idolization of this mad tyrant, the German people had surrendered their lives to him; some had worshiped him like a Messiah and followed him into apocalyptic disaster. Surrender to a human being? What utter insanity! Yet it is my most profound joy and the greatest blessing that I was able to surrender my life to Maharajji.

The very idea of surrender evokes fear in many people, and rightfully so. Naive surrender carries extraordinary dangers. But even more dangerous is the belief that we are the ego. When we see our human reality as little more than body, mind, and personality, then out of that limited perspective, an act of surrender, whether to a person or an idea, must look like self-delusion and an invitation for abuse. It is our unfortunate tendency to want to follow a strong leader out of immature motives, which leads to disasters like Jonestown, the Nazis, fundamentalism, and terrorism of all kinds. It also leads to the countless personal self-betrayals people suffer in their relationships at home and at work. Who hasn't surrendered at one time or another to a demeaning job, a tyrannical boss, a loveless relationship, or a limiting idea or belief?

However, the surrender to the satguru is not an act of blind submission. Far from it! *True surrender is always surrender to the essence of Truth and Oneness in us.* It is the conscious yielding of the mature soul to guidance by our inherent divinity through the agency of the guru. The true satguru is *antaryami*, the "knower and guide, who resides in the heart," who knows all our thoughts and emotions. But when we have difficulty accessing our internal wisdom, it manifests in the outer world as the human form of the guru.

Certainly a devotee may project feelings and needs onto the guru, but to see the relationship only through the lens of such transference is to miss its true potential and purpose. If we have the rare good fortune to find a true guru, we can receive the critical guidance we need to overcome our dependencies and expectations. A true guru offers the *chela*, the devotee or disciple, what is needed for his or her growth. In the guru's clear mirror, we can see our unrealistic projections and fears, and greatly accelerate our awakening. My surrender did not come from an expectation that Maharajji would save me or fulfill my needs; it came from an awareness of who he was to me, a remembering that must have grown over lifetimes. I recognized myself in his light—a recognition as unshakable as the light itself. In that deep place, I wanted nothing from Maharajji; it was simply an opening into love. In that sense of oneness, I had everything I could ever want. "The guru is not external," he said.

To this day Maharajji's unconditional love uplifts me in countless ways, helps me, and gives me deep, lasting joy. But while his presence continues to have a profound impact, I've always known that he is not going to "fix" me. Instead Maharajji showed me my own potential for love and transcendent wisdom. *If he can be like this, then so can I.* This is not conceit; it is simply recognition of what is possible for all of us. Surrender to the guru means that I have to be true to myself. I have to access the intuitive wisdom at my core, the inner guru, and learn how to let that, and not my ego desires, direct my life. His love gives me the strength to change, while the work of opening to grace is my own. By continuing every day to surrender my self-will, my self-importance, and my entire being to him—who is now alive in me as the inner guru—I come to know his presence, the taste of the Absolute, in all things.

Those who love and revere me,
who surrender all actions to me,
who meditate upon me
with undistracted attention,

whose minds have entered my being—
I come to them all, Arjuna,
and quickly rescue them all
from the ocean of death and birth.

Concentrate every thought
on me alone; with a mind
fully absorbed, one-pointed,
you will live within me, forever.

--Bhagavad Gita, Stephen Mitchell tr.

9

Under The Blanket

OVER THE NEXT DAYS AND WEEKS and months my heart opened more than I could ever have imagined possible. It was miraculous. There was no end to Maharajji's ocean of love. It was not the kind of love we usually experience in life—the kind that comes wrapped in attachment, need, and rejection. Unconditional love wants nothing; it is the most fundamental truth of our being. Carried by the life-breath, this love flows from the Source out of which we are born into the Oneness in which we dissolve.

What an extraordinary time! I was like a parched sponge soaking up the water of life. I could not get enough. Maharajji was playful, intimate, and always at ease, yet filled with enormous power. We westerners hung out with him all morning and afternoon, absorbed in his being, singing kirtan and drinking chai. We called it *the five-limbed yoga*: aimlessly walking about, telling stories of the Beloved, eating, drinking, and letting our love flow into song. This is what lovers do. It is the path of the enjoyment of divine love, bhakti. Dissolving in love like this is the ultimate yoga, leading to final union with the Beloved. Rumi spoke of this state when he sang: "Not until someone dissolves can he or she know what union is."

Maharajji didn't teach like other gurus; in fact, he didn't teach at all. It was simply being with him that transformed us. Our reality was his and he met us there inside our thoughts and emotions. From inside our hearts, he led us into our own depth through a simple gesture, a look, a smile, a frown, a few direct words, and much laughter. There were no speeches, no theology or philosophy, nothing to learn but this love. His love was his teaching. He didn't give us anything that could feed the mind and separate us from the heart. Day by day the ego let go in the exhilarating joy of devotion. Simply to be in the presence of such absolute love changed us completely. It showed us how to live in the perfection of the Now.

As I sat before him day after day, gazing up at him, my mind became still. My eyes and my heart devoured every line in his face, every expression, every one of his movements and sounds. His form, his presence, his every gesture fed my hungry heart, and little by little I lost myself in this love. Years later I saw a young mother gaze at her newborn child, immersed in the unfathomable miracle before her eyes, and I realized that this was the way we had looked at Maharajji, thrilled to no end by the miracle before our eyes. When we weren't with him, we told stories about Maharajji to each other. It was a way to keep the heart open and focused on what was most important. Feasting on love was our yoga, our practice of union. We are doing it to this day.

The days went by in a flow of intense grace. The depth, texture, and degree of this love were simply not known in the world we came from. We had found a piece of heaven on earth. In the timeless space of his presence, my heart filled up and my mind emptied out. I didn't speak his language, and it didn't matter to me at all. Actually, I consider it a blessing that I didn't understand what was being said, as my deep communion with him took place as a wordless union of souls in which I understood everything I needed to know.

> *I am filled with you*
> *Skin, blood, bone, brain, and soul.*
> *There's no room for lack of trust, or trust.*
> *Nothing in this existence but that existence*
> --Rumi, Coleman Barks tr.

It went on like this for many weeks, until one evening, as we all sat together after darshan, someone said, "Wasn't it amazing what Maharajji did today?" And with sudden astonishment, almost shock, it registered in my mind that there were things going on other than this silent absorption. I had been too immersed in loving him to reflect on anything other than our undisturbed union. From that day on, little by little, my mind came back. I didn't fall out of love. No, it was far too late for that. Come what may, I was going to dissolve in this love, because I recognized that nothing less than this is the true state of the soul. And so everything that still stood in the way of my freedom began to rise to the surface: my desires, judgments, and fears.

As the purification of mind and emotions began, my sense of separation, my feelings of jealousy, rejection and anger started to surface again. Maharajji loved me in exactly the same way; I was the one who could not love me. For moments or even unbearable hours, these feelings would separate me from Maharajji and from my own heart. In the presence of such great love, even the smallest disturbance of the heart weighed me down like a profound darkness. At times I would feel completely cut off, abandoned, hopeless, or angry.

VISHNU DIGAMBAR AND RAMGIRI BY MAHARAJJI'S TAKHAT, 1973

In the light of the love that surrounded me, these thoughts and emotions felt incredibly out of place.

Once I was sitting right next to Maharajji with my friend Vishnu Digambar. Baba had not paid any attention to me for maybe two days and my attachment had overwhelmed my unconditional love. It was dreadful. Waves of rejection and jealousy stirred into a mighty tsunami, and I was drowning. Externally, everything seemed so peaceful; here I was sitting at the guru's feet surrounded by my closest friends in the world, yet inside I felt alone and abandoned. And all Maharajji had done was not feed my sense of self-importance for two days!

Vishnu, on the other hand, was receiving all the attention. This plunged me into the bowels of hell. There he sat, his face beaming and his lap full of *prasad*, blessed fruit and sweets that Maharajji would distribute among us, while I had received nothing from the guru's hand. Obviously I was completely unloved and unworthy. There was no hope for me. If I had any sense, I figured, I should just go and kill myself. Suddenly Vishnu, who sat right next to me, took one of the apples Maharajji had tossed into his lap and gave it to me. I had a strange experience: his arm reached through an infinite tunnel that spanned from heaven into the hell of my loneliness. It was as if Vishnu and happiness had been thousands of miles away. Out of that distance of my self-imposed isolation, the apple dropped into my lap and the light went back on in my heart.

> Where there is a great amount of light, any darkness becomes very noticeable.

Where there is a great amount of light, any darkness becomes very noticeable; the shadows seem deeper and darker. Self-realized beings emanate a light of truth that allows us to see our internal obstructions with great clarity. We need to become aware of these dark places before we can become free of them. But no matter what negative thoughts or emotional dramas possessed me, as soon as I was ready to let go of attachment to my most current tragedy, there Maharajji was again, looking at me with that same unwavering love, and I would melt as the walls of my prison dissolved.

By far the most remarkable moments came when Maharajji would look directly into my eyes. These glances were usually short, but they took me completely outside of time. They allowed me to gaze into the presence of absolute love and complete emptiness, like falling into the eyes of God. More than in any other way, it was revealed to me here how the personal and the Absolute coexist, how the eyes of a sage are the gateway into the totality and the fullness of being. It was a direct view into enlightenment, the most intimate encounter with freedom.

My thoughts stopped and my mind came to complete attention. From my small conflicted world, I could look directly into the magnificence of the non-dual Absolute Self. Then I was able to sense in me a very small part of what I saw: absolute bliss, power, and consciousness in infinite space. It was a taste of eternity, of complete presence, a dissolving into Pure Being, beyond all concepts and boundaries. I tasted the absolute intimacy of guru and chela, the vision of oneness. Each time I held his gaze, my individual self died a bit more and the true "I" came to life. It was a blissful death—a letting go of the burden of maintaining this puny individual me with its self-importance and drama. There was no sense of loss, but a taste of infinity, of the immeasurable presence of the Self. In this space there was no longer a difference between individuals, because there were no individuals. There was only pure Being, only God. It was the vision of oneness.

And yet, in this relative world there were two individuals, the lover and the Beloved, and this dance of love between us, the dance of guru and chela. Again, the metaphor of the magnifying glass: All around us is the presence of Universal Love. It is in everything, everywhere, but we cannot feel it, and so we cannot know its absolute preciousness and that it is completely available to us. The guru, the sage, is the magnifying glass that concentrates this cosmic love onto us. In the unwavering gaze of this love, we slowly "heat up," our impurities rise to the surface and go up in smoke. Eventually, when the time is right, we burst into flame. Then we know the light in us and can pass it on.

But I was not yet "ripe," not yet ready to dissolve the "I" in this space, and so the very depth and power of the attraction also scared me. Nevertheless, I kept seeking his gaze. Like a moth circling the candle flame, it was irresistible. The separate "I" could not survive in this state. And even though I wanted this dissolving more and more every day, I wasn't ready for it; I could not yet surrender completely. I thought I needed to hold on to some identity or I wouldn't be able to function. I didn't yet know that the deeper wisdom of the heart, the intuitive mind, could run my life perfectly, and so I still clung to the very source of my suffering—the sense of "I."

Before their oneness is realized, the dance of lovers moves between two poles: the bliss of union and the agony of separation. I would sit in front of Maharajji with my heart wide open, basking in the pure bliss of his presence. Then a stressful thought would arise in my mind, perhaps a judgment, a desire, or self-doubt. As soon as I believed that thought, I had plunged from heaven down into hell, from timelessness into time. Sometimes this descent was so intense that it took my breath away. Then I would look at Maharajji and the clouds would dissolve again. By simply being the love that he was, he woke me up again and again out of these illusions of pain.

I saw clearly how stressful thoughts and emotions ruled much of my life. Any negative impulse would shut down my heart, even while sitting right in front of my guru. It was an intense purification through the ruthless fire of love, which incinerated anything in its way. I wanted my ego-mind turned into pure white ash, held by yogis to be a sacred substance of utmost purity. After anything other than the truth has been burned away, ash is a symbol of what remains of the mind in one who is free. Such a mind does not stand in the way of love; it has merged with the heart.

When the mind has merged into the heart, what's left is oneness—the union of the universal Self, of lover and the divine Beloved. When I was in my right mind, I wanted nothing other than this union. But when the burning was intense, I fell into all the usual reactions: I complained, felt sorry for myself, and made feeble attempts to escape. But whenever I realized how much lighter I felt, I would ask for more burning.

The love, the purification of mind, and the moments of playful teaching continued. Each day followed the next like precious pearls on a string. I had almost forgotten that a world existed outside this Himalayan valley with its sacred chanting, its temples and bells, and this liquid essence of love that melted all defenses and fears. Despite the process of purification, I knew that if there ever was a

Shangri-La, this was it.

Maharajji had become the unshakable core of my world. I looked into his eyes and felt absolute peace. I noticed the way he was present in his body and I understood unlimited power. I saw how he played and joked with us with perfect ease and felt his infinite kindness. I knew about the stream of miracles that routinely happened around him,[1] but it was the love that touched me most deeply.

One day I sat before him, peaceful and deeply absorbed. All of a sudden he roused me out of my contemplation and, with a silent wave of his hand, sent me over to the nearby temple of Durga, the Divine Mother. His simple gesture came with a power that shook me to my soul. I walked the few steps to the temple of the Goddess, sat down and gazed deep into her brilliant eyes. In that silent communion, I realized that the adoration of the feminine aspect of God would be a vital part of my journey. In one moment, one wordless and potent motion, Maharajji had put me under the protection of the divine feminine and given me a focus and source for my worship.

Another day he turned to me and asked, "Who are you?" The question struck me at my core. It was not about my name, my history, my personality; he was asking if I knew my true identity, my Being. I said simply and truthfully, "I don't know, Maharajji." Clearly, I had to find the answer. "Who am I?" is the essential question of *jnana yoga*, the ancient path of self-inquiry[2]. Maharajji inspired deep devotion or *bhakti* in us, the path of loving surrender to God, but he was the master of all yogas. His question pointed me toward the yoga of knowledge and to the integral yoga of HeartSourcing.

TAKING A WALK AROUND THE ASHRAM WITH MAHARAJJI

At yet another time Maharajji opened the floodgates of my heart by showering me with special affection. He praised me and heaped fruits and sweets into my lap. But more than that he gave me a taste of himself, of his state of awareness. The effect was staggering. I felt powerfully charged and completely open, like a flower drinking in the sun. A vast happiness flooded through me and I walked through the valley two feet off the ground. I was in a heaven much more exquisite and thrilling than anything I could have imagined: divine bliss, the realization of freedom, the ability to love the whole world. It didn't cross my mind then, but this experience of boundless bliss was one answer to his question, "Who are you?" We are this bliss.

We *are* supreme happiness. It is our true essence; it is what we exist to discover. This state of pure ecstasy lasted for a few days. I had the sense that Maharajji had granted me a taste of his world, the realm of the *siddhas*, the great enlightened ones who, from time to time, grace our physical world. When we are oppressed by darkness, they come to spread the light of their Being and to show us the ancient pathways to freedom in new ways so we can understand. True Siddhas are very rare in this world. They move effortlessly beyond what we consider to be the immutable laws of creation; what we regard as miracles are the natural ways they express themselves. They appear among us for one reason alone: to lift us up through their compassion. Maharajji, the mahasiddha, granted me as much of a taste of bliss as I could contain. After a few days, I slipped back into my more limited state and began to forget. But I was not going to forget completely! I became even more determined to realize the freedom Maharajji was showing me.

Maharjji was simply love. Through the cleansing effect of his presence, through the inspiration of being with him, he relieved us of a great deal of our burdens, but he did not take them all. Now our most important task is *to love ourselves as he loves us*. A part of me still sits by his takhat today, with a still mind and an open heart, breathing in the rhythm of my Beloved. Timelessness never ends.

10

The Universal Self

TOWARD THE MIDDLE OF AUGUST 1973, the deep space of love we shared became extraordinarily peaceful. All we could think of was spending every minute with Maharajji, drinking the nectar that flowed without bounds from his inexhaustible well. We sat around him, lighthearted, completely open, in a world of bliss. Maharajji had stopped "working" us as he had before, playfully churning up our old pain so it could be set free in the light of his love. Now he was giving us a little taste of the inner state of his being, completely free of all wants and worries. We basked in his presence for many hours every day and sang kirtan. Sometimes he would sing with us, laughing and glowing like a child in bliss, although in an instant his face could change into that of a sage of timeless wisdom and limitless power. The energy in the ashram—this high-powered shakti—was absolutely exhilarating.

I swam in this great ocean of love and drank as much of it as my heart could contain. What I saw in Baba was far beyond what I was able to comprehend. I gave up even trying. I was living through an extraordinary experience and simply let it take me. What was there to do but surrender every part of myself to my beloved?

One day we walked with Maharajji across the courtyard to the Hanuman temple. Hanuman is the symbol of perfect service, humility, devotion, and strength. To express true humility, the story goes: the Divine took on the humble form of a monkey. The untrained mind behaves with the fickle unsteadiness of a monkey, jumping around all the time, but when the divine spirit in us has mastered the mind, it assumes the majestic power of Hanuman. So Hanuman the Monkey God, faith incarnate, teaches us in complete simplicity how to master our lower nature by devotion and selfless service.

His form demonstrates the power that arises from sadhana when pursued with single-minded devotion. As we strolled with Baba toward the temple, I walked next to him. Suddenly, through one of those mind transmissions I would occasionally get, I understood that he wanted me to have a marble plaque engraved with the *Hanuman Chalisa*, a forty-verse hymn to Hanuman, to be put into the wall of the temple. He, who had never asked anything of me, sent me this message clear as day.

A few days later he told us to leave the valley and come back in two weeks. After packing our few belongings, we went for a last darshan. We sat with him for a while as he gave specific instructions to various people, telling some to return to America and others to visit local temples or towns. I had no intention of ever leaving India again. And most importantly, I couldn't imagine missing a single moment when I could be at his feet, so I became as still and "invisible" as I could, hoping he'd ignore me even though I sat right in front of him. After a while the most extraordinary thing happened. As I looked at Maharajji, I saw his human body in cosmic dimensions, beyond form, beyond scale, beyond any possible description. It was as though his body was of infinite size, transparent to eternity, containing vast galaxies of uncounted worlds, a vision far beyond our customary view of reality. It was completely impersonal, vast beyond imagination, and yet the most intimate moment I have ever experienced.

In India there is a description of the Divine as *sat-chit-ananda*. This term divides the One Reality into three aspects: *Sat* means divine Existence, pure Being; *Chit* stands for divine Consciousness; and *Ananda* is divine Bliss. Pure existence, unlimited consciousness, absolute bliss—these words rolled into one, *satchitananda*, is the closest I can come to describing what I saw that day. Mere words fall pitifully short of the awe-inspiring enormity of the experience. What I saw in Maharajji was like looking into the clearest mirror imaginable, the mirror of Being. I had a glimpse of the magnificent scope of who we all truly are. Once more my concept of reality, my ideas about how things are, my map of reality, turned out to be far too small.

I don't know how long my vision lasted; it was timeless and it shook me down to my bones. As soon as it was complete, Maharajji turned to me and tenderly said one single word, *Jao!* Go! Yes, he was sending me away, but he made this single word, Jao, sound like an intimate declaration of love. I got up, trembling and dazed by what

I had just witnessed. I took a few steps and turned a corner. My knees were shaking so badly, I could not go any further—and lo and behold, there was a stool right where I needed it! In all my months in the ashram, I had never seen a single chair or stool. With the exception of Maharajji's *takhats*, everyone sat on the ground. And now, sitting down on that simple three-legged stool, I had another epiphany: everything, everything down to the last and smallest detail of life is directed and orchestrated by the infinite caring of the Universal Mind. It is the dance of the Divine Mother in her infinite manifestation, which have one thing in common: Her absolute love. This stool was not a stool; it was Her caring made manifest. It is the same with all of life. Now it was my task to come to realize the presence of that immense love in all things.

As I waited for my ride on the road, I looked back across the mountain stream to the ashram and saw Maharajji sitting on a low wall by the far side of the bridge—a small figure wrapped in a blanket, the radiant heart of the universe. I stood still, gazing at him, my heart overflowing. Never in a million years would it have entered my mind that this was the last time I would see his physical body.

Finding the Guru Inside

A week later I was walking through the marketplace in a nearby town and a stranger came up to me, visibly upset, waving his arms in the air and yelling, "Maharajji has died! Maharajji has died!" *Oh God*, I thought, *you Indians, the crazy stories you come up with all the time!* How could the core of the universe disappear? Baba was the center of my universe, absolutely rock solid, its heart of hearts. That he could leave his body had never crossed my mind, and therefore it was impossible. I shrugged it off. Five days later the very same scene repeated itself. Another man, in another place, highly upset, waving his arms in the air, "Maharajji has died! Maharajji has died!" This time there was a twinge of pain in my heart. Could it be true? How could it be possible? I was in shock.

AT MAHARAJJI'S FUNERAL PYRE

Two hours later my friends and I caught a train to Brindavan. In the evening we arrived at the ashram; there was a large fire burning in the courtyard. I sat there gazing numbly at the flames, silent and stunned as the fire burned on. I watched as Siddhi Ma, Maharajji's closest devotee, the woman who now holds a large part of his legacy, fell to the ground in front of the fire in a gesture of devotion and total grief. It touched me to the core. Only then someone told me that Maharajji's body had already been burned in those flames. I had been looking at his funeral pyre.

What do you do when the heart of your world has been ripped out? I was disoriented and numb, but still alive, still breathing, still moving around, which was somewhat surprising. It took seventeen years before I was strong enough to feel the extent of my grief. Only then, in an outburst of sorrow that shook the walls, was I able to shed the pain of missing him. At the time, however, I had no idea what to do with my life without Maharajji.

I went back to the mountains, found a cave in the jungles up river from the ashram, and moved in. Here I immersed myself in a new way of life, that of a sadhu. Without intending to, over the last months I had increasingly turned into a wandering monk. Since ancient times these mendicants have roamed the landscape of India, renunciates on their way to God. They live outdoors most of the time without possessions and sustain themselves by receiving alms. The whole of Indian society supports these sadhus so they can devote themselves fully to the quest for enlightenment; in return, the sadhus share with people the wisdom and bliss they have found.

I had not planned on becoming a sadhu; I had only done what seemed natural at the time. My mind was so absorbed in Maharajji that I had to simplify my affairs radically in order to not be distracted. I had given away most of my possessions; all I had left was a shoulder bag and a blanket. As Janis Joplin sang, "Freedom's just another word for nothing left to lose." Of course, I wasn't that free. My mind still held on to countless confusions and judgments, wants and needs, but this simple spiritual lifestyle, close to nature, without the entanglement of possessions, fit me perfectly. My day was pristine simplicity: get up, take a bath in the river, stir the embers of the *dhuni* fire that burned day and night, meditate, do nothing, eat a little, collect some firewood, meditate, breathe, feel one with the jungle, go to sleep. My job was to remember Maharajji, to try to feel him in every part of my being. Such luxury to have all day to do nothing other than to sink into the loving presence of God!

The jungle—my friend, my mother, my protector, my lover—held me in her verdant embrace. Monkeys and other wild things came to visit. The mountain stream had a life of its own that intertwined with my waking and sleeping. And in this great stillness I noticed that Maharajji wasn't gone at all; I simply had to change where I was looking for him. When I turned my attention inside, there he was—a feeling of infinite tenderness, a solid sense of presence and power, and, of course, vast love. The challenge now was to remember him all the time, to live in his internal presence, and to live his love as my own.

> The enlightened ones provide a doorway for us into the intimacy of the true Self.

Perhaps you will have a meditation like that: you sit quietly in the wild jungle of your messy and stressful thoughts and emotions. At first it may seem overwhelming and hostile, but then you notice the dhuni fire that burns in your heart of hearts all the time. It warms you and gives you shelter. And as you focus on it over time, the jungle becomes peaceful. What appeared hostile turns out to be not more than a dream and you are waking up.

On the day he died, Maharajji said, "I am leaving Central Jail." Yes, Maharajji's body was gone from the physical plane. But while his body had vanished, where could he go? Since he had transcended the limiting prison of identification with body, ego, and mind, he lived in oneness with Source. He was satchitananda. He was fully aware that he was—and is—not a body, but the vast field of consciousness in which all creation appears and passes away. Is there a place where unlimited consciousness is not? Every day it became increasingly more obvious to me that only his body had disappeared, while Maharajji himself continued to be amazingly present.

I had learned first hand from Maharajji that the vastness of the Universal Self can also be extraordinarily personal. The enlightened ones provide a doorway for us into the intimacy of the true Self. They give a human face to the infinite, and their hearts are interested in our particular plight. They show us by their example how we can live in the blissful meeting place of emptiness and form, of vision and heart, of God and Goddess, and how we can dance in the dream of this world while fully awake.

Maharajji laid down his body like an old blanket that had done its duty, but He, the Essence of Being, personal and impersonal at the same time, is always present in the deepest place of the heart and in all things. Although we can no longer locate him in a body somewhere outside of us, he is here and can touch us, like all enlightened masters of the past, as awareness and love. In my heart, he is still sitting there, by the bridge over the mountain stream, a small figure radiating his immense blessing into the universe.

MAHARAJJII SITTING BY THE BRIDGE

11

Devotion

DEVOTION IS THE DEVELOPMENT OF THE living intelligence of the heart. It enables us to penetrate the confusing multiplicity of life and distill from it what really matters, our awakening, the discovery of our identity with the absolute Self.

There are two aspects to the supreme intelligence of the heart: the pure bliss of limitless universal love and intuitive intelligence, the wisdom mind. Both originate not from the ego-mind but from the Self. They are the expression of Universal Consciousness, satchitananda, in this world. Every human being has the capacity to experience the supreme gift: the purity of the heart.

> Devotion is the development of the living intelligence of the heart.

Purity of the heart is the highest form of intelligence.

The innermost nucleus of our being is always immaculate in its purity. It means that the heart itself, our deepest identity, is always pure. The question is whether we know that and have access to it. If not, then it is the unruly mind that needs to be purified. It is the confusion and turmoil of the mind and its sense of separation from God, that the Western traditions mean when they speak of "original sin." This confusion is real enough for all of us, but interior to it, in what is known as the *Cave of the Heart*, the core of each being, absolute, timeless purity reigns. The cave of the Heart is the seat of the Self. It is a nonlocal reality, free of the presence or absence of objects. To abide in the cave of the Heart is enlightenment, the realization of Oneness. It enables us to drink continuously from the unlimited well of pure love and to share its abundance freely.

Devotion is of two primary types, with form and without form. In both of these manifestations, devotion is essential for the path. *Formless devotion* is pure dedication to an abstract ideal, like truth, liberation, higher knowledge, wisdom, or enlightenment. It is to follow the attraction of such a conceptual goal with intensity and express devotion to it through commitment to spiritual practice. I see great devotion for instance in the practice of Zen Buddhism with its profound dedication the realization of formless truth. To sit in zazen meditation for days, weeks, even years, as many practitioners do, takes formidable commitment and great strength of heart. Such devotion is evident in everyone who is dedicated to a sustained and focused spiritual path.

Devotion with form orients itself toward a fully realized being—a form of God, a deity, a saint, a guru or sage—as a focal point with the aim to merge our individual consciousness with Consciousness itself, by merging with the all-encompassing awareness of the object of our devotion. This is how our mistaken identity disappears into oneness with all things through the yoga of the heart.

This type of devotion has been likened to a relationship with a being in whose heart the love of God is burning brightly. To be in the presence of such a being is like placing a freshly cut, green log next to one that is fully ablaze. Give it some time and both logs will be on fire with the love of God. This is the power of satsang, of spiritual association, which enables the transmission of the devotional sentiment. For this practice you do not need to be in the physical presence of your Beloved. The inner relationship is all important. This love transcends the limits of time and space.

> Our mistaken identity disappears into oneness with all things through the yoga of the heart.

Awakening by association occurs through the transmission of love, the merging of the heart-mind of the lover and the Beloved. Nothing can dim that love because it is the reality of the soul; its light is brilliant in those who are *consciously one with the Source*. Being in relationship with them in any way possible is an invaluable gift.

As long as we cannot yet detect the light in us, we can see it in the face of the Beloved. Opening to the Beloved brings us into relationship with the great love that is dormant in us. The ancient way of the heart empowers us to overcome negative impulses based on fear. The opening of the heart turns our attention away from all the distractions that keep us in bondage. Such devotion brings more blessings than one could ever imagine.

Perhaps the simplest practice to create a connection between the soul and God is the use of a mantra. Mantras are sacred words or simple, short phrases that have a special power to clear the mind and open the heart. Repeated silently, in a low voice or in song, a mantra brings our thought waves into a single, harmonious focus that nurtures devotion.

Lord Jesus Christ, have mercy on me—was repeated by pilgrims for centuries on their long travels, mile after mile, day after day, month after month. Mantras are known to all religions. They are verbal formulas for the adoration of God, for protection, and for the transcendence of the lower self. They are a lifeline that can save us from drowning in a world that knows little of the higher aspiration of spirituality. With each repetition, we give ourselves a precious gift that the world cannot give us and which no one can ever take from us.

In all parts of the world there are sacred places where a tradition of devotion has been cultivated for a long time. When I lived in Brindavan before meeting Maharajji, two hermits took my American friend Shyamdas and me into their hearts and under their wings. We knew nothing of their ancient traditions, but our hearts were open and hungry. These two old men took us to their favorite places that hardly any westerners had ever seen—temples and towns that had lived in a continuous celebration of Krishna for centuries. They introduced us to the "inner technology" of devotional love, helping us understand that the heart can be developed, just as the mind can learn and the body be trained.

Awakening by association occurs through the transmission of love.

One of the first things that struck me was the way they spoke of being a servant. To my great astonishment, it appeared to be something they aspired to. This sounded crazy to me at first. *What is wrong with these people?* In the way I was raised, being a servant was demeaning and low-class, the very last thing you wanted to be. But when these two old hermits spoke of being a servant, their eyes filled with light and their love of God was more palpable than ever. They showed me what a blessing it is to be able to serve God in all beings. They spoke of the way Krishna taught *karma yoga*, the way of selfless action in the *Bhagavad Gita*, and slowly I came to know that being a true servant is an enormous accomplishment, a way to make all our actions in this world sacred and elevating.

What touched me the most in those days was the spirit of the people we met in these holy places. Almost everyone around us was deeply immersed in loving God, and their God was a lover. Krishna, as he is worshipped in Brindavan, is the pure archetype of the Beloved. This *avatar* inspires passionate love along an ecstatic and sublime path to the divine. I saw old men shamelessly crying in their love for Krishna, aware that their tears were pure bliss. Groups of women walked to the temples singing with voices of such powerful purity that my hair stood on end. An old blind beggar walked by my window every morning singing Krishna's praise with such power that the walls shook. These extraordinary people awakened in me an irresistible yearning that had to be stilled.

The Forms of God

Maharajji said, "The best way to worship God is every way." We find devotion equally in the dance of the Sufis, the stirring psalms of the Jews, the powerful ceremonies of indigenous peoples, the sacraments of the Christians, and the meditative stillness of Buddhists. It is present in the pursuit of truth through the mind. It celebrates love and wisdom in all forms and all places, for everything is part of the One. The many forms of deities and God-realized beings are windows into that oneness. Devotion to them dissolves our limitations and blindness.

A moment of such realization is described in the tradition of Krishna. One of his lovers, a *gopi*, comes to the river to fill a pitcher with water. As she is going about this mundane task, her mind is filled with her love and yearning for Krishna. She hasn't seen him in days and her heart aches for his touch. *Where is my Beloved? Why does he hide from me?* As she lifts the water jug to the top of her head and begins to walk home, suddenly she sees her Beloved everywhere—in each leaf of the trees, in the birds that sing in the branches, in the clouds in the sky, in the earth under her feet, and in every person she meets. How can she ever feel that He is absent when He is in all things?

Another story tells of the different levels of understanding that co-exist at the same time. Hanuman is the great devotee of the divine incarnation of Sri Rama, the hero of the *Ramayana*, one of the most beloved Hindu epics. In one point of the story Lord Rama asks Hanuman, "How do you see me?" And Hanuman responds, "On the physical level, when I identify with this body, You are my Master and I am Your servant. At the level of deeper insight, I know myself to be a spark of your Divine Self, a reflection of your light. And at the level of truth, I know that You and I are one and the same."

> The Universal Mother is the oneness of life itself, a doorway into the awakened state.

There was a point early on in my life when I could no longer deal with what I called "the God business." Bewildered by what I experienced as irrational, conflicting, or even heartless religious teachings, the irreconcilable aspects of religion became so intolerable to me that I simply closed myself off to the whole thing. I lived without God for a while and He, She, or It didn't seem to mind. Instead of seeking God, I sought freedom and truth and peace. This was the formless type of devotion; I worked on elevating my consciousness. These concepts were clean and value neutral. They freed me from the burden of my misgivings and my confusion about religion.

I was drawn to study Tibetan Buddhism. The Buddhist teachings do not use the concept of God, which made Buddhism attractive to me. What confused me at first is that Tibetans have a vast pantheon of colorful deities. Then I learned that these deities represented *symbolic aspects of the enlightened mind.* This caught my attention and helped build a bridge for my understanding.

The deities aren't gods up in heaven who control life with fire and brimstone. They are but personifications of attributes of the ultimate nature of my own consciousness—qualities such as completeness, wisdom, insight into emptiness, equanimity, unlimited power, compassion, and unconditional love. That's why they are not foreign and aloof, but intimate, compassionate, whole, and exciting. Encountering the deities allowed my studies to go beyond mere mental understanding to become a real and full-bodied experience.

The masters are part of us, found in the innermost place in the heart.

In India there are even more forms of the divine—all representatives of aspects of the one absolute Self, the one ultimate Truth, the one and only God—an enormous expression of the vast generosity of the Indian mind. As soon as I arrived there, I began to have spontaneous visions of the Hindu deities. Like so many facets of light emitted by the infinite diamond of the Self, these deities are aspects of the enlightened heart-mind in all of us and are completely alive. If we open to this supreme psychology of the higher mind, the deities can interact with us (with our everyday ego-bound consciousness) in grace-filled ways.

When consciousness merges through devotion with a deity such as Shiva,[1] the Lord of the yogis, we discover that Shiva is much more than a form. He is a path to enlightenment, and the Unified Mind itself, *brahman*, our own enlightened awareness. Shiva is the ideal yogi, and manifests in us as our highest ideal. Devotion allows our consciousness to gradually merge with the essence of the deity, the essence of the enlightened heart-mind.

At one point I stayed in Haridwar, a town at the foot of the Himalayas where the sacred river Ganges flows into the plains. Marble steps lead down into the swiftly flowing current and all day pilgrims bathe and pray in the holy waters. In the evening, a large crowd gathered for a ceremony called *arti*, honoring Ganga Devi, the Goddess of the river. I stood in the crowd and noticed the feeling was intimate, permeated by tenderness and devotion as all these souls merged into prayer. Ganga Devi is a motherly, nurturing presence who manifests in multiple ways. On the physical plane, she is the Ganges River that fertilizes and waters the fields and so feeds the people. In the divine realm, she is a goddess of magnificent beauty, who possesses such absolute purity that she can absorb and dissolve the impurities (or "sins") of the world; when pilgrims come to bathe in the river, they seek to awaken this purity within themselves. In the night sky, we can admire her beauty as the Milky Way, the "river of milk." In the human realm, she manifests as pure vitality and as the liquid flow of grace that connects us with each other and allows us to feel our fundamental oneness. In mystical reality she represents the union of wisdom and devotion in us. And finally, as one of the many forms of the Universal Mother, she is the oneness of life itself, a doorway into the awakened state.

> When our mind is clear, when we have cleansed the mirror of our heart, our love will be constant.

About forty yards from me a priest waved flames over the river waters while about three hundred devotees sang an ancient hymn honoring the Goddess. The atmosphere was tender and deep and drenched in devotion. Suddenly, as I swayed along with the song, the image of a resplendent female figure appeared in my mind like a flash of lightning. I don't know how I knew this was Ganga Devi, but there she was, brilliant, dazzling, unmistakable. The vision ceased as quickly as it had appeared, but it left an after-image on my mind and a profound imprint on my heart that has continued unabated for almost four decades now.

The same awareness of divinity manifesting in form exists in most traditions. Those who are open to direct mystical experience can intimately encounter their Beloved in the here and now. *"Where two or three come together in my name, there am I with them"²* is not a figure of speech, it is literally true. The masters and higher beings come to uplift us. They are part of us, found in the innermost place in the heart.

The Beloved

True devotion is fervent dedication to all forms of the divine. Such love is all-encompassing, transcendent and present everywhere at all times. It is the true state of our hearts. Like looking into a clear mirror, we can see our own expanded state of Being first in the external Beloved. And when, through extended practice, we experience this love fully blossoming in our hearts, we know ourselves fully. With that devotion has found its fulfillment.

My Beloved is Maharajji, and my love for him continues to open me more and more. I can experience him in two ways: as a human being and as the all-encompassing, sublime presence of love and awareness itself. The guru is the spark. I am the tinder. *Let my heart burn in its devotion to him until all my separateness and confusion are consumed and all that remains is the oneness of love.* This is *Guru Yoga*, a way to merge with the enlightened mind and heart of the master. This practice has two aspects:

- To fall ever more deeply in love with the guru—until the chela's true identity is revealed in the union of the heart essence of guru and chela.
- To systematically remove the obstacles that stands in the way of love— negative emotions, stress-producing thoughts and the fundamental ignorance of the ego of suffering.

At first the Beloved may seem distant, someone we think of every so often, but soon our love grows stronger. As the desire arises to be more connected to the Beloved, we discover that he or she is a trickster who plays a game of hide-and-seek. We fall in love and taste of the bliss of union, but then the mind interferes and it seems as if he hides from us again. This repeats many times and it is maddening. Why can't we capture his essence and hold him prisoner in our heart? Why is he so elusive? Why do we fall back

> We are awakening together.

again and again into delusion and separation? Slowly it dawns on us that our struggles and our longing for union—even while we are seemingly separated—is also a form of love. The bliss of union and the ache of seeking the Beloved again are both expressions of love. The opposite of that love is not separation, but forgetfulness and indifference, one of the greatest poisons we know.

When our mind is clear, when we have cleansed the mirror of our heart, our love will be constant. Then we will no longer get distracted from love. The fabric of life becomes transparent and reveals the presence of the Beloved in all situations. As our heart matures, we see that he or she is not limited to one body, one being. We discover this presence everywhere and in all beings and things. This is the goal of devotion, to live in permanent union with the Beloved, who turns out to be everything. The Beloved is the guru, the Beloved is every being, and most intimately, the Beloved is what we are.

Lost in Love

One time one of us asked Baba how we should meditate. It was obvious that Maharajji knew the secret to liberation and we were ready to do whatever he said. Whether it was sleeping on a bed of nails, watching our breath turn into icicles in a Himalayan cave, or standing on one leg in an icy stream, repeating a thousand-syllable mantra for fifty years—whatever it was, we were ready.

He said, "Meditate like Jesus."

Meditate like Jesus?! We were stunned. What did that mean? How did Jesus meditate? That had to be the secret of secrets! So we asked, "Maharajji, how did Jesus meditate?" He closed his eyes. Everything became extremely still, as though the whole world had stopped. In that complete stillness a tear flowed down his cheek. We had never seen him like this. We waited breathlessly. Then he opened his eyes and said, *"He lost himself in love!"*

> Everything that increases our love is welcome. An open heart knows no barriers.

No specific practice, no great heroic feat that we could set out to achieve. "He lost himself in love."

How can we lose ourselves in love? By drinking deeply from the well of the heart, by feeling our way into our depth. By yearning for the Beloved, the Self, with every part of our being. By being persistent. By removing the obstacles of anger, fear and depression. By becoming less and less distracted. By filling the empty spaces within. By seeing the Beloved increasingly in all beings everywhere. By realizing that all the pain of the world has only one purpose: to point us back to the heart, to the Source, to the healing and the wholeness within, and then allowing this fullness to flow out from us into the world. This is the purpose of the relationship with the Beloved. This is the purpose of being alive.

In this love for God we can appear slightly mad to the world; we may not be understood. When the wonderful "madness" for the divine takes hold of us, the rational mind takes a back seat to the heart. Those who have been infected by this love will follow their path against all the well-meant advice of the world. They have an inner knowing they must follow, sometimes blindly trusting in guidance, at other times with keen determination. Those who are "suffering" from that same madness will understand. Many of us have caught the "disease" of devotion: housewives and engineers, bus drivers and grocery clerks, doctors and servants of all kinds—all mystics in everyday life and seekers after the truth in our own right. We are awakening together.

Love for God in any form is the most powerful transformative force in human experience. Some fall in love and instantly gain a life-long relationship with the Beloved; for others, the experience is more gradual. One of my German friends arrived in Maharajji's presence and saw nothing but an "old man in a blanket." She felt nothing special about him and thought he had to be some kind of charlatan. She got very upset, thinking, "I have been duped. This is what I have come halfway around the world to see?" She wanted to leave instantly, but she couldn't get a ride out of the mountains that evening. As she was going to sleep, she noticed a tiny, almost imperceptible twinge in her heart. It meant nothing to her. Somehow, circumstances didn't allow her to leave the next day either, and that night there was another twinge, still tiny, but a little more noticeable. And so it went, day after day, until she had fallen completely in love with that old man in a blanket. This love has remained the single focal point of her life.

Everything that increases our love is welcome. An open heart knows no barriers. "The best way to worship God is every way," Maharajji said.[3] There is no need to switch religions. Invoking the Beloved in any form opens us to the blessings of all enlightened beings— past, present and future—for they are one. And while we know this love to be universal, it's also completely personal and intimate. To know this kind of love is an incredible gift.

The Beloved is the mirror image of our inner truth, the light within us that dispels darkness, the place inside to which all the great teachers have endeavored to guide us. And while love never forces itself, it does want to be known, fully and completely. It waits for us to wake up and pay attention to what really matters. It waits for us until we are ready to lose ourselves in love.

12

From Molehill To Mountain

Aﬀter Maharajji's passing, I lived in the soft embrace of the jungle. Every day in this silence and peace untangled the knots of my confused heart a bit more. Maharajji came to me in many ways, helping me to understand that he was not gone at all. His presence in me was so strong that very often I could feel him unmistakably inside my body, inside my heart. He came to me through dreams and visions, or appeared as a vivid presence I could feel all around me, powerful and instantly recognizable, always helping me to reconnect with his love and guiding me to new levels of understanding. I realized that he could show up anywhere, at any time, to anyone, and so I continued to experience him in the present tense. And being a consummate trickster, he could take any form—a beggar in the street, a man on the bus, an unexpected guest, even an animal. Sometimes I would know him when he appeared in such a form; more often I would realize who it was only later on.

One of his Indian devotees said it this way: "Maharajji was actually the biggest saint. He had done all the yogic austerities… The true devotees of God never wear saffron[1], carry malas (prayer beads), or put on sandalwood. You can't know them unless they want it, and then you can only know them as much as they allow."[2]

Often, when I looked at a picture of Maharajji, he would appear in the image. There is a distinct difference between looking at a picture of a face and having those eyes actively look back at you. His eyes would come alive and sometimes his facial expressions would change as he communicated with me in this silent way. To communicate directly with the Beloved through pictures or statues is one of the skills of advanced devotional practice.

As I lived in my cave, I kept a small picture of Baba with me. One day, as had happened many times before, the picture came alive and we met in the silent communion of the deep heart. Then something new occurred: his face in the picture changed into the face of another person, and then another, and another. First slowly and then faster and faster, face after face looked directly at me—men and women and children, old and young, of all races and times—a mighty stream of humanity flowing through this small picture frame[3]. I saw hundreds of faces in what seemed like a few minutes. Then the flow of images slowed until it stopped on the final face: Maharajji had turned into . . . *Hitler!* I panicked. Hitler! This was the face of absolute evil to me. What was it doing in Maharajji's picture?

And then I realized it: while he was still in his body, one of the sayings we had bantered about among ourselves was *"Maharajji is everything!"* We said it as though we really knew what we were saying. Well, now I was being shown just how true it was, and it hit me like a lightning bolt.

This epiphany contained three very important insights. The first was that Maharajji's being is not confined to the person I had come to know and to love. He was the old man in the blanket, yes, and at the same time he is a transcendent state of awareness that is not limited to the confines of a particular body. Everything is included in this awareness. During the time I spent in his presence, this had become clear to me beyond any doubt. Enlightened beings have realized their oneness with the universal Self (*Brahman*). They are no longer identified with the limitations of a body and personality, but with that limitless ocean of being out of which everything arises, every moment anew. All beings, and the inanimate world as well, are part of this field of transcendent and everpresent awareness, the Self. It shines as the light of God. Again and again creation arises, is sustained, and then dissolves in this field. This field, this primary awareness, is what we all are. And all manifestations of darkness, including Hitler, are contained in that light.

> Only by skillfully facing our fears can we become fearless.

The second insight was the realization of how powerless darkness is in the presence of Light. Yes, it can appear to rule the world for a while, but darkness and the absence of love are merely a fleeting dream that is always dispelled as soon as the Light of truth shines again. Picture an ancient Egyptian tomb that has been sealed in absolute darkness for 5,000 years. Open one crack in the door, or light a match. What happens to the darkness of thousands of years? It is instantly gone! The primary reality is the Light of consciousness. This consciousness is the satguru. It is everywhere and we can see it once we have developed eyes that can see, the eyes of the soul. Then we see it as what we are.

The third insight triggered a profound release of some of my deepest fears. If I knew anything at all in this world, it was the reality of Maharajji's love. I remembered the three-legged stool on which I sat after the vision of the Universal Self. What complete attention this loving consciousness has, even for my smallest human needs! It encompasses all of creation, with its vast beauty and its confounding darkness. Everything that life brings comes out of this Source. Now

I understood that the guru's vast being and unlimited love surpass everything I had feared, and I knew I was safe in this world.

At first I perceived this sense of safety as though it came from outside. I felt lost and had the extremely good fortune to be able to attach myself to a great being, to Maharajji. Being with him awakened my own higher potential. Then he did what gurus do: he removed his form and with that the focus of my attachments. Now I had to find that safety in me. I had to realize this vast love in my own heart and stand in it firmly. This is done by skillfully handling our fears and recognizing them as the pathway to freedom. It is the journey through darkness into the light. At every step of the journey the guru is present, at first for some as an external guide, and then increasingly as the inner essence, the consciousness in the cave of the Heart.

Only by skillfully facing our fears can we become fearless. The cycles, the hills and valleys, continue. As we pass through them, the inner presence, the Self, the source of bliss, becomes increasingly known. We progress to the extent we are willing to no longer run away from our fears, our stressful emotions and thoughts. Can we stop to hide from what is here to show us the way? Even the greatest challenges exist for only one purpose: to guide us to our freedom.

Mountain of God

Maharajji had given me a new name, Ramgiri, which means "Mountain of God." Although I usually felt more like a molehill, that name gave me a hint of what I could be. The Giris are part of the ancient order of Swamis, founded in the 9th century by the great saint Shankaracharya.[4] Most of the Giris are ascetics, wild and earthy, living outside in the jungles and hills, trusting the universe to supply their needs, and given completely to their quest for God realization. How did I, this perplexed kid from Germany, end up with a name like that?

When Maharajji gave a spiritual name to someone, it was an act of great substance. Along with the new name came a new spiritual identity, a specific way to travel the path and to serve. It is the principle of *namarupa*—*nama*, the name, describing the spiritual essence, and *rupa*, the form this essence takes. Receiving a new name symbolizes a second birth into the spiritual realm. The name is a sign of the guru's protection and connects you to the essence or lineage of the guru. If it is developed, the power of such an initiation can grow from lifetime to lifetime until liberation.

Soon after my experience with Maharajji's picture, it became cold in the mountains, so I went down to the plains and began to travel the Indian countryside, moving from one holy place to another. I slept outside under the stars, people fed me, and I was cared for by the softness and abundance of spiritual India. Western travelers are often appalled by the poverty, pollution, and noise they encounter in India. But look deeper and you will see that within the physical landscape of India there is a living land of the Spirit. I met saints and holy beings of amazing realization, their eyes brimming with light. Just as impressive was the devotion and love of so many ordinary people. Almost daily I came across exquisite temples and sacred places of all kinds. India is full of such sanctuaries that hold the life blood of the country. The life of a sadhu is simple and it was good for me. Being supported so fully in my quest for liberation freed me from worldly cares and allowed me to focus inward, to begin to realize in myself some of the depth of being I had tasted in Maharajji.

In the winter of 1974 I was again in Haridwar to attend a huge spiritual festival, the *Kumbha Mela*[5], which is held every twelve years. Everyone was there—gnarly yogis who left their mountain caves only for this event; sects of all kinds that erected tents and blared their sacred music over scratchy loudspeakers; naked sadhus, the Nagas, smeared in ash; swamis in all shades of orange and red; and a vast sea of pilgrims. A few of us Western sadhus stayed in a nearby forest.

RAM GIRI, 1974

Maharajji had given three of us the name Giri—Hanuman Giri from Holland, Shambu Giri from Canada, and me. Purana Giri, an older Indian sadhu with long matted hair and weather-beaten skin, had set up his camp close by under the trees. He was tough and skinny from living a life of spiritual austerities in the jungle. In every one of his movements, looks, and words I could sense that he was completely committed to this life of self-realization. Since Maharajji, who was universally known and respected as a realized saint of the highest kind, had given us our names, Purana Giri offered to initiate the three of us into the order of Giris.

The initiation in the jungle was simple and carried an ancient power. We were sent off to take a purifying bath in the Ganges, only a few steps from our camp. Then Purana Giri performed a short ceremony, fed us, gave us the orange cloth as a sign of renunciation, and whispered the secret mantra into our ears. During the ceremony, my perception opened up, all sense of separation dissolved, and the world was one seamless whole, without delusion and fear. The experience lingered on in the jungle night. Even though I was still just a neurotic kid from the West who took himself much too seriously, I had now become a conduit of the ancient path of Shiva, the ultimate yogi. It was good to be welcomed into the company of this noble lineage, stretching back to antiquity, and to benefit from the power and inspiration such association brings.

I had now become an initiate into the traditions of Shiva, Ram, and Krishna as well as the path of the Divine Mother; it was my task to unite them with my Western legacy.

The Parting Gift

As I continued to roam around India, I occasionally didn't feel well. I would get fevers and pains but ignored them. Finally they became so persistent that I went to see the best physician I could find in New Delhi. He saw my orange robes and matted hair, the entire holy man get-up, and he must have realized that he had to be really straight with me so I would listen. He told me I had cancer and that I would die if I didn't return to the West for treatment, because there wasn't a way to treat this particular kind of cancer in India. In fact, as I later found out, this was a deadly cancer and there was no treatment for it anywhere.

I was 23 years old and the thought of dying soon had never occurred to me. I walked around in a daze for two days, fearing for my life. Then, and I remember this very distinctly, I stood in front of a Hanuman temple in the middle of Delhi and heard a voice ring out loud and clear in my mind: *"He loved you so much; this will not be wasted!"* I had never heard such a voice. It spoke with absolute authority and it could not be doubted. Instantly all my fear was gone and it never came back. I knew right then with complete certitude that I was not going to die from this illness. Clearly, Maharajji's love was not going to be wasted. And as I realized that my life had just been handed back to me, the very next thought that arose was a fervent prayer that some day I might be able to share with others the magnificent gifts of this love. This has remained the deepest motivation of my life. HeartSourcing is its manifestation, the way this love can awaken us from within.

> HeartSourcing is the way love can awaken us from within.

The fear of dying was gone, but the symptoms were still there. Larry Brilliant, a physician in our satsang, examined me and came to the same conclusion: I had cancer. To be certain, he took me to see another specialist. The diagnosis was the same. Although I had been determined to live out my life as a sadhu in India, I now had no choice but to go back to the West. It was like the old joke: How do you make God laugh? Tell him your plans.

Larry bought me an airplane ticket to Munich, but before I left I had to complete the task Maharajji had given me. I sent a marble slab engraved with the Hanuman Chalisa up to the mountains where it was immediately installed in the temple at Kainchi. When I arrived in Munich, physicians performed a biopsy. Then they stood around my hospital bed for two weeks, scratching their heads. My symptoms were gone and they couldn't find any cancer. Finally they let me go—one of those cases of an unexplainable disappearance of a disease. It was only later that I found out that Maharajji had very often used the Hanuman Chalisa[6] to effect healing. He had known that I would have this disease, and had set the stage for my healing before he died.

Every moment of my life is his gift.

THE THIRD SKILL:
EMOTIONAL HARMONY

13

Spiritual Community

Back in Germany and no longer ill, it dawned on me that I was meant to live in the West. Apparently I was supposed to face what I feared rather than run away from it. I experienced it as a terrible bummer. The experience of Maharajji's love was enshrined in my heart, a treasure beyond all treasures, but despite that peaceful and loving presence inside, I was still conflicted, confused, and easily angered. The ocean was deep, but there was much turbulence on the surface. I wanted nothing more than to share this deep love, but I was not at all ready to do so. I spoke to many people about my experience with Maharajji, about this amazing love, but nobody could hear me. After I uttered two sentences, their eyes would glaze over and they stopped listening. What I told them was beyond their experience and imagination.

I felt like a stranger in a strange land. I meditated a lot to maintain some level of clarity and continued my devotional practice to keep my heart open, but I felt stifled by the materialism around me. And as the visions and dreams I had of Maharajji diminished, I missed him more than I could say. After several months of this kind of alienation, I was drowning, gasping for spiritual air, for the great loving support I had known at the feet of my guru, for satsang, the living community of devotees. I had no one to talk to about what was most important to me.

During all stages of the spiritual path, the support, encouragement, and protection of satsang are of crucial importance for maintaining *sadhana* and a connection to the Beloved. When we are spiritually young, we are like a seedling just poking its first tender leaves up out of the forest floor. This new life is easily destroyed. We need a fence around us for protection. Satsang is that fence. Later, when this little tree has grown into a large oak, the fence is no longer needed. We can stand alone and are able to offer protection to others. Had I been surrounded by satsang, I could have avoided much of my pain.

A short while later I heard that His Holiness the 16th Karmapa, the great Tibetan teacher, was coming to Europe. I had studied Tibetan Buddhism and met some extraordinary lamas. I was not going to miss the opportunity to be in the Karmapa's presence. I went to Copenhagen, spent several days with him there and then traveled around Europe as part of his small entourage. He seemed as solid and as deep as Maharajji. At one point we were in a retreat center close to Hamburg where His Holiness performed an ancient Tibetan ritual known as the Black Crown Ceremony.[1] Afterwards, our little group traveled into the center of town to go shopping. As I stood outside a department store waiting for our bus, with people milling around on all sides, suddenly I saw His Holiness walking through the crowd toward me; he was absolutely present, a Buddha totally at peace with himself.

Two things struck me immediately. First, nobody noticed him! Here was a heavy-set Tibetan monk in maroon robes and a shaved head, who in those days looked extremely out of place in a German shopping mall, yet he appeared to be completely invisible to the crowd of people. No one stared; no one even noticed him. Secondly I was struck by the stunning difference between the crowd and His Holiness. While he was completely present and free, everyone else appeared glued to the physical environment. They were preoccupied, their attention was tied into the displays in the store windows, tethered to the material plane by desires, worries, and tensions. In the presence of this completely free being, their lack of freedom became visible like a physical substance. No matter how autonomous they imagined themselves to be, they were clearly not at all free. I saw them as "hungry ghosts," seeking to fulfill their hunger through material things, which of course can never lead to fulfillment.

> We cannot choose what we have become, but we can choose what we will be.

I watched all this as I stood by the side of the road waiting for our bus. When the Karmapa came up to me, he looked at me and asked with a twinkle, "No bus?" As I answered him, I suddenly *saw* myself. Next to his absolute freedom and the solidity of his being, I was a tall, lanky kid, full of attachments, and bound to the physical world just like the people around me. I too was a hungry ghost, but my hunger had turned in the direction of freedom. It was startling to see myself this way. His Holiness showed me that enlightenment can be lived not only in Indian ashrams or Tibetan shrine rooms, but also in the complex, noisy, distracting environment of the West. It was profoundly encouraging.

We cannot choose what we have become, but we can choose what we will be.

Soon I was again by myself, trying to survive as best I could and not doing a very good job of maintaining access to the clear air of the spirit. I had moved to Heidelberg and held a marginal job teaching meditation and kirtan that kept me in the city during the week.

Every weekend I escaped the nervous energy of downtown and took refuge in a Benedictine monastery. The kind-hearted monks gave me a cell and fed me, and I sat still all weekend, repeating my mantra. The sacred words of the mantra were my lifeline, like a snorkel that brought me just enough air from the higher realms so I wouldn't suffocate. I deperately needed this spiritual nourishment of the love I had known in India, and I had to fight for it, as I had yet to find the source of this nourishment within myself.

The Goddess with the Mouth of a Sailor

One morning I received a postcard from a friend in New York. On the back was a photograph of her spiritual teacher, a woman named Joya. I looked at her picture and immediately realized that Joya was definitely not my cup of tea. Without a doubt she was the least likely candidate for a spiritual teacher I could imagine. I was yearning to return to the simplicity of the warm heart of India; instead, here was a 30ish woman from Brooklyn, eyes rimmed with heavy black mascara and gold jewelry dripping from wherever she could hang it. Maharajji had warned us not to get entangled in worldliness, which he playfully called "women and gold." Well, here I was looking at both and I intended to heed his warning.

I had heard stories about Joya. She was a Jewish housewife from Brooklyn who had had a powerful vision of Jesus that set in motion a great inner transformation. Soon she was having ongoing visions of Sri Ramana Maharshi, Sai Baba of Shirdi, and most often Baba Nityananda of Ganeshpuri—all *avadhutas*, Indian saints of the highest caliber. After about a year of this, Maharajji appeared to her and she recognized him as her guru, her deepest heart connection. Soon after that people began to gather around her and she began to teach in her own unconventional style. Many of my friends, including Ram Dass, said that Maharajji was alive in her. I was not impressed. I wanted Maharajji and the peace of India, not some gaudy, overweight housewife from Brooklyn. I put the postcard down and went about my business. That evening, just for the heck of it, I took another look at the picture . . . and to my amazement her eyes turned into Baba's eyes. There he was, completely present, fully alive and filled with love. Maharajji was looking at me through her false eyelashes! Damn! He sure is a trickster. And there was nothing else to do but to pack my bags and go to New York.

My first day in Brooklyn was a shock. Still jetlagged, I was thrown into a bizarre world with a soundtrack of wailing sirens and the relentless thundering of an elevated subway train that passed right in front of the window. I sat on the floor of a large living room full of people packed together like sardines in a can. There was a garish red velvet throne on the far end of the room, a huge leap from my simple cave in the jungle. What in the world was I doing here?

Many of my old friends from India were here. It was a relief to be with satsang again. Singing kirtan we waited in the cramped heat for a long time until someone yelled, "Make a path!" Everyone exhaled and crunched together even more tightly. Then the Temptations' hit song "My Girl" erupted, obviously on cue. With the song in full swing, an apparition entered the room: long flowing black hair trailing behind her, gold flashing in all directions, and a double set of false eyelashes weighing down her eyelids. This complete exaggeration of a woman came striding down the path to the throne, laughing and screeching in a shrill voice. Before I had time to shiver, and much to my surprise, I noticed that despite the loud drama and her brassy appearance, so tasteless to my snooty European sensibilities, *there was nobody home!* Damn again! In a flash I had a vision of the internal reality inside the person named Joya: a great inner stillness and an enormous heart. And she was having a lot of fun. I was thunderstruck!

Here was the play of *persona* or "mask" in its full glory. Personality is merely the packaging, the particular way a soul moves through the world. The question is whether you can get to the gift inside the wrapping. Seeing her as so empty of ego took less than a second, but it gave me a timeless view of the gift of all gifts, the Self, the reality of the indestructible freedom and peace we all carry in us without knowing it.

It was an experience of an intensity and clarity that was unforgettable. I had seen it in this "most unlikely candidate" and it created a bond between us that would guide me well for many years. It was not like falling in love. It was deeper than that; it was the revelation of an ancient soul connection between us and the recognition that an awareness of the Self was alive in this woman that I could trust completely. All my preconceived notions of what holiness had to look like were ripped to shreds by my encounter with Joya. I didn't like the tornado of her manifestation, but after I had seen the still eye of that storm, the winds didn't blow me away. I was able to sit back and enjoy the show. And what a show it was!

Joya brought along Ram Dass. Hilda Charlton, who had spent many years in India with her guru Baba Nityananda, trailed after them. As Joya's teacher, Hilda helped her make sense of the bewildering barrage of blissful experiences she was having daily. Ram Dass and Joya sat on the throne together, Hilda on a chair nearby; everyone else sat on the floor. Joya began to teach in a very personal and fiercely direct way. Her perception of people was acute, and it was obvious that she cared deeply, but her style was brutal. She spoke very direct and personal, pointing out the shadow side of people and enticing them to set themselves free. No one warranted special treatment, least of all Ram Dass, who was constantly in her crosshairs.

Through it all, Hilda made screeching sounds with her fingers as she rubbed the glass on a framed picture of Joya in an effort to "keep her down" with psychic powers. The word was that Joya was in such a high state that it was difficult for her to stay in her body, and all kinds of magic had to be used to keep her here and functioning properly. Surprisingly little of this eccentric spectacle bothered me; it was simply "the show."

The more I came to know Joya, the more outrageous she became. She spoke—mostly yelled—in a heavy Brooklynese accent liberally spiced with the F-word. She flaunted herself as the Divine Mother, spoke unceasingly about sex, and had absolutely no pretense about being anyone other than who she was. She was born to be the boss; self-doubt seemed completely unknown to her. She was the Brooklyn *dakini*, and enjoyed her role immensely. And while my mind vacillated between amusement and outrage at her drama and noise, I couldn't deny the great love we shared for Maharajji. . It was immediately obvious between us. She was, and always remained, " the least likely candidate" to be a teacher for me, but with her love and her tough dedication to her student's freedom she helped me gradually carve my true image out of the raw rock of my being.

Not long after my arrival, the whole New York scene fell apart as Joya and Ram Dass created impressive fireworks in their separation. After having been deeply devoted to her, Ram Dass now felt he had been duped by a fraud; he wrote an article in *The Yoga Journal* called "Egg on My Beard." [1] It would not be the last time Joya would be accused of being a fraud; her brash, unsophisticated ways made her an easy target.

The Indian tradition tells of a mythological sage named Durvasa. He has a particularly difficult personality, in fact his name literally means "one who is difficult to live with." He has a habit of showing up when it's least convenient and demands to be fed and taken care of. According to Indian tradition, hospitality is the highest duty of a host, and anyone whom Durvasa visits better make a great effort to please him. But the sage doesn't make it easy; he is extremely demanding and hard to please; he insists on the fulfillment of completely irrational requests and he can be insulting and completely unreasonable. He does everything to upset you and if you incur his wrath he is very quick to pronounce a curse on you. This is not to be taken lightly, because Durvasa is a sage of the highest order and what he says will always come true. On the other hand, when one does manage to please him, he can give unprecedented blessings and boons.

Durvasa is the personification of trouble and pain, of all the annoying, frustrating, and destructive situations we encounter every day. But why would this difficult energy manifest in a sage? It is because Durvasa represents the aspect of reality that teaches patience, endurance, and wisdom, and how to keep a balanced mind in even the most aggravating circumstances. He is the form of God who is testing you. When your goal is to control the mind and the ego, then rationality and irrationality do not matter. In fact, only by encountering challenging situations can you develop the willpower and insight that can triumph over all obstacles. When we learn how to welcome such a teacher and serve him at any time and at any cost, then the grace of Durvasa can come and we can realize that we haven't lost anything in such austerity, rather we become abundant in the wealth of spirit and gain a serene mind.

There is a small or large aspect of Durvasa in any good spiritual teacher, simply because creativity and destruction are both aspects of life. Good things can come only after the bad has been removed. You can build a new house only after you wreck the old one. Construction and demolition must go hand in hand. Such a teacher destroys our illusions in order to fulfill our wishes. When life sends us hardships and adversity, it is easy to develop a sense of humiliation, despair, or anger. But when we look through clearer eyes, we can come to understand the purpose of such experiences. We can realize that we are being trained, that life, or the teacher, is shaking us awake out of our ignorance and illusions.

Naturally to learn from a challenging teacher such as Ma is not right for everyone. There has to be a deep devotional connection that allows the student to see the teacher's compassion even in the most difficult moments. This is not easy, and many came and left her teaching after a while. There is no blame in that. Joya's fiery drama was just not what they needed. I was consistently amazed that it didn't seem to affect me that much. It must have been our shared love for Maharajji that sustained me. It allowed me to see her heart behind her Durvasa nature and her great internal calmness even in the greatest frenzy.

In the wake of Ram Dass' article, Joya's jealous Sicilian husband divorced her after beating up some of the yogis. Hilda and her picture scratching were soon left behind as well.

Joya had a way of either involving you in "the show" or making you run as fast as you could. I noticed to my surprise that I was along for the ride. A few of us left New York with her and settled into a rented house on Florida's East coast. Soon the rest of her students joined us and we founded an ashram in rural retirement land. The locals were sure we were freaks.

Once the dust settled, I was amazed at the extent of the love. I continued to feel uncomfortable with Joya's blatant intensity, but she had an earthiness that was delicious and a ruthless devotion to Maharajji that never seemed to waver. Quickly the deep connection we had became clear and I came to trust her. There were moments of unbelievable tenderness between us, when she turned off the Brooklyn tornado and showed a profound sensitivity, inner calm, and human warmth. Most importantly, in her presence Maharajji came to me without fail. I could breathe deeply the clear air of the spirit. Life had been soft and filled with profound kindness in India, oppressive in Germany, and now in the U.S. it had become a wild and thrilling adventure.

Joya changed her name to Ma Jaya[2] and kept the drama moving at a brisk pace. About 200 of us moved into a few tightly packed houses on a raw piece of land—our new ashram, a pressure cooker situation. Our personalities grated against each other like sandpaper, gradually smoothing out our sharp edges. Ma remained the still center as well as the perpetual provocateur, constantly pouring fuel on the funeral pyres of our egos.

As more of my uptight beliefs dissolved about how a spiritual teacher should look and behave, I came to appreciate Ma more and more. She remained outrageous, unpredictable, and definitely dangerous to my ego. At the same time her tremendous ability for compassion was the medicine that helped heal the raw places that remain after the ego has lost its defenses. In this way her teaching was extremely personal; her relationship with each one of us was the agent of transformation. Yes, we practiced the different branches of yoga, primarily meditation, devotion and karma yoga; that is what can be spoken about. But what was really transformative was the direct transmission of shakti and love, heart-to-heart, soul-to-soul, and that is not a teaching that can be put into words. True spiritual teaching is like that, it is the insight that happens in inner stillness in association with another soul you trust to the extent that you let them get under your egos defenses. Any good teacher must be an agitator for his or her close students or the teaching will be powerless and ineffective. Chogyam Trungkpa used to say "The job of the spiritual friend is to insult you." And Pema Chodron added that, "when you really start working closely with a teacher, that teacher becomes the greatest troublemaker in your life." The reason for that is of course that in order to become free and to experience the full capacity of the heart, you have to come to know where you still get hooked by your old reactions. A teacher who loves you is a supreme vehicle for that internal house-cleaning.

And that was what I wanted: a teacher who was tough yet loving enough to shake me out of my sleep and my habitual pain. To survive around her required a ruthless desire for freedom to match her equally ruthless habit of stripping the ego of its pretenses. She ran the community with great caring and an iron fist, a constant offense to my sense of personal liberty and a challenge to my willingness to surrender. Just when I thought I was safe and settled into a cozy ego-routine, she would be in my face again, deconstructing this latest version of my mistaken identity, burning my attachments to ash. It was as though her being could not tolerate falseness in anyone close to her. The constant challenge for me was to hold onto the love and not get lost in the drama.

14

The Emotional Roller Coaster

Living with Ma in the ashram was an emotional roller-coaster. It gave me the best possible laboratory for my inner work. Ma was always as passionate as she was deeply loving and supportive. But that was not always obvious on the surface. She used any opportunity to shake us awake through usually unconventional means, pulling us out of our slumber of complacency and indifference. Like a Zen master who slaps a student with his stick to awaken attention, she would use any trick to show us where we were still asleep in duality. We never knew what to expect next. Anyone not willing to be stripped in the most direct way of their self-importance would be well advised to avoid this type of teaching.

Ma knew with high precision how to push our buttons. Whatever unsavory part of my psyche I was trying to hide, she would see it with laser-like accuracy and bring it out so I could free myself. She had a tireless devotion to my awakening, an earthy energy, and we shared a great love for Maharajji - but she sure wasn't easy to deal with! Often I wanted to leave to find a more comfortable way, but even more I wanted to be free, so I stayed. Ever since my first experience with her, this flash of a vision of the divine presence at her core, I was able to trust that I was connected to this aspect of her being and that it would guide me. But as I soon found out, she did not always act from that inner wisdom. She would go in and out of this profound attunement and when she was in her Brooklyn personality she did many things that weren't skillful.

MA JAYA, THE BROOKLYN DAKINI

Soon there were two camps, those who were devoted to her and thought she could do no wrong, and those who saw her as a failed teacher on an ego trip of gigantic proportion. Sitting between these two camps, what could I do? I could only look at my own experience and listen to my own heart. And time and again my heart told me that she meant no harm and my experience taught me that I made progress. Ma had profound gifts, and she was also profoundly human. Being in relationship with her was the fastest train I could find.

Really, Ma was like life itself, only more direct. Life also brings up relentlessly what we want to hide, our weakness, shame, and conceit, but it does it slowly and without showing you that there is an intention to set you free. With a teacher like Ma, the process can be more intense, but also transparent. In the back of your mind you know that the objective of every moment is to set you free. The underlying love is apparent. Without a teacher this universal love is of course also always present, we may just have to look more closely to see it. The ashram was a place for *tapasya*[1] in the West, the hot fire of liberation, the burning of the seeds of karma. I could use it for that purpose—or I could get myself burned. It was up to me.

It is natural for us to try to hide the negative aspects of our personality. But what is the result of that? They become more engrained and harder for us to see—even though they may be quite obvious to the people who know us. To counteract our wish to hide what has to come to light, Ma helped everyone with their issues openly in front of the whole group of about 200 people. After we overcame our embarrassment and shyness, we learned very quickly that we were all dealing with the same stuff. Nobody's problems are special; our delusions and fears, our pettiness, anger, and jealousies are common to all of us. Soon there were no secrets among us. We came to know that we were not our "stuff," and realized that we were very courageous people, determined to be free . . . no matter what. It taught us wonderful compassion for each other and created a deep bond among us.

Time and again Ma brought to my attention my two major blind spots: my imagined weakness and low self-esteem and their flip side, the way I covered up my insecurities with arrogance, pretending I was better than anyone else. Twin delusions, mirror images. Why would I believe that I was better than anyone else? Because in some hidden place I felt I was not good enough, that something about me was terrible.

Ma would work on me from both ends. She refused to accept the fantasy of my weakness and kept popping the balloon of my arrogance. Whatever needed to see the light of day, she would flush it out of its hiding places. Slowly she broke up the unconscious patterns of my pain into manageable pieces, and the raw places always healed in the love we shared. At first I used to be mortified when caught in moments of arrogance, anger, or lack of awareness, and I would collapse into self-condemnation. But the love from Ma and everyone around me would flow just as before, and I realized that I was the only one who condemned me. Love is always the best medicine and before long I was able to say, "Oh, that's that again, I know that. It's on it's way out." And gradually I saw the old habits dissolve.

15

Healing Emotions

OUR EMOTIONS SWING ON A PENDULUM. We move back and forth from pleasure to pain, from attachment to hatred, from grasping to rejecting. This is what binds us to the world of duality. This is how we suffer. And because it's a pendulum, whenever we attain the pleasure we seek we put in place the seed of the pain that will follow. To find peace, to be in emotional harmony, we must find the still center, the pivot point. This is the non-dual mind, the place of emotional peace, the deep Heart.

> Whenever we attain the pleasure we seek, we put in place the seed of the pain that will follow.

We all have to deal with emotional challenges. They are not a curse, but rather something we can encounter in new ways, something we cannot only heal, but mine for wisdom. That however will take some readjustments in the ways we deal with pain. When we make these adjustments, our emotional challenges can be a door to freedom, a means to find the end of suffering.

Emotional wounds can fester for a lifetime. This is not only painful; it creates a profound confusion in the mind, since we unconsciously assume that our pain is part of what we are now. This is why emotional healing is an indispensable part of awakening.

What are emotions? *An emotion is a combination of thoughts and body sensations.* Think of someone you believe hurt you, someone you have not yet forgiven completely. Then become still and mentally scan through your body. Somewhere there is a stressful sensation that represents that emotion—a knot in the gut, a tension in your shoulders, a lump in the throat. It can be anywhere in the body, subtle or gross, but it will be there. If it's not obvious to you, become more still and you will be able to feel it.

> Emotional challenges can be a door to freedom.

We are defended against our emotions. In childhood, many of us learn to disassociate and not feel them. That makes sense when we have no way to resolve them—better not to feel at all than to feel frequent pain—but it also makes sure that these wounds don't heal. Repressed emotions have amazing resilience.

When toxic emotions are repressed, they hide in the body and can become a serious emotional complex, a behavior problem, or make us ill. Our emotions can literally kill us. Did you know that there is a spike in heart attacks on Monday mornings? People who can't stand to go through yet another hectic or humdrum week, doing meaningless work and feeling like an insignificant cog in the machinery of an uncaring world, kill themselves right on time, at nine o'clock on Monday morning. Emotions are that powerful!

By repressing our pain, our unconscious mind fills up with all sorts of toxic waste—anger, low self-esteem, self-hatred, arrogance, and so on. We are so used to our self-depreciating or self-aggrandizing beliefs that we mistake them for reality. *I'm not good enough. People don't love me. I'm not worthy. I can't get it right. I've made too many mistakes. I'm not capable.* Or we flip them around and become arrogant. *I am better than they are* is nothing but a thinly disguised defense against *I am worse than they are.*

Like an ancient curse, these beliefs burden us and manifest internally as mental turmoil, depression, anxiety, or stress, or externally as anger, relationship conflicts, accidents, and so on. "Out of sight, out of mind" is the motto. But when these complexes are hidden, we cannot deal with them, and it takes a lot of energy to repress and cover them up, minimize and deny, forget and ignore them.

Finding the Key

Stressful feelings wash over us in waves or patterns we recognize. We say we are "prone to" depression, anxiety, anger, or fear, as if this is simply the way it is and we can do nothing about it. Our toxic emotions are like a pair of glasses through which we see the world. If we are sad, the whole world is tinted grey and dreary. If we are scared or angry, we are certain that other people are out to get us. Whatever we project, we perceive—a self-fulfilling prediction. Over and over again, we fail to create harmony or success. No one taught us how to heal our emotional wounds.

> Our toxic emotions are like a pair of glasses through which we see the world.

The choice we have is quite simple: Either we put forth the effort to free ourselves, or we continue to live in pain.

Time does *not* heal all things; they just get buried deeper. I have worked with people whose childhood pain was still acute . . . eighty years later. The pain may get less but it doesn't go away until we free ourselves. Our first obstacle is that we're looking in the wrong places for the solution. We accuse the people and situations that bother us, or, behaving like victims, we manipulate others in the hope of getting their love, acknowledgment, and appreciation. We convince ourselves that we are like this because of our unhappy past, the chemistry in our brain, the uncertainty of the future, or an uncaring God. All this is hopeless.

Again: the cause of our pain is never what we are reacting to, *it's the fact that we are reacting*. It's not the world, but the unskillful way in which we react to the world that is making us miserable. We believe we are hurt by external events, by other people. But where do we experience our emotional stress? Inside, in our body and mind. So in our search for the cause and the cure, *let's look inside*. Not with blame or shame, but with curiosity, compassion, and the desire to wake up to the truth.

> The choice we have is quite simple: Either we put forth the effort to free ourselves, or we continue to live in pain.

It was a shock when I first realized that I had caused all of my pain myself—*all of it!* Then a wave of relief washed over me. Clearly, if I create my own pain, then I can learn how not to create it!

The Blame Game

First we have to stop casting blame. By blaming, complaining, and judging, we hide the truth about our pain and unhappiness. We place our attention outside—*They did that to me! They should be punished. It's not fair*—which blinds us to what's actually going on inside and turns us into victims. Of course we can also blame our body, our illness, our disability, and so on. All this is fruitless. As long as we project blame, we are stuck in a victim mindset, and victims become victimizers, of themselves and of others. If we want to be free, we have to be free of emotional reactivity. That is self-mastery. That is peace.

But we love to blame. When we blame, we don't have to take responsibility. We are so accustomed to this victim position that we build a large part of our (mistaken) identity around it. The ego says: *People are cruel. People are wrong.* (In other words, I am not to blame, I am better than they are.) *I am weak. I can't stand up for myself.* (I don't have to make an effort.) *I'm not good enough. I am damaged.* (How's that for an identity?) *The world is not safe.* (True—as long as you believe it.) *I have to teach them a lesson.* (Attack is the best defense). The ego wants to remain a victim. There is a certain comfort in the type of suffering we are used to. The devil we know is better than the devil we don't know. But in truth the devil we don't know is the angel that will set us free.

We have to turn to where the pain actually is. It takes courage, or just being really tired of the pain. We can't change the world to eliminate all external sources of stress, but *we can change the way we react.* The world is simply the way it is, we can love it or hate it. Blaming never solves anything; it is simply a destructive habit, nothing else. Once we become aware of our habit of blaming, the door to emotional harmony opens.

16

The Pain Body[1]

HAVE YOU EVER NOTICED HOW CERTAIN problems seem to follow you around? Maybe you have had several intimate partners who betrayed or abandoned you. Or you may feel invisible to your superiors, no matter where you work. Or no matter how hard you try to ignore it, childhood abuse keeps haunting you. Or your kids don't listen to you. Or you're always worrying about something. You try your very best, but your issues won't go away.

We have the tendency to unconsciously cling to our suffering. The reason for that is our *pain body, our deeply engrained unconscious habit of suffering*. We have it because pain is part of our ego-identity. Yes, it's a mistaken identity, but it is what we experience every day. If we could give voice to the ego, it might say: *"I am the one who has this much joy and this much pain in my life. That is what I am used to and who I know myself to be."* In other words, out of long habit we live in a zone—and for most of us it's to some extent a *dis-comfort*

> Pain is part of our ego-identity.

zone. It is the way we have been. And although consciously we want to be happy, unconsciously we cling to this discomfort zone, because it's what we know. The unknown scares us, even if the unknown is the happiness and freedom we seek.

As long as it rules us in ignorance, the ego is unconsciously deeply insecure, because it is not real. The ego is a collection of assumptions and habits based on ignorance of our true divine Being. Because of this fundamental insecurity the ego-mind wants stability at all cost and rejects change. It clings to the image it has of itself and sabotages our attempts to get free of pain. This is the root of all self-sabotage.

And so this tendency to *remain who we have been* creates the force to remain asleep. It sabotages our happiness and our enlightenment. It asures that we repeat our old patterns, and we will be helpless against their influence, as long as we remain unaware of this mechanism. To free ourselves of our unconscious habits we have to become conscious of them. As the light dissolves darkness, awareness dissolves unconsciousness.

Have you ever been in the middle of a pleasant conversation with a friend and suddenly you notice she is no longer fully present with you? Something in the conversation, or in her thoughts, triggered whatever now preoccupies her. And soon enough you will see her in some pain. You've just witnessed how the pain body took over your friend. Suddenly it seemed "she was no longer herself." This is correct. You were no longer talking to your friend, but to her pain body, her old habit to suffer. The pain body aspect of the ego is a deception, an illusion. It is not at all interested in our welfare, but in its own survival. And the pain body needs pain to maintain itself.

People with powerful pain bodies are constantly tense; they walk around with a permanent frown and experience stress so consistently that they consider this the normal condition of their lives. I was like this much of the time in my earlier years. But for most of us the pain body remains dormant at least some of the time, and then life is good. When it awakens to feed itself, then there's trouble.

Here is another example of how you may have noticed the pain body in yourself. Perhaps you remember a time when you began an argument with someone you love. Your pain body had just awakened, yet you still had enough awareness to notice a thought, "Why am I saying this? I know this will lead to a conflict, and I don't want conflict." But you said it anyway, the other person reacted, and soon you were embroiled in an argument. Even though you saw it coming and didn't want it, you couldn't stop it. That is why the pain body is like a psychic parasite, who overcomes and posesses us. When the pain body wants to feed, it creates something to get upset about and then feeds on your pain or your anger. When it's had enough, it goes back to sleep. Then you lick your wounds and try to contain the damage. You may say, "I don't know what possessed me!" Well, now you know. It was the pain body, the force of unconscious self-sabotage. You will be at its mercy until you dissolve it.

A Correct Way to Deal with Pain

The problem is not only the pain body. It is also because we don't know how to deal with pain in a sensible, healthy way. For thousands of years we have repressed painful sensations, as soon as they appeared. Our rejection of pain has become automatic; it is an instant, instinctive resistance. We don't question it. It is impulsive, unconscious, unrealistic and destructive. Our compulsion to escape all pain condemns us to an unsettled life full of nervous distractions. It gives us the sense that we live in a "valley of tears" and that heaven is elsewhere. We do not know that we are the creators of our own suffering and believe suffering to be inescapable. Therefore we live in constant terror of the next calamity. Yet there is a wonderful way out of this.

Whatever we experience is part of Earth School. If we encounter it correctly, each experience turns into a gift of grace. Even pain brings liberation; it is a portal into the Here and Now, to the dissolving of ego and to the end of suffering. Pain has something crucial to give us, but if we fend it off, we cannot become aware of its value.

> The past is over and we carry it now in us as an illusion, like the snake we see in the rope.

If we do not encounter pain correctly so it can dissolve, we collect an enormous amount of old hurt in our subconscious. As soon as you play one tone on a piano, all the corresponding strings vibrate in resonance. In the same way, old, repressed pain is activated in us by new pain. This internal morass of pain is the soil in which the pain body grows. It keeps us from going inward to attend to the pain where it is and so to find our peace, because we fear yesterdays unresolved pain. But it is exactly there, toward the pain, where we have to go to free ourselves of pain. It can seem daunting to encounter the thoughts, images, and emotions of our traumas. But the past is over and we carry it now in us as an illusion, like the snake we see in the rope. There is no need to wrestle with the snake—instead we must look closely so we can see the truth of the rope! The power of our true Self is infinitely greater than the shadows of the past. It can free us of anything that separates us from our healing and our awakening.

As we learn to carefully turn to our stressful emotions—our pain, fear, anger, or guilt—they will dissolve due to their unreal and impermanent nature. Then we no longer collect our hurt and no longer carry the pain of the past in us—the pain of our own past, the pain of our families, our gender, our nation, and the pain of all of humanity.

We have four tasks before us:

1. To retrain our brain, so we are able to encounter pain in the right way, as soon as it appears.
2. To dissolve the reservoir of old, repressed pain, so we become free of the past and capable to live in the Now.
3. To question our beliefs about suffering, in order to radically change our view of ourselves and the world.
4. To let our pain guide us to open the gates of the heart and let the hidden love heal what ails us.

The following chapters will help you accomplish these tasks. In particular I want to invite you to question any beliefs about the inevitability of suffering. Yes, as the Buddha taught, sickness, old age and death are inevitable, but do we need to suffer about them? Is it inevitable that we identify with the body, mind and personality that will eventually perish? Our stressful thoughts and emotions are deeply ingrained, but they lose power over us the more conscious we become. The Self in the cave of the Heart is the inner ruler (*antary-amin*) and it creates our world out of love. It guides us to liberation from confusion, which makes us unable to recognize our own greatness and our freedom.

The War with a Part of You

As we react impulsively to painful emotions, the mind reflexively interprets these sensations as threats or enemies and tries to escape from them or to fight them off. This is known as the *fight-or-flight reflex*, an ancient instinct that is a function of primitive parts of the brain, including the "reptilian complex." Let's make sure it doesn't send us down the same path as the dinosaurs.

The fight-or-flight reflex is crucial to our survival. It automatically kicks in when there is an immediate threat. You're crossing a street and out of the corner of your eye you notice a car coming toward you at great speed and you leap out of the way before you have time to think. Congratulations, the fight-or-flight reflex just saved your life! But since the time of the dinosaurs, evolution has added a few more parts to the human brain; we have developed an inner life with a kaleidoscope of emotions, something utterly unknown to reptiles.

The reptilian brain, however, was never informed of the difference between real *external* threats and the *internal* sensations caused by emotions. The mind interprets them as threats and this creates serious problems.

> Changing our reality will not happen through emotional war.

Your teenager says something edgy. You instantly react and get on her case with that *tone of voice* (externalized fighting response). She stomps off in a huff and now you feel bad about your reaction (internalized fighting response, you're attacking yourself), so you smoke a cigarette, pour yourself a drink, distract yourself by watching TV, or reach for the ice cream to numb out the emotion (all flight responses; you're trying to escape from your feelings). Your pain body just loves this! In the course of a few minutes you've fed it three different kinds of pain. Yummie!

Much of the time we are in a state of war with our emotions. You fight your feelings by repressing them, by pretending they don't bother you, or by displacing your inner tension onto conflicts with others. You flee from your feelings when you try not to feel them. All addictions are part of this, including those that are hard to spot, such as overwork, time-consuming distractions, the need to be right, or the compulsion to worry or judge yourself. The problem with these strategies is that the emotion and its corresponding body sensation is *a part of you* at that moment. Who wins when you are fighting a part of yourself? It's an inevitable lose-lose situation. And trying to escape from a part of you is equally hopeless since *wherever you go, there you are.*

Being ever so inventive, the human mind has developed two other ways of dealing with our emotions: indulging and complaining. We indulge through self-pity. *Oh, it feels so good to hurt so bad.* Through the sweet sensation of *"poor me,"* we cultivate the mind of a victim. We don't trust the good feelings, so we settle for bad ones. As troubling as bad feelings may be, they give the ego what it wants: a sense of identity. I'm with a friend at the beach. Two elderly ladies spread their towels beside us and begin to discuss everything that is wrong with their health. They are having a marvelous time describing their suffering in great multi-colored detail. Eventually my friend and I pick up our stuff and move down the beach. Two hours later we walk back to our car. The two ladies are still at it, discussing now how they were mistreated by doctors in various hospitals. This is true mastery of the fine art of indulge-and-complain.

When we are at war with our emotions, stress hormones flood through our bodies, making us miserable. They lower our immune system until we're exhausted or sick. We hate it and tomorrow we'll do it all over again. Whether we grumble out loud or silently in the mind, it's a self-destructive habit to want things to be different than they are. Fighting, fleeing, indulging, and complaining about the way we feel—in short: "FFIC"—is a trap. It has no effect other than making us miserable. Changing our reality is possible of course, but it will not happen through emotional war. How we live is up to us: in the mastery peace and clarity bring, or in a war we can only lose.

17

Open Attention

W E CAN SEEK RELIEF FROM OUR suffering in two ways: by seeking comfort and personal wellbeing as an end in itself, or by aspiring for liberation. Among the countless methods offered in the spiritual supermarket of today, many promise Self-realization, but cannot deliver. Comfort is important for our good functioning, but as long as the ego is engaged in its unending search for pleasure and the avoidance of pain, it simply recycles its habitual patterns with slight and only temporary improvements. This is a great, but hidden, problem with many of the approaches to better living today. Any relief from suffering that comes from efforts toward improved ego functioning will not only be temporary, but will more firmly imprison us. A more comfortable ego will tend to resist awakening. Only the *dissolving* of the blinding aspects of ego and its confining emotional patterns can lead to permanent freedom from pain. A

> Only the dissolving of the blinding aspects of ego can lead to permanent freedom from pain.

comfortable ego can spend a lifetime in the delusions of the immature spiritual wonderland of early Earth School. From the perspective of truth, this will be a life where nothing is gained. Psychology is usually honest about that. It promises better ego functioning without pretending to be more than it is. Many other sources make confusing and fraudulent promises.

Lasting emotional harmony can only come as a *by-product* of spiritual practice, the dissolving of the prison of ego. This is an important distinction. On the path to Self-realization, emotional healing will occur naturally and become complete. When freedom is the goal, our work will be honest and deep, the ego will function well, and we will be able to generate the ruthless commitment to truth that is necessary to overcome the deeply-rooted emotional patterns that keep us in bondage. We will become still, and open to our inner wisdom, the profound healing power of the Self, the inner guru.

> The deep healing Open Attention brings is therefore not something we do. Rather, we set the stage for the healing power in us to dissolve the emotional patterns that stand in the way.

The deep healing Open Attention brings is therefore not something we do. Rather, we set the stage for the healing power in us to dissolve the emotional patterns that stand in the way. Disturbing emotions are like clouds in the sky. The Self is the sun. When we direct our consciousness at the clouds, they soon dissolve.

It may not come as a surprise that in order to free ourselves of emotional pain, we must do exactly the opposite of fight, flight, indulge or complain (FFIC). We must find an attunement to our feelings. The strategies of FFIC have one thing in common: they keep us unconscious and in conflict with our emotions. This is true for the habit of indulging as well, because it makes us drown in negative feelings. What then is the opposite of FFIC?

The strange thing about healing emotions is that *we already know what to do, but we don't know that we know*. That means we cannot use the knowledge we already have. Let me illustrate this with a story. Imagine you're walking someplace, minding your own business, having a good time. You turn a corner and there, by the side of the road, is a little girl who is crying and crying. She is about four or five years old and sobbing terribly. There's no one else around. What do you do?

You know what to do. You walk up to the little girl and try to console her. You may ask her what's wrong, but she cannot answer because she's sobbing too hard. So what you do? You put your arms around her and hold her. While you're holding her, feeling her little body shaking from head to toe, are you thinking about the movie you might go see tonight? Of course not! You are fully present with her. You are open and present and your attention is fully on her. This is the way of kindness. After a while the girl's sobs die down and soon she wiggles out of your arms and is off playing again. You may never know what was wrong. It doesn't matter; her pain is resolved.

What resolved it? The pain of the little girl was released because you added something she could not yet do for herself: you added your conscious presence, your *openness*, your *attention*, your caring.

That little girl stands for the feelings inside you. Her crying represents the stressful body sensations you've been treating with FFIC. Now think for a moment about how you have reacted to your own feelings in the past. If your feelings were that little girl, how have you been treating her?

Re-imagine the scene: You're taking a walk, minding your own business, then you turn the corner and see and hear the little girl crying (which means you become aware of a stressful emotion and body sensation). As soon as you notice her, you run the other way. *I need to get out of here! I don't have the time for this! Or, Help! If I deal with her I might get completely overwhelmed by her pain.* This is the flight reflex.

Does it make sense?

But wait, it gets worse. You might pick up a big stick from the side of the road and beat her into the ground until you can't hear her cries any more (that's the fight reflex: you repress your emotions), or you hand her candy (or a beer, joint, or pill) to silence her (the flight reflex to escape from feelings, the root of all addiction). We have a name for this kind of behavior—"criminal insanity." You would get locked up if you treated a little girl like this, and rightfully so. But we routinely do this to ourselves and consider it normal.

Here are a few other mad responses to the little girl—your feelings. You could feel sorry for her, yet do nothing to help her. This is self-pity, the common passive surrender to unhappiness, a way of indulging. Another option is to complain about her. *She is terrible, crying and carrying on like this! Why can't she just shut up and go away?* Internally such self-rejection and self-hate simply increase pain, and by repressing it, they asure that it stays within us.

Then there is *letting go* and *bypassing*, two immensely popular escape strategies. The concept of letting go of a thought or emotion that hurts appears like a good idea. But it is not the same as being done with something. When you let go, you feel better, but a small seed of the pain stays within you. Give it some time and from that seed it will sprout again. Bypassing occurs when you deny a problem and escape to 'higher ground.' Because a husband watches porn, he neglects his wife. When she asks for some attention and intimacy, her husband, who thinks of himself as very spiritual and open-minded, withdraws and says, "I don't have a problem. You shouldn't be so needy. It's all an illusion anyway."

These unconscious and unthinking defense strategies against your negative emotions cannot set you free. Instead they assure that you will continue to carry them inside you. Over time they will cause you to fall into other, ever more painful emotions, into chronic defensiveness, rage, self-hate, hopelessness and despair. As long as you treat your emotions unconsciously as if they are a threat or an enemy and wage war inside you, you suffering will only increase.

And you do not have to learn what to do, because you already know. You know intuitively how you can console a crying child or help an adult in trouble. We all know that friendliness of the heart. We are not starting from zero. We all have helped others intuitively and with Open Attention without knowing it. It is just simple sane human behavior. Now we can use our capacity for kindness for ourselves and treat us with the inborn benevolence of the heart.

Thoreau spoke of the unhappiness we have amassed since our childhood when he said that "Most men lead lives of quiet desperation." The reason for this desperation lies in the fact that we have not known how to be kind to us, but have waged war against a part of us, our own emotions. If we do nothing, this habit will continue and become more pronounced over the years. Without knowing it, we are feeding the inner pain while we remain distracted on the surface of our lives. The feelings will fester and appear even more frightening or upsetting. Freedom and mastery can come when we open to our emotions and pay attention to their body sensations.

This is Open Attention:

When you sense a negative emotion, begin by becoming still and bringing your attention to the here and now. Feel what is going on in your body. Mentally scan through your body and identify the exact location of the body sensation(s) that express the emotion. If there are several, focus on the one that is strongest. Open to that sensation. Notice if you're pulling back or tensing up, out of old habit. Open again. Breathe. Relax while maintaining your focus. Simply be present with the sensation the way you would be present with a child that is in distress and needs help. Recall that the body sensation is a part of you that needs help. Feel what is going on in you, feel it as deeply as you can. Be aware of your fundamental caring and love, expressed through this inner awareness. Maintain your inner focus and notice what happens.

Whenever you want to free yourself from the grip of stressful feelings, gently repeat this process of emotional healing. Do it with kindness. If you suffer from trauma or are emotionally very sensitive, you may not be able to do this practice for very long at first. As I've said before, sometimes just a moment of Open Attention may be all you can do and it will be enough. It changes the pattern of repression. It brings love and the light of awareness into the darkness of old pain. Always be gentle with yourself, even as you strive with a highly focused mind to become free. Make sure you have a good support system and seek the help of a licensed therapist or counselor if needed.

The practice of Open Attention is cumulative and builds on itself. If you have practiced successfully for a while and then more difficult emotions arise, know this to be an excellent sign of progress! Your increasing skill, awareness, and strength allow you to deal with these feelings; they are coming up because they want to be released. Gradually you will notice how your attention sharpens and you can focus onto the more subtle disturbances that used to escape your mind. You will be able to free deep-seated pain as well as the elusive emotions of unease, discontent, resentment, denial, shame, and resistance that form the usual background static of our lives. The purpose of this practice is to free yourself of *all* the disturbing emotional patterns that form a crust of obstructions around the heart. With Open Attention you can systematically dissolve this crust and gain access to the freedom and unconditional love that you are. Nothing is more exciting, and nothing is more beneficial.

Open Attention is clear and straightforward. Could it really be that simple to free yourself? Yes, it is magnificently effective and simple, but resistance will invariably arise. Sooner or later the pain body will vigorously try to sabotage your attempts to practice Open Attention. *What nonsense, I am just wasting my time. I have much more important things to do, or, This doesn't work. I'm not good at it. Let me find something else.* Watch for these thoughts and others like them; watch for boredom, distraction, and lack of commitment. You don't have to fall for these obstacles; they are simply how the pain body tries to maintain control by automatically repeating your old defense strategies. Don't fall into the trap.

> Opening up and paying Attention are the fundamental building blocks and the essential characteristics of love. Love is the best medicine.

Please see Appendix II for a detailed description of this practice.

Healing with Love

Why is Open Attention so effective in dissolving the pain body? The secret is really very simple. Open Attention enables us to use the power of love consciously for our healing, and love is always the best medicine.

When we realize that stressful sensations in the body are not an enemy or a threat, but *parts of us that need help*, then we can stop waging war against ourselves. We do the opposite: **open** up to that which hurts and pay **attention** to it. Opening up and paying Attention are the fundamental building blocks and the essential characteristics of love. Love is the best medicine.

When you treat yourself with the practical kindness inherent in Open Attention, you experience the main factor in healing emotional pain: the power of pure unconditional love. **Open Attention is the concrete application of love for emotional and physical healing and Self-realization.** This tangible practice of self-love addresses one specific area of stress or pain at a time. As that concern resolves itself, your focus then can rest peacefully in the heart or move successively to other areas of discomfort. Your attention can reach increasingly deeper, moving throughout the body and mind, guided by the great intelligence of your innate healing potential. You do not have to identify the causes of all the stressful emo-

> Love is the real and eternal state of our being. It is the perfect antidote to everything that grows out of fear.

tions you encounter. Simply know that the cause now lies within you and that it is fear-based. Nor do you need to know what each feeling is. Simply feeling it deeply until it dissolves will take care of it. The task is to allow the force of love to penetrate through the symptoms and dissolve the cause because *the cause is always a place void of love.*

Love is the real and eternal state of our being. It is the perfect antidote to everything that grows out of fear. With Open Attention we actively bring the presence of conscious love into the body. There it heals, and becomes rooted and true, and from there the presence of love in us will radiate into the world. This is how we heal the world by healing ourselves.

Surrender

Turning inward in stillness and getting in touch with deeper levels of our being is of profound importance. How else are we going to come to know ourselves? But this is not the end of the story. As our capacity for self-awareness and self-love increase, our ability to surrender will also deepen. It does not matter to what symbol or understanding of wholeness we surrender, as long as it represents to us an all-inclusive, universal goodness. We have complete freedom to turn to whatever manifestation of God or Truth most appeals to us. As Maharajji said, "The best way to worship God is every way."

And we know how to surrender! Even as infants and children we automatically surrendered our pain and worries to our mother, who was the representative of a caring universe. Any problems we may have experienced in this relationship came later. The ability to surrender is hard wired into us on a deep level of our being, and we know from experience that surrender works. Therefore it is of enormous value for us to develop a deep and trusting relationship to reality. We can do this by opening and surrendering to the Source of Love or Truth that most deeply attracts us.

This is how surrender works: Imagine you're dreaming and in your dream the dream ego is attacked by hostile forces and in great fear and pain. The more it struggles to find a way to solve its predicament, the stronger the evil forces become. Not realizing that it's the dreamer of its own dream, the dream ego imagines itself lost in a hostile and uncaring universe. But eventually it comes to the end of its rope and gives up the fight, usually only after exhausting itself in a struggle it cannot possibly win. At that point of surrender, it wakes up and with that all its troubles instantly dissolve. This is the realization that an awareness exists that creates the dream ego as well as the monsters, a supreme awareness that can and will dispel the troubles of the dream ego, which are all self-created.

Applying this view to our waking life may help us gain a sense of how we can make use of the absolute kindness of the cosmic mind through surrendering our self-will and humbly asking for help. It is good to remember in our struggles that we are struggling within the mind of illusion and that the solution we seek is found in non-dual awareness and in the love we are. For instance, fear: there is (1) the observing ego (the subject), there is (2) what it is afraid of (the object that is observed) and there is (3) the relationship between them, the thoughts and sensations of fear. And there is something else: there is an awareness that is conscious of all that; it contains the subject, the object and their relationship. This awareness is timeless; it has no limit; it contains all things. All of life occurs within this awareness like a dream occurs within the mind of the dreamer. All surrender ultimately leads to an awakening as That. In that recognition all struggle and all suffering come to an end. It is the infinite love of existence in and for itself.

18

Unity Consciousness

ONE DAY, OUT OF THE BLUE, all sense of myself as a separate entity disappeared. Spontaneously, suddenly, I was free! Words cannot describe it but only point toward this most primal and transcendent of all experiences, and I must use the word "I" even though my awareness was no longer confined to the small prison of an "I." This awareness was vast, limitless, and as intimate as only absolute love can be. No one around me noticed anything different about my state of mind; I was functioning normally in the world, but there was a powerful hidden undercurrent of constant bliss.

> I was one with the sky, and the house, and the song of the birds.

I was one with the sky, and the house, and the song of the birds. The world was exactly the same as before, but now I saw it with the clear eyes of truth. Gone was the impression that I was a small separate entity, locked into a body of flesh, an ego confined in a bag of skin. I had merged into oneness, which was especially obvious when I looked at the people around me. The words "you and I" had lost their meaning, as I saw that the same consciousness animates all apparently separate beings; that all exists in one single field of awareness, and that *I am* that consciousness. It wasn't that I loved the people or that I loved the world. It was much more intimate. "I" had disappeared into love; I had become love. This is the realization of the true Self, of the Oneness of Being, the recognition that *I am unlimited freedom, wisdom, knowledge, compassion. I am supreme kindness, the Universal Mind, the creator of all the worlds. I am absolute happiness.*

This experience of union is the goal of all spiritual yearning. Experiencing this state of "not-I" taught me more than all the spiritual books and teachings combined. It brought to life everything I had heard or seen. It was a dissolving into that limitless love that I had sensed in my best moments to be the heart of the world, the core of reality. It was a merging into oneness with what we call God.

No matter what name you give your deepest yearning, this absolute Oneness is what you are thinking of. It is the matrix that creates everything and into which everything again dissolves. It is the Great Mother of Being, creating all the worlds and all creatures in them. Within Her womb beings arise and become unconscious of their true Source, like falling asleep. You dream that you are not free, that you are limited and bound, and that there is something to fear. But that can never be true because you are always one with the Source and the Source is love.

All the great wisdom traditions point to this realization of Oneness. The gateway into this experience is the Now.

How do you enter this gateway? When you can see through your thoughts and emotions, you come to live in the wisdom mind, the supreme intelligence in the Heart. Then you can see *through* the one who sees. Then you are one with all things. The world is revealed as a dream, and you are aware you are dreaming. With this awareness all fear melts away. Reality, as it is, is abundance. Happiness is complete.

The vast ocean of awareness contains all the worlds. The material world is not an unyielding reality; it is consciousness appearing in a solidified state.

Awareness is the primary and essential reality.
Awareness is the Source.
The essence of consciousness is infinite unconditional Love,
Therefore Love rules the world.
Worlds arise and pass away, but the Self, the matrix,
is always one and the same.
This Self is what we are.

The Universal Form of the Guru

Wherever I looked, I saw unlimited consciousness appearing as the world. Yet this vast and majestic creation had a personal feeling to it. Everywhere I looked, I saw and felt the essence of Maharajji. His love and his unmistakable presence permeated everything. It was surprising at first, but then I realized in this oneness with the divine Self that for me he is that Self. He is one with all things. As I entered this oneness, I merged into his cosmic form, universal and personal at the same time. It was beyond any notion of an "I" and, at the same time, carried the sweet flavor of the most personal love.

Everyone and everything is the Beloved.

Swami Muktananda said, "When you love the guru as you love the world, the world is filled with the Guru." If you are devoted to a realized being—to Jesus, to Krishna, to Shiva, to one of the many forms of the Divine Mother, or to a liberated guru or saint—then the experience of the Self will have for you the familiar taste of the form through which you fell in love with the Self. "Everyone is a reflection of my face," Maharajji said. And so, naturally for me, everything was of his essence. Everyone and everything is the Beloved.

This is what complete love does: it makes you come alive down to the last fiber of your being. It thrills you to no end. In that love you need nothing else, for this love is complete unto itself. This love animates all of creation. It is fearless and deathless. In this love, you honor the body as a temporary vehicle, as the great servant it is, no more and no less, but you, in your true identity, are pure awareness that has no limit and will never die. At the moment of physical death, the body is left behind, but what can happen to this exalted awareness? Where can it go? It is the Source of all things. Those who have realized this while still alive have already died to any illusion of limitation. As Ramana Maharshi declared, "You will know in due course that your glory lies where you cease to exist." And in Maharajji's words, "The body passes away. Everything is impermanent except the love of God."

On the fourth day after the disappearance of the sense of an "I," a thought crossed my mind, *Wow, I am having an incredible experience.* "I" had come back. My awareness descended once more into the limited sense of self. It began with the thought of an "I," which is the first error, the first confusion. This basic "I"-thought gives birth to all the stressful thoughts and emotions that separate us from what we are. They are the veil that hides from us the truth, and the last frontier before bliss.

I had been given a preview of the enlightened state, but I had more work to do. The "I" that came back was filled with the most profound gratitude for the glorious view of Reality I had been granted. A deeper devotion than ever before surged through my being, and I wanted nothing more than to return to this state of realization. What I needed to do would become clear in time.

THE FOURTH SKILL:
PEACE OF MIND

19

Moving On

I HAD LIVED ON THE ASHRAM FOR 24 years. During this time we had created a sacred community on what had been a raw patch of sand and palmetto scrub. We built houses and beautiful temples amidst a flowering landscape next to a slow, gentle river that meanders to the Atlantic. We were a close-knit, loving community of 200 people and hundreds more who would come and go, all deeply focused on our awakening. It was an amazing spiritual family, and this communal living had taught me a great deal about the practical art of compassion. But everything has a beginning and an end and it became clear to me that my stay here was over. Now it was time to share the gift of Maharajji's love with the world.

For a while I had felt a growing sense of unease on the ashram. I had loved Ma's earthy passion for God. Her intense style accelerated my awakening and there was a great deal of love. This had worked well for me, but now I felt out of place. In many ways it was simply time to leave. I had taken all I could receive from Ma's teaching and had to look for new challenges and a more independent life. And things had changed.

Increasingly I saw how Ma's personality got in her way. One day she could radiate an immensely powerful, light-filled presence and was a magnanimous and gracious leader. The next day she was struggling and did things that hurt her. At moments I saw fear in her and the anger of a bruised ego.

I never experienced Ma being abusive, but the stories of my friends who left hurt and embittered were disturbing. What made it much worse was that this could not be discussed openly because a culture had grown on the ashram which forbade any criticism of Ma. It made her blind to her own shortcomings and it robbed the community of some of the vitality it could have had. I was close enough to see, but not too close to be blinded. Time and again aspects of her personality got in the way, but she could not be open about it. She could not let her students ripen by sharing her own struggles. The power she had over the community was corrupting her to some extent.

By some grace I was able to see this clearly and without judgment. And why would I need to judge? Her way worked as well as it did for her and the group, but no longer for me. Judgment would cloud my perception. It is painful and unnecessary. Recognizing this I can keep my heart open and direct my life with clarity and understanding. I could grant that this exceptional woman, who helped so many thousands of people, had her own work to do. I certainly could forgive the fact that she was not perfect—no personality is. But when she pretended that all her actions were guided from a higher source, she lost credibility in my eyes. Since the community had joined her in this pretense, most could not see that at times the emperor had no clothes. When I tried to address some of these issues directly with her she was not open to feedback. So I started a discussion group trying to break down some of these unhealthy tabus in the community. But as soon as we had some success, Ma made it impossible for us to continue our meetings. At that point I knew that the ashram was no longer the right environment for my growth.

Many have criticized Ma Jaya. Many others have gained tremendously from their association with her. What is the truth? Is there one truth, or many? Fully realized beings like Maharajji are exceedingly rare, and people judged even him. It is the nature of the unenlightened mind to judge. We can tell when we judge because it is stressful. When we observe with clarity, then there is no stress and our insight allows us to act with wisdom and love. Most spiritual teachers are excellent and compassionate, and can help us for some stretch of the way. This is a great blessing. Can we see the light of the Self in them without demanding their personalities to be perfect?

To project our ideas of perfection onto anyone is a recipe for disappointment. Can we not appreciate the gifts they share with us and allow that they are still on the way, just like us? That seems to be a much more balanced and compassionate attitude. We need to make our own lives right, not anyone elses. What we seek is within us; it is the Self. The teacher's personality is just the packaging and it is never perfect. In that imperfection it serves us greatly. Its job is to show us all the places where we're still stuck. The only question that is important is: how true and one-ponted is our own search? To the extent that it is, our own sincerity will guide us perfectly from within.

Right around that time an event occurred which I later recognized as the culmination of my time with Ma Jaya. As the main *pujari* (priest) on the ashram, I used to perform large fire ceremonies several times a year—a yogic form of worship of the Divine Mother, grand theater of the soul. At this particular time we had all gathered around the sacred fire and during the high point of the celebration I began to chant the 108 names of the Divine Mother. To my surprise I noticed that I didn't have a single distracting thought during the entire length of the ritual. My mind was clear and my heart fully engaged. I had become an empty vessel, honoring Ma as a representative of the Goddess. Maharajji had said: *Bring your mind to one point and wait for grace.* It was a flawless ritual, an ideal moment, and the culmination and end of my time as Ma Jaya's student.

While I sensed it was time to move on, I had to be sure that the impulse came from the higher mind, not from my ego. I had followed inner guidance in all major decisions, but now no guidance was coming. So I stayed and every day I felt more out of place at the ashram. Finally I said to Maharajji, "It feels like you want me to leave this place, but I am not leaving on my own. If you want me to leave, you will have to send me someone in whom I can recognize the same enlightened consciousness I have known in you." It was just a passing thought.

And again the unfailing, but usually hidden guidance became visible. A friend told me about a woman from California named Byron Katie who had developed a method to free the mind from confusion and stress. I became interested in this practice and wanted to meet her to get a firsthand impression of the quality of her approach. She had a tight schedule of events all around the world, but none anywhere close to Florida. I offered to organize a seminar for her, and in the course of a sequence of seemingly impossible "coincidences," she agreed to come to the ashram, where I hosted her a mere three weeks later.

> The sat-guru is the road we travel on.

That day I went to meet her in the ashram parking lot. Her car drove up, she lowered the window, and I instantly fell into the bottomless depth of her brilliant blue eyes. Nothing had to be said. It was clear: here was the messenger I had asked for. Everything fell into place. Two days after her visit I moved out of the ashram. A week later I joined Katie for her training in California. The transition was seamless. Later Katie told me that her advisors had strongly urged her not to go to an ashram in the boondocks of Florida. "They said I should go to the large cities where I can reach many more people. But," she added with a smile, "I go where the heart calls."

Many have asked me since then: "How do you leave a spiritual teacher?" My answer is that we should leave a spiritual teacher the same way we should leave any important relationship: with much love, appreciation, and gratitude for everything we have received. Everything is a gift, the support as well as the challenges. It is up to us how we react. If we have anger or regrets, it is our opportunity to become free, to complete the learning we can receive from this relationship. Everything we experience is perfectly designed by the deepest intelligence in our heart to assist us in our awakening. If we remember this, we will understand the profound kindness of the world we live in. Rumi spoke of the ability of our heart to transcend the quarrels of the mind when he wrote, *"Out beyond ideas of rightdoing and wrongdoing, there is a field. I'll meet you there."* The question is never if the other person shows up on that field, but if we do.

> When our search is genuine, it leads us to everything we need, whether we know it or not, and always exactly on time.

Throughout these changes Maharajji's presence in me was unshakable. After all, it is the presence of my very own Self. This is the difference between a sat-guru and a spiritual teacher. The sat-guru may appear as a person, but is much more than that. He or she is in essence the consciousness of Brahman, the Divine Self. This consciousness is the gate we pass through in the process of our awakening, which is the realization that we are this consciousness. A spiritual teacher points out the way. The sat-guru is the road we travel on. Prompted by the purity and power of our yearning, the road to the heart emerges from the heart and leads us unfailingly home into the heart. Therefore there is only one sat-guru for every soul, the outer manifestation of the Self that dwells in the heart.

It is not necessary to meet such a guru in physical form. What is necessary to receive such guidance is single-minded devotion and commitment to freedom. Teachers on the other hand can be many. We must cherish them for they show us the way to the heart. But I was not looking for another teacher—so why was I being guided to Katie and her practice of clearing the mind? Because when our search is genuine, it leads us to everything we need, whether we know it or not, and always exactly on time. Katie's form of self-inquiry was a revelation for me. She calls it simply "The Work of Byron Katie." I found it to be a highly effective way to clear the mind.

Our conditioned mind can turn into a scary, uncomfortable danger zone. *I've made many mistakes. Something terrible is going to happen to me. I don't have enough money. There is too much to do. People hurt me. I am not good enough...* It's like a mine field where we never know what can blow up next. But once we examine these thoughts through the inquiry of The Work, we may find them to be completely untrue. Thoughts are simply thoughts—articles of belief and not necessarily correct. The more we question our stressful beliefs, the more we will discover a deeper truth, and this truth shall set us free.

20

Clarity of Mind

DURING THE TWO LOWER LEVELS OF Earth School our conditioned mind and emotions rule us, but since we identify with them, our awareness of our bondage is limited. It is not until we reach the third level, that we see more clearly and can free ourselves of their tyranny. Now we are called to evolve the wisdom mind, the intuitive intellect. It enables us to understand and gain a view of our true goal—the Self—and opens the door to Self-realization.

The Target

Let's get an overview. In our conditioned state of mind, we believe we are the body and the ego-based personality. We identify with its layers: thoughts, emotions, behavior and physical manifestations and believe that's all there is to us. It is a view our culture reinforces constantly. We can picture these layers like a set of Russian dolls with an empty space in the center. Even more simplified, it looks like a doughnut.

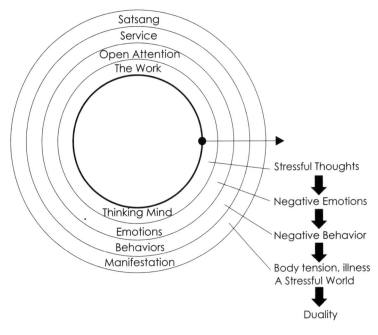

Satsang
Service
Open Attention
The Work

Thinking Mind
Emotions
Behaviors
Manifestation

Stressful Thoughts

Negative Emotions

Negative Behavior

Body tension, illness
A Stressful World

Duality

The Way of Suffering

The Doughnut - the Layers of the Human Personality ™

This is our temporal and mortal self, which we develop in the course of a lifetime and shed at death. For the short span of a life it serves us well. It is good and necessary to take care of it. *But body and personality is not what we are.* This becomes tangibly evident when we are in the grip of a stressful thought. Not knowing how to free ourselves of this thought, it becomes negative emotion, unskillful behavior and a stressful world. This is the way of suffering. The mind, connected to the senses, has an outward flowing tendency (the arrow pointing to the right) that causes us to get lost in attachments, aversions and confusion in the world of duality and multiplicity.

From the soul's point of view, identifying with this temporary vehicle makes as much sense as saying, "I am my car." What would you think of someone you're dating, who proudly states, "I am my Ford, my Toyota, my Maserati." Would you have another date with the guy? (Well you might consider the Maserati, right?) Of course it's good to take care of your car, to change the oil and give it a wax job every so often, but hey, after a few years it's an old clunker and you junk it or trade it in. Yes, even the Maserati. The same is true of our treasured body and personality. After a few more years—or maybe less, who knows—all that will be left is a small pile of ash. This is not a morbid view at all; it is extremely empowering. It can liberate us from the fear of death. I am not saying we should not enjoy our cars. No, let's enjoy our cars by all means, let's enjoy the experiences of this life! Let's take excellent care of it. And let's realize we are the one inside the car, the one who is taking the ride, not the car. Body and personality, as nice and useful as they may be, are no more than a vehicle we get to use for a while before we move on. From the soul's point of view, identifying with them is crazy.

So let's get this straight: we are not a doughnut. We are not the vehicle, neither the body nor our behavior, emotions, or thoughts. All these are what dies. We are the immortal and blissful consciousness that inhabits this vehicle for a while, a consciousness embedded in a limitless, timeless awareness in which all form, the entire creation, arises. This is the Self, the presence of the Absolute, beyond all form as well as immanent in every part of creation at the same time. We can access it in the cave of the Heart, the very core of our being. It is the eternal presence, the peace that passes all understanding, the well of true, unconditional and universal love that never dries up. By seeking to realize our identity as the Self, we come to end our confusion and suffering and allow the restless mind to merge into the heart. That is enlightenment. We are guided in that, pulled into ourselves, by the intuitive mind and the pure love of the Self.

We can picture it all like this.

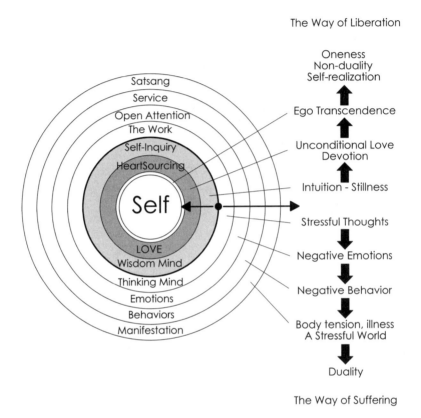

The Way of Liberation

Oneness
Non-duality
Self-realization

Ego Transcendence

Unconditional Love
Devotion

Intuition - Stillness

Stressful Thoughts

Negative Emotions

Negative Behavior

Body tension, illness
A Stressful World

Duality

The Way of Suffering

Satsang
Service
Open Attention
The Work
Self-Inquiry
HeartSourcing
Self
LOVE
Wisdom Mind
Thinking Mind
Emotions
Behaviors
Manifestation

THE WHOLE HUMAN BEING

The Self is at the center of this graphic, the bull's eye, accessible in the cave of the Heart. Of course the Self is not a thing; it is pure consciousness, present not just in the heart, but everywhere. In terms of our little picture, the Self is both the bull's eye (the inner presence) as well as the paper on which the entire picture is printed (unlimited awareness, the cause and matrix of everything) and the consiousness in you, which reads these words.

The mantra Om is the bow, the soul is the arrow,
and Brahman or the Supreme Self is the target (that must be pierced
by the arrow).
This target must be sought with great vigilance.
Then one merges in Brahman even as the arrow merges in its target.
-- Mundaka Upanishad

Now let's see how the Self creates our inner reality. The first veil that separates us from the Self is ahamkara, the "I-making tendency" of the mind, the ego, which has to be made transparent by the process of sadhana. It takes form in each thought which reinforces this mistaken sense of a separate "I." The next layer is the bliss body. It is the tangible experience of the infinite Love of the Self, the Love of God, in which we all participate and exist. Through HeartSourcing and devotion we attune to this layer and let it ferry us to the awareness of the Self. The wisdom mind or intuitive intellect is the next layer. It manifests as the "inner voice" that knows; it does not have to reason or doubt because it participates directly in the Truth of the Self. Self-inquiry (*jnana yoga*) opens us to the direct experience of the Self. These two innermost layers attract our consciousness to the center; they move us inward (the left-pointing arrow) to the recognition of the non-dual and blissful reality of the Self.

Stillness is the entry ticket to that inner reality. It enables us to see the subtle truth of what we are. It becomes intuitive perception (*jnana*) and flowers into unconditional love and devotion (*bhakti*). When these ripen, the illusion of ego separation becomes completely translucent in the unity of our being. This is the way of Liberation, non-duality and Oneness. It is the realization of immortality and the end of all fear.

As it is, we stand in two worlds; we call them inner and outer reality. They are not separate, they are one in our perceiving. We are the conscious, unconcerned witness, who observes both with equal ease: the outward-flowing sequence of manifestation from thoughts to physical manifestation, and the inward flow through stillness, intuitive knowing, all-inclusive love and ego-transcendence into our true enlightened identity.

Being increasingly aware, we have the right response to any challenge

In the forgetfulness of the Self, the externalization of consciousness creates confusion and ignorance. As long as our thinking and pain body are conditioned into this outward progression, we go through cycles of suffering that reinforce themselves with each repetition. Doing nothing to change, we inadvertently increase the density of the pain body. Like a shadow that seeks darkness, externalized consciousness becomes more and more obscured. But when we attune our being to the truth and the love at our core, the shadows dissolve. Our awareness naturally enters a process that flows to the Self and leads to awakening.

The causes of suffering are not the events in our life,
but that we feel cut off from our wholeness
by our stressful thoughts and emotions about these events.

What are the skills that dissolve the causes of suffering and aid in Self-realization? *Meditation* gives us fundamental stillness and inner awareness; it counteracts the mind's conditioned tendency toward distraction. A potent antidote to clear the mind of specific stressful thoughts is *The Work. Open Attention* directly frees us of negative feelings. The resulting stillness and emotional harmony allow us to get in touch with the wisdom mind. Classical *Self-inquiry* poses the question, *Who am I?* It results not in intellectual understanding but in a deep peeling away of all false notions and emotional attachments, which culminates in the spontaneous, intuitive perception of the Self. *HeartSourcing and Devotion* activate the bliss body (which replaces the pain body) and allow the ego to melt in the love of the Self. As intuitive perception and devotion culminate, the ahamkara (subtle ego), the last barrier before Self-realization, becomes translucent and eventually dissolves. This is enlightenment.

The integral approach of HeartSourcing Yoga brings together these potent skills as antidotes to our suffering for each level of our being. They find their completion through selfless service (karma yoga) and satsang (spiritual company). Being increasingly aware, we have the right response to any challenge and can resolve it by realizing it as the opportunity and blessing it is.

Clearing the Mind

How then can we most quickly overcome the stressful habits of the thinking mind? To make a computer analogy, we can say that we are born with extraordinary hardware—our brain and nervous system. But as infants, we don't yet have the "software" needed to use the hardware. That software, the deeper mental conditioning—*how we think*—along with the contents of our files, our thoughts—*what we think*—is installed by society—our parents, siblings, friends, teachers, TV shows, books, and so on. As we grow up, we examine our surface beliefs, keep some and discard or install others, but that only alters the content of our thoughts, the subject matter in the files of our computer. It doesn't change the all-important deeper mental conditioning, *how we think*—and we keep using the same old templates, the same old patterns of thinking, to solve the problems of life. Stress signals us that our thinking isn't working well. So we try again.

We input new data into our mental computer and seek to solve our problems in a different way. Again, failure! Again and again we try, but some areas of our life keep malfunctioning. Rather than looking at our malfunctioning software, we blame the world. Finally we hire somebody else to input new data (a specialist who tells us *what* to think), only to notice that things turn out as bad or even worse than before. Stress again. Then we turn against ourselves: *What's the matter with me? Why can't I ever get it right? I'm such a failure!*

Not true at all. Our suffering is not caused by us or the world, but by *the software we've inherited from society, which is defective and no longer useful!* But it is still supported by the collective (un)consciousness. All the people who are caught in this way of thinking share the same mental dysfunction and the same blind spots. This is what we call "normal." We have no perspective on the software with which we think. That software does well with relatively simple tasks, like putting men on the moon. When it comes to more difficult things— freeing a human relationship of conflict for instance, or bridging the longest distance in the known universe, the space between the head and the heart—then that software routinely fails us.

We can tell when viruses have infected our software by one simple indicator: we experience stress. But part of the old software is the belief that stress is an unalterable and necessary part of our existence. As long as we use the old operating system, we will think, feel, and do hurtful things. The effect of that can be seen every night on the TV news. Does what you see there appear to be the outcome of sane human thinking? Hardly. What you see and experience there is the consequence of completely flawed human software.

It's time to upgrade our mind to a better operating system.
It's time for Human Mind 2.0.
We need to clear the bugs out of our thinking.

That is exactly what The Work of Byron Katie can do. It is a very simple, elegant, and highly sophisticated anti-virus program for our brain. This process, which can be learned in about 30 minutes, will enable you to find the ways your thinking malfunctions, recognize them as faulty and fix them. It can be used systematically to examine entire complexes of stressful thoughts and clear them one by one, helping you to overcome problems that have plagued you for decades. And once the bugs are resolved, the problems do not return. Once you know a deeper truth, you will be unable to believe the old lies your mind has told you for so long. You will be operating on a much higher level of competence.

Practicing The Work is not a linear process of learning new stuff. It occurs in a series of *Aha!* moments, qualitative jumps into a greater truth. It is a shift into the perception of non-dual reality, into the wisdom of the heart. At first it can be a bit perplexing, because we come to think thoughts we never thought before. As we learn these new ways, we must be patient. Everything will become clear in good time.

Moving into a New World

The Work[1] was a true eye-opener for me. Every day was filled with astounding discoveries. I learned that I could question any belief that caused me stress— my tirades about all the things I didn't like, the thoughts that drove my negative emotional patterns, and especially the false gods I worshipped, the core beliefs I held to be unquestionably true: *suffering is an inevitable part of life; every high is followed by a low; people can hurt me; life is difficult*, and many more. To my utter amazement, I saw that these were not truths but mere beliefs. When I examined them, they turned out to be completely mistaken. Like almost everyone around me, I had taken my beliefs to be facts and suffered the consequences. Why? Simply because I had taken birth on this planet and this is the way we humans (still) think.

I realized that every stressful thought I could investigate was another door into freedom, the freedom of the non-dual mind. *Suffering is indeed optional.* Our suffering and confusion are caused by the flawed software of the mind, a disease of wrong thinking that is so predominant that we take it for granted. It never occurred to me that I could question it, but now millions of us are breaking free of the chains, and by freeing ourselves we change the world. This is the true revolution of our time!

On a smaller, personal scale, The Work worked miracles on my everyday complaints. Now I could actively liberate myself. Questioning my negative thoughts I saw the truth: they were lies. Seeing them as false instantly depletes these thoughts of all their power. Whether it was my upset about people, about traffic, about money, whether it was in the moment or ancient conflicts, The Work worked its magic with it all. In a few minutes of practice, I could often free myself of tensions I had held for many years.

With The Work and Open Attention, we have two master skills that free us from pain and bring us great peace. They empower us to take the quantum leap from duality into the unified mind. Once we have learned these practices, we can use them for the rest of our life. You've heard the saying, "Give a person a fish and you feed him for a day. Teach him how to fish and you feed him for a lifetime." Now we can teach us to fish.

> *With The Work, suffering is now optional. It doesn't have to last for years. It can get down to months, weeks, days, minutes, seconds. And that's what it does. You undo one [thought] and next time it arises, you may just not notice. And I say that's phenomenal. That hasn't been available before—on purpose for so many.*
> --Byron Katie

For a brief introduction to The Work, please see Appendix III

21

Snakes Into Ropes

A S CHILDREN WE INNOCENTLY TRY TO learn who we are and what the world is all about. We take our cues from our environment, and then we live within the beliefs we absorb as though they were true. Negative or positive, our beliefs are self-fulfilling prophecies; we are enslaved by them until we can see through our stress-producing thoughts to find the truth. Many of our negative thoughts settle into the subconscious mind and can stay there for decades, slowly poisoning us. We believe them with great conviction and subconsciously repeat them like dark mantras, until we wake up. They are the source of low self-esteem, unworthiness, anger, shame, and much fear.

Part of the beauty of The Work is that we do not have to go digging for hidden problems; we simply use the practice to liberate stress in the mind, day by day, moment by moment. We work with the little annoyances and the darkest of thoughts. Every so often a powerful belief might come up, a belief that is at the core of a lot of old pain. This happened to me one day when an ancient memory arose: I was perhaps four years old when my mother yelled at me in anger, *"You are a terrible child!"*

The resurfacing memory hit me like a bullet. The instant it burst into my awareness, my back went into a painful spasm and I fell to the floor. When I regained my bearings after about three seconds, I was thrilled. Although the thought had come up with intense emotional and physical pain, another part of my mind knew instantly that this was a pure blessing. I recognized it as one of my core beliefs and I could set myself free.

I am the one who is responsible for what I think!

On the surface it seemed that my mother was to blame for the fact that I didn't feel good about myself. She looked like the perpetrator, and I could make a life-long career out of being the victim. But my mother was innocent. How many thousands of times had she told me how wonderful I was and how much she loved me? And then there was one moment of frustration when she lost her calm . . . *and I believed her!* I am the one who is responsible for what I think! Then, as a child, I was not yet able to do that.

Now, if I take responsibility for my beliefs, I can change them. But as long as I blame someone else, I will remain the victim of my thoughts in which I create an uncaring world, and I will re-create this uncaring world in my mind over and over again. I cannot even be sure that my mother said those words; they were simply stored that way in my memory bank, along with all kinds of other fictions and nightmares. Perhaps I made it up. It didn't matter. What mattered is that I could now see it and set myself free.

During my childhood this particular thought was the unspoken belief of most people around me. *We are terrible* was the hidden conviction of the German people after the collective nightmare of World War II. Unconsciously, the mind seeks "proof" of its beliefs and the Holocaust was the perfect evidence that the nightmare in our heads was true. We were guilty and our shame followed us at every step. This is how the sins of the fathers are passed on for generations. "We are terrible" was the mental matrix in which everyone lived—the suffocating horror that lay over the land. This is not only a German problem; it is the collective shame of all of humanity. It is related to, "We are not safe," one of the core beliefs of our age of terrorism, and, "People are trying to hurt us." As long as we see any of us as monsters, we must believe that we have a bit of monster inside us, and we secretly suffer self-rejection and fear. The more pain our stressful thoughts cause, the more determined we get to deny and repress them—and the more we do that, the more we must inevitably live in the pain these thoughts generate. We're caught in a vicious cycle. The inner tension invariably expresses itself until we break the spell and set ourselves free. (For a meditation on Setting the Monster Free, please see Appendix IV).

> The more pain our stressful thoughts cause, the more determined we get to deny and repress them—and the more we do that, the more we must inevitably live in the pain these thoughts generate. We're caught in a vicious cycle.

Of course, we *must* repress such thoughts as long as we don't know how to free ourselves of them. We have no other option. Who wants to live in pain? Without the right skills, we have to defend ourselves against our painful beliefs, and then we wonder why we are not happy and have ulcers, back pain and bad relationships. But with the right understanding and skills, we no longer need to hide our distressing beliefs. We can set ourselves free of them once and for all. This is a fundamentally different approach to life.

When this idea that I was terrible came up, I could have pushed it down again, hoping it would go away. But repression leads to expression, condemning us to live out our nightmares. And who of us is not a perpetrator? I certainly was. I tortured myself for years. I never missed an opportunity to feel badly about myself.

While nursing my painful back, I took this thought—*I am terrible*—into inquiry with The Work and used Open Attention to free up the emotions in my body. The sharp spasm in my back was intense; the pain of the thought was like a knife in the gut and the heart. But the most definite feeling was a thrill of joy that shot through my whole body, accompanied by deep gratitude. I had been completely unaware that I held this belief; what an opportunity now to set myself free!

I began the inquiry. It is so easy to learn, even children can do it. It consists of four simple questions (Is it true? Can I absolutely know it is true? How do I react, what happens, when I believe the thought? And: Who would I be without the thought?) and a process called "turnarounds." As an example, let me just walk you through my experience. Perhaps in some ways it may reflect your own.

The first question: "I am terrible," *is that true?* It felt scathingly true in the place that had held this nightmare for so long. So in that place my answer was Yes.

Can I absolutely know that it's true that I am terrible? This is the second question, and in the light of truth I knew that it was not true at all.

How do I react, what happens when I believe this thought? I recounted the ways I had felt terrible about myself, the decades of self-torture and shame. My perceived weakness as a child. What I told myself about low grades in school in subjects that did not interest me, *"I can't do it, I'm not good enough."* My torturous first adventures with the opposite sex. The millions of times where my self-esteem imploded into depression. How I had felt forever unsafe. The cover-up of arrogance and prideful posturing. I visited every part of my private hell and, wherever I brought the light of awareness, my self-loathing dissolved. I was meticulous, not wanting to leave behind any part of this delusion, this hidden shameful identity. After some time, no other associated painful thoughts surfaced. I waited. I looked again.

Nothing.

So I went on to the fourth question: *Who would I be without this thought?* I tried on my answers to this question like slipping into a new suit for the very first time. It fit well. I could be comfortable in this new way of being. Even after being loved so completely by Maharajji, self-love had been hard to come by. Without this thought I could love myself and do what I had yearned for: love others more deeply. A huge sense of relief began to spread through my bones. My breathing became deeper and the tension in my back began to release.

Then I *turned it around*. "I am not terrible." Feeling this truth was a caress to my soul. I let myself enjoy it, gave myself many examples. A wave of deep healing spread through every cell of my body. I took my time. I was in no hurry to cut this experience short. Among all the evidence that I was not terrible one stood out—the way I had been loved. It was especially sweet to notice my mother's deep love for me and, of course, Maharajji's love above all—the perfect reflection of the enormous love that is hidden within all of us. It makes a lie out of anything that tells us we are less, not capable or deserving of this great divine love.

> The stress-producing thought we believe is like a poisonous snake. It comes up and we react immediately, without thinking. We act as though it were true. The Work gives us an opportunity to stop this blind reaction by taking a closer look at the snake.

Then I examined a variation of this turnaround, "My thinking is terrible." Indeed, that was the only terrible thing I could find. My thinking was the only source of terror. The thought that causes fear is the terrorist.

Next I turned around the word terrible: "I am wonderful." Ah, the relief, the self-recognition went even deeper. I was free at last of the deep-rooted distortion of a belief that had never been true. I saw myself as wonderful at every age—as a baby, small child, adolescent, young and older adult—and the pain of all those years washed away. Now I could see more clearly what Maharajji had seen when he looked at me with his abundance of love; I could let in the love that had been given to me so lavishly by so many. We are all wonderful beyond our wildest dreams. How could it be otherwise? What an amazing gift it is to end the spell of negative thinking! Far worse than all the evil witches in fairy tales, our minds hold us hostage in a web of lies and we forget that we are animated by the loving presence of God.

The entire process took about two hours. I was in bliss. "You're glowing," my friends said. "What happened to you?" Now I can no longer believe this "terrible" thought. I see it for the lie it has always been.

The stress-producing thought we believe is like a poisonous snake. It comes up and we react immediately, without thinking. We act as though it were true. The Work gives us an opportunity to stop this blind reaction by taking a closer look at the snake. "Ah," we see, "there is no snake!" What has tortured us for so long is nothing more than a rope! Once we see the rope, it will always be a rope... and the fear is gone.

If you don't like to suffer, the Work is available to you. It is not difficult to do, certainly much easier than suffering. There are many forms of guidance available when you want to go deep. It works when you work it. *But*, you think, *my particular pain is so real!* I used to feel the same way. Trust the process. Dare to question your most cherished stressful beliefs and see what transpires. Only you can set yourself free.

Sanity doesn't suffer, ever. A clear mind is a beautiful mind and sees only its reflection. It falls at its own feet. It's illumined, it's beautiful. It's clear, it's God. It doesn't add anything or subtract anything; it simply sees clearly what is real and what is not. And in this, suffering is not possible.

--Byron Katie, The Parlour

The Mind of God

While we work on ourselves to peel away all the layers of pain and confusion, it's helpful to step back every so often to get a larger perspective and an ever clearer view of where we are going. My experience with Maharajji created a quantum leap in my understanding about what is possible for us humans and about the incredible miracles we are.

When Baba met people for the very first time, he knew their name, who in the family was not well, who needed help, what their deepest desires were, and what they ate for breakfast. Often he would welcome a new arrival like a long-lost close friend or relative, whose entire life he knew well. At other times, for reasons known only to him, he would hide what he knew.

That was astounding enough, but what was even more amazing was that when he made predictions—and he did so quite sparingly—they always came true. For example, in the early '60s the Chinese army was massed at the northern border of India, ready to invade. Nehru, the president of India, came to Maharajji to ask if he should evacuate millions of people from Delhi, a near impossible task. Maharajji told him not to worry because the Chinese would withdraw without further fighting. This is exactly what happened.

He knew every aspect of our lives, and he set the stage for events in our future, like my healing from cancer. There was no doubting his abilities. While past and future lay before Maharajji like an open book, to think of this power as a psychic ability would be entirely misleading. Baba was not psychic; he was enlightened. He was not an ego, looking from within the world of illusion at the world of illusion. He was—and is—observing life from the absolute clarity of the Self. What flowed out of him was directed by one motivation only—it was the expression of the absolute love of the Self.

That someone could know past and future with such precision seemed impossible to grasp. So I asked Maharajji for understanding and took that question into deep meditation. I saw that in the heart-cave, the innermost part of what we are, all time has already happened; the past and the future are completely present, and the story of existence is already complete. Intuitive insight doesn't feed the mind's desire to reason and speculate. It simply drops a direct revelation of the way things are into our lap, then we can do with it as we please. I felt no desire to do anything with this insight other than bow to that revelation, to recognize in it the sacredness of creation, and to let it inspire me to shed the obstructions that hide that enlightened perspective from me.

The knowing of the heart is beyond all thoughts, fears, and desires. There is a much greater intelligence running the show of our lives than our puny everyday minds. What a relief!

THE END OF FEAR

22

Finding the Light in the Darkness: Auschwitz

W E CANNOT TRULY REACH OUR FULL potential in any area of our lives as long as we are captives of our old ways of thinking and feeling, trapped in the dualities of good and evil, right and wrong, what is to be feared and what is to be loved. In order to fully unfold and to know true and unchanging happiness, we must make peace with our fears. Only then can we truly love. To make peace with fear, we have to face it. Only then can we live in the fullness of the heart.

> To make peace with fear, we have to face it. Only then can we live in the fullness of the heart.

My deepest fear arose from my perception of evil. If I was to make friends with reality, I had to come to grips with that fear. All the ancient mythologies speak of the great battle between good and evil. It is an internal battle and it had gone on inside of me for too long. Slowly, through grace and my everyday spiritual practice, I had nurtured in me a resolute confidence and real compassion to set myself free. Such compassion is as sharp as a knife; it can cut through everything that bars the way. It gives the heart its unique song to sing.

So clearly it was not a coincidence when I met Roshi Bernie Glassman in Hawaii when we were both visiting Ram Dass. He is a highly respected Zen teacher, founder of the Zen Peacemaker order (www.zenpeacemakers.org), a being of extraordinary heart. For a few days we shared Hawaii's delightful balmy love. I knew then that I would join Bernie and several dozen meditators, yogis, and regular folk on his yearly "Bearing Witness Retreat" in Auschwitz. I didn't have to make a decision. It was time, time to go into this frightened, shameful, and grieving part of my mind in order to dissolve it into the heart.

Arriving at Auschwitz

On a bitterly cold and grey November day I arrived in Krakow, Poland, to journey into the very heart of everything I had feared all my life. An arctic wind was blowing down from the North and I shivered from the bone-chilling anticipation of what I was about to witness. I met the members of Bernie's group in a Jewish restaurant in the Kazimierz district, the old Jewish quarter of Krakow, filled with pictures and memorabilia of Jewish life. Klezmer music filled the place with great joyous energy. What a flourishing haven of Jewish culture and spirit! Then I found out it was all pure imitation. Yes, the restaurant had once been a thriving center of culture and commerce, but now it was run by Poles as a tourist attraction. Of the three million Jews who lived in Poland before the war, hardly any are left. The restaurant is a mere shadow, a ghost of the vibrant Jewish community that used to exist here—a special kind of museum that speaks of the Nazis' effectiveness in their brutal extermination campaign.

I wondered if I was mad to enter Auschwitz, the most notorious of all the death camps of the Nazis. No, I was here to free myself of fear, this terrible affliction that is born out of ignorance of the true nature of Reality and reinforces in us the perception of separateness and vulnerability. But now, as I was about to come face to face with that unimaginable suffering, all theories of liberation seemed lifeless. All I could do was to center myself and open to whatever was going to come. For all my life I had seen images from the camps. They had become deeply engrained in my mind. I could not defend myself by telling me that they were about other people's experience. At the very core of our being we are all profoundly connected, we are one. There is a sense of compassion that transcends our separate existence and in that place we cannot help but feel for the suffering of others.

> Our fears are like the vivid nightmare of a child. They are resolved by waking up.

But before we gain such kindheartedness, the same energy is present in us as fear. When fear is overcome, it matures into compassion.

In an effort to understand the incomprehensible magnitude of what they might have experienced, and to come to grips with my fears, I had often imagined myself as a prisoner at Auschwitz—naked, cold, hungry, with shaved head, beaten, and on the way to the gas chamber. How would I deal with an experience like that? Of course it all happened in my imagination. Obviously I did not have the real experience. But all fears play in the mind and this was as real as it got for me. And it was not just my fear I tried to face, it was my part of the fear of humanity. What happened at Auschwitz is part of our common fate, our common terror, that something like this could happen to us as well. We like to keep such terrors hidden away deeply in the subconscious, but from there they secretly suffocate our hearts.

Although you never feel ready to face the unknown, I did not come unprepared. I had with me the grace of my teachers, my skills, and the strength accumulated from my past practice. I trusted they would help me here. But all my preparation did not dispel the deep chill I felt in my bones.

The next morning I awoke strangely disoriented and in terror. I felt completely numb and confused and had to repeat to myself several times, *"No, you are not going to perish here. The killing stopped decades ago. You have come here as a tourist. You are going to the camp in a comfortable modern bus, with friends, voluntarily. You will get out alive…!"* When I got a grip again on my present reality, I realized that for a moment I had lost touch of my sense of connection to Maharajji's presence.[1] It is as natural now as the very presence of my heart and is usually constant. It felt like falling into a state of black nothingness, like being cut off from the source of love, imagining myself to be nothing more that a body-bound ego that can be destroyed. How terrifying this state of mind is, and who doesn't know it? It is the ego's fear of annihilation and it causes us to live in a continuous, unconscious escape.

> The story of fear and discomfort is the story of the victim "me."

We are terrified that, if we were to approach the inner hell of our imaginary fears, we would be tortured, overwhelmed, swallowed alive. However, once we muster the courage to enter the menacing places inside, we see that the darkness is not a dead end, but a tunnel, a passageway to the brilliant light at the other end—the light of the Self and freedom from pain. Emerging from this dark tunnel of our own birth canal, we are born anew into increasing freedom and peace, into divine presence, into unconditional love. Until we travel through that tunnel, our blind urges to fight, flee, indulge, or complain will force us into hopeless, unthinking reactions. That means we will have to continue to live with our pain and we will unconsciously spread it. In truth however all our fears arc like the vivid nightmare of a child. They are resolved not by fighting the monsters or by escaping from them, but by a completely different movement we cannot imagine as long as we are hypnotized by our fears. They are resolved by waking up.

I want to pause here for a moment to asure you that there is a good purpose for you and me walking together now into and out of my life-long hell in these next few pages. To say it better: we are about to pass through the valley of the *shadow* of death – *not* the valley of death! In order to become fully alive, we cannot avoid crossing this valley. The story of fear and discomfort is the story of the victim "me." The discovery of the Self that conquers all lies on the other side of that valley. Will you stay in identity with the pain body, or realize the timeless Self? Will you be a victim, or will you be victorious over the mind? Just like mine, your own personal hell is not a destination, but a passageway into the light. Some of your own

> We must free ourselves of our dark past. We must look into the eye of the monster and bring it to peace, or we will condemn ourselves to stay in its power

fear or past pain may be stirred. If you want to become free of it, I invite you to welcome it and know it to be *a part of you that needs help.* This is how our jouney together is serving your freedom. Have that courage! Proceed slowly, deliberately, and with great compassion for yourself. And then, after we have shed some of the weight that burdens us, we will together celebrate the heart's invigorating glory in the last chapter. As Maharajji used to say: "If you don't make it empty, how will you fill it up again?" Honor yourself deeply for your desire to become free.

I was going to Auschwitz because I was determined to win my freedom. Of course, not only Germans and Jews have a dark past to clear. We all do, because we are all part of humanity and all humans carry a shadow. The deep memory of centuries of violence, abuse, neglect and pain of all kinds are an Auschwitz of the mind in all of us and it has many counterparts in the physical world, filled with vast horrors. This is our common heritage and we are here to overcome it.

Even though there have been many other genocides[2] and atrocities before and since, Auschwitz is still the most momentous symbol of hate and brutality. Nowhere else has the sadistic, industrialized human slaughter reached such grotesque depths.[3] Nowhere else has humanity erected such a chilling monument to its darkest side. And it is not only out there somewhere in Poland. It is in us, part of our human condition. It is part of our bondage and terror and it can become a gateway to our freedom. The question that faces us all is this: Can I stop the killing, the horror and shame *in me*? And therefore: Can I open to my own true potential for love?

We must free ourselves of our dark past. We must look into the eye of the monster and bring it to peace, or we will condemn ourselves to stay in its power.

For a meditation on Setting the Monster Free, please see Appendix IV.

The Nightmare

For quite a while we sat in complete darkness. Then the old footage began to flicker onto the screen of the Auschwitz theater and I was confronted by a sea of corpses, decomposing skeletal forms with twisted limbs, hollow extinguished eyes and gaping mouths, lying about in large heaps. These films were made on the days immediately following the camp's liberation. The bodies were tossed into mass graves, first by civilians and soldiers, then finally pushed by bulldozers, a sickening, bone chilling display. My mind froze, horror-struck. As a child in school I had seen footage of the Nazi atrocities many times, but nothing to this extent. I could taste and feel my body reacting, but I could not form thoughts. What happened at Auschwitz and in so many other places was, and still is, unthinkable.

PAINTING BY MARIAN KOLODZIEJ, AUSCHWITZ SURVIVOR

After the film, I entered the camp under the infamous sign AR-BEIT MACHT FREI (Work Makes You Free). I walked on the ashes of one-and-a-half million people. One-and-a-half million people like you and me, with hopes and dreams, with laughter and love, and with pain. Their humanity ripped from them, they had become walking skeletons with burning deep eyes, numbers, statistics, their sheer multitude numbing the mind. Here, in this museum of death and brutality, some of them came back to life. Pictures of their faces lined the walls as we crossed the barracks. I looked at them, silently, seeking some resolution, some hope, some flicker of peace in what I saw. I could not find it.

I walked past mountains of hair shorn from their heads, some of it still neatly braided by some woman's hand. Their hair and other parts of their bodies had been shipped back to Germany to be used as industrial raw material in support of the war effort. There were mountains of suitcases, mountains of toothbrushes, eyeglasses, shoes. Then the rooms of torture, chambers of cold concrete, each with a specific purpose: the starvation cells, the suffocation room, the *Stehbunker*[4] —a concrete cell, less than 3 x 3 feet, into which four men would be locked all night with barely enough room to stand, only to be sent out again the next day to their backbreaking work. The strategy of feeding people less than they needed in order to stay alive—an entire inventory of unbelievable cruelty. The execution wall. The gallows. The people continued to move through my mind's eye, women, children and men, multitudes upon multitudes, unspeakable pain, much of it neatly catalogued and recorded by the Nazis' penchant for order, even here.

It was more than I could process or comprehend. This depth of suffering, this ocean of pain. My imagination could not encompass the extent of this cruelty. It had to capitulate. All I could do was to be still and enter a place of unknowing. My mind made feeble efforts to regain its bearings, but in vain. There was only a wordless, thoughtless, incomprehensible sadness in the recognition of the abyss of depravity and suffering humans are capable of—and that means me.

> *I am not different, not separate from them.*
> Sh'ma Yisrael, Adonai Elohaynu, Adonai Echad
> *Hear, O Israel, the Lord our God, the Lord is One.*
> *We are one.*

We are one in our love and our beauty; we are one in our cruelty and our madness. What was left was a sense of profound reverence in the face of such suffering. It felt like a prayer without gesture or word, a prayer that we humans will be released from our own folly, from the blindness of the heart and the madness of the mind that created such horrendous hatred and confusion.

Now I understood the words of H.G. Adler, who survived the Theresienstadt, Auschwitz, and Buchenwald concentration camps and wrote: "Who has not personally experienced this destruction, does not know, will never be able to know. He has to be silent. He has to listen and to examine his life's purpose for himself and as a human being in the world." I realized that all my attempts to come to grips with my fears by making the experience of others manageable in my mind had failed.

> Slowly, ever so slowly, compassion took hold where unknown terror had ruled.

This insight came with a sense of relief. I can never understand someone else's pain, nor can I free them of it. I can only free myself, my own heart and mind. Only then will I be fully capable of giving to the world my compassion and my understanding. Only to the extent that I am awake can I be of help to anyone elses' awakening. I fell into silence and a profound awe before the immensity of what transpired here. I could only bow my head in humility in the face of what I saw. This is how Auschwitz became a sacred place for me, challenging me to go beyond everything I thought I knew and to open unconditionally to what it was teaching me.

I had seen more than I could handle in one day. That's when I knew I had to work with my feelings. I went deep into this numbness with Open Attention. It felt as though a part of me was not alive. I searched and found it. Hard as a block of ice, the numbness reached from deep in my gut up to my throat and radiated outward into my limbs and head. It was composed of fear, dread, panic, and terror. It seemed that if I were to let myself feel these sensations fully, I would be annihilated. At the core of this numbness, a tremendous nausea wrenched my gut. Then a violent shaking, heaving, great streams of uncried tears. I met them all as parts of me that desperately needed help. I could no longer hide it. I could no longer repress it. I dove deep into this dark hell, deeper and deeper, radiating into my terror the breath of human kindness, meeting that deadly coldness with the warm rays of awareness.

Release did not happen quickly. Again and again I had to dive into this death-like numbness, deeper and deeper each time. Slowly insights began to unfold. Clearly, by killing the Jews and other "undesirables" (gypsies, homosexuals, people with disabilities, those with different political views, and more), the Germans had 'killed' themselves as well. What we do to another, we do to ourselves. This is an absolute rule, whether the deed is small or enormous. In that cavernous dead space in my body, I found that which had been killed in me. I kept descending into that icy cold, further and further, determined not to miss even the smallest bit of my ancient horror. Even as I descended, I felt a great strength in the courage of this descent. I knew that I had to either live with this pain, or find my way through it into freedom.

> Love is the great antidote to the madness. It begins with you and me. It always begins now.

Slowly, the deadness relinquished its power. Slowly, a sense of life returned. Slowly, ever so slowly, compassion took hold where unknown terror had ruled. I continued the practice of Open Attention every day I was in Auschwitz, and every day I discovered a greater depth of feeling, as pain dissipated and freedom naturally arose. Little by little the fear melted away as a the inner resilience we all have took hold. We indeed come alive by going into that which we fear, into the dead and terrified parts of us. Every day on this journey I welcomed myself back to the land of the living a little bit more, giving birth to myself in the city of death.

We went to the second camp in the Auschwitz complex, known as Birkenau or Auschwitz 2. This camp is gigantic. Alongside numerous large gas chambers and crematoria, it held barracks for 50,000 prisoners. The crematoria were designed to kill and "process" 5,000 human bodies in a day. But that wasn't enough. The Nazis meant to double this camp in size, their plans foiled only by the end of the war. Here the trains of cattle cars disgorged innocent people from all parts of Europe onto a selection site where they were separated, men on one side, women on the other. Then their fate was decided by the infamous Dr. Mengele or one of his men: a small gesture sent each one either to the right and the gas chambers, or to the left to slave labor and an almost certain slow death by starvation, cold, sickness, torture, and brutal work.[5]

I fell into deep silence at that selection site. As some in our group read aloud from the list of the names of the dead, I descended beyond listening into the great stillness inside the soul. No nightmare has the power to disturb this sacred stillness within. Coming to stillness here was not an escape. Quite to the contrary, it was a return to the reality of who we are. *We are this silence that cannot be disturbed.* In the face of such cruelty, the purity of silence takes on a special significance—it is the absolute peace at the core of the heart. Here every nightmare is revealed in its true form, as a passing dream, unreal and transparent, even a nightmare as big as Auschwitz. Along with the peace, an enormous sense of compassion arose in me, carried by a clear view of my real purpose in this world: to learn how to love. Love is the great antidote to the madness. It begins with you and me. It always begins now.

The Heart of Death

Surrounded by the history of so much killing, I had to reconsider my understanding of what death really is. We fear death because we identify with our temporary body and personality. But they are like the clothing we wear for a while until it no longer serves us. In truth, we are pure awareness; everything else dies into the light. We die out of time and the illusion that we are this temporary body/mind/ego into the immortality and the bliss of the soul.

Even while we live in these bodies, we die whenever we shed an old way of being and open to a greater, more light-filled perspective. What dies is the smallness, the limitation, the darkness, the fear and separation—everything we are not. If we closely observe this ever-present process of dying and being reborn, it becomes clear that death is very familiar to us, because in small ways it happens all the time, and that it is a good thing, a gradual waking up from illusion into reality. And reality is our freedom; it is infinitely kinder than our stressful beliefs about death.

When I was in India, I spent time at the burning ghats in Kashi, the most sacred city in India (also known as Benares or Varanasi). Here, on a set of wide steps leading down to the sacred Ganges River, the bodies of the dead are burned on wooden pyres. This has been going on around the clock for about 5,000 years. These burning ghats are even more permeated by death than Auschwitz, yet the feeling in these two places could not be more different. The burning ghats are a sacred place for those who follow the *sanatana dharma* (the Hindu philosophy and religion), the eternal law of Self-realization. It is considered a great blessing to die in Kashi and to have one's body cremated here; it is said that as the body burns, the soul is released from the bondage of the endless cycle of birth and death into liberation. Consequently, the streets of Kashi are filled with the old and the dying, many of them poor and sick with leprosy and other diseases. Many spend their last days begging for the money to buy food and the wood for their cremation. Despite the sorry state of their bodies, they are elated because they know that after uncounted lifetimes of wandering in *samsara*—the ongoing cycle of birth, death, and rebirth based on ignorance of the true Self—they have arrived at the last way station, about to be released into the light of God. They know they are about to be unshackled from illusion and pain. There is a vast sense of peace here that the dying share with the living, an awareness that these are the last moments before final beatitude.

Even Auschwitz serves peace.

One dark, moonless night I stood by the river surrounded by over a dozen open fires, each consuming a human body. Breathing in the smell of burning flesh (which smells just like a backyard barbeque), I looked up into the black nighttime sky. There was no moon, no stars, not even space, just an infinite depth of immense, unbounded, black nothingness. So much death here had eaten away the limits the human mind builds around life. Here existence was infinite, beyond the cycles of birth, death and rebirth, containing nothing and everything. At first I was shocked by the power of this revelation. An existential fear gripped me. But almost instantly the fear subsided and a great stillness took its place, and in that stillness I discovered that death has a heart. Emptiness and fullness are one. One instant we are struggling, and the next we are released into a freedom so vast it extinguishes the fearful mind. And then the heart—as big as all existence—can reveal to us that we are one with the bliss of the Heart of God.

In Auschwitz, death also has a heart, the same heart, but it is hidden from us by the immensity of fear, pain and brutality. Death, nevertheless, is always the passageway out of the dream of duality and separation into oneness. The *Tibetan Book of the Dead*[5] contains lucid descriptions of the states between death and rebirth, called the *bar-dos*, around the central encounter with the "clear light of reality." In the Western traditions, we would describe this experience as coming face to face with the presence of God or Absolute Love. In this presence, the truth of the soul is known. It is the complete release of all suffering, fear, and pain of the recent lifetime. At this point it is possible to merge with the light.

If you have done your inner work, if your soul is ripe, it is the end of the journey, the release into oneness. If you are not done with attachments, the journey continues into a new existence in which you will be given yet another opportunity to learn the lessons you have yet to grasp. There is also a third option: if your soul has matured in its ability to love, you can consciously choose to return to this world again for the benefit of all beings. This is the path of a *Bodhisattva*— a "wisdom being" who has enlightenment for all as his aim.

If we are unaware of the release that is coming before we die, we surround death with fear. The possibility of a clear and peaceful view is overwhelmed by this fear, by our belief in danger and evil, by our clinging to ego. What can we do? We can put our entire fear-based perception of death under inquiry and let the emotional prison dissolve. Yes, this is not a little thing. It means to overcome some of our deepest conditioning, but this conditioning for fear is not the truth of who we are. When that truth dawns, when we awaken and light comes into our perception, darkness naturally, and easily, disappears. Who would we be without our fear of a terrible death, of abuse and of terror, our dark stories of villains and victims? Do these stories serve us? Can they set us free? Do they make the world a better place? And most importantly, is there an alternative?

Within the horror of Auschwitz, I found the liberating truth, that once we have surrendered our attachments, death is a dissolving into peace. When we know that our path leads to the great peace of enlightenment, we come to know that each event in our lives takes us closer to this supreme goal. And so we come to understand that everything serves our freedom. *Absolutely everything!* This is why even Auschwitz serves peace. It is, and remains, a stark reminder of how wrong we can go, what the mind can do when it is disconnected from the heart. It is a wake-up call out of the negative extremes into which the ego-driven mind can fall, and thereby it serves as a powerful inspiration toward its opposite—it is compelling us to turn inward to harness the power of love.

> *Someday, after we have mastered the winds, the waves, the tides and gravity, we shall harness for God the energies of love. Then for the second time in the history of the world, we will have discovered fire.*
>
> --Pierre Teilhard de Chardin

23

The Doorway Into The Light

THE NEXT DAY I NOTICE HOW my mind attempts to slip away. Even here it does not want to face Auschwitz. It wants to escape, to minimize, forget, and repress. On the surface our ancient habit of mental escape into distractions appears to keep us safe from unpleasant experiences, but it does exactly the opposite. It keeps us from facing ourselves and therefore from healing our internal pain. This of course serves the pain body. It feeds itself from the putrid mix of subconscious fears, self-recrimination, shame, and self-hate. But meditation has taught me to observe the mind with the mind. I am deeply grateful for that, because self-awareness is the key to awakening. And as I look inward, I see how the mind does it all: Fight, flight, indulge, and complain. I repress the hidden fears in my mind, distract myself so I don't have to face them, indulge in depression and anger, and complain. But I have decided to no longer feed this insanity. I have come here, into this life, to this place, to be free. And I know that nothing but my own mind has the power to keep me imprisoned.

As long as I am asleep, the quality of my life will be ruled by a seemingly unsolvable conflict: I am caught in an unseen internal war, the conflict of perpetrator and victim. While in the external world I can distinguish them and call one person perpetrator and another victim, internally, as states of mind, they are intimately linked. I am always my own perpetrator and my own victim. From my actions I reap my own karma; when I hurt someone I hurt myself. And whenever I see myself as a victim, I hurt myself by perpetrating the victim mindset on me. This madness will only stop when I cut through this duality and see all beings as one.

Of course it's not easy. Trauma has a long reach; it is passed on from generation to generation. But the truth is that the past is gone; it is finished. It lives on as thoughts and images in the mind, but it has only the power we give it. It cannot stop us from being present now. Being fully present completely disempowers the past and restores power to us, where it belongs.

> The past is gone; it is finished. It lives on as thoughts and images in the mind, but it has only the power we give it. It cannot stop us from being present now. Being fully present completely disempowers the past and restores power to us, where it belongs.

How is it then that events of the past still cause us pain? How can we be victims of what happened before we were born? Is it genetic? Is it a racial or national memory? Is it imagination? All of these may be factors, but primarily pain from the past is caused by powerful, deep-seated, stressful beliefs. *People are cruel. This is a dangerous world. It's not safe to trust people. I have to protect myself. Horrible things could happen to me.* As though we are looking through a pair of colored glasses, we experiencee the world through our beliefs. As long as we believe such thoughts, they repeat reflexively in our subconscious mind, creating a trance state of unhappiness and of fear. Our stressful thoughts victimize us, and it is we who perpetrate them on us. We are victim and perpetrator in one. Unaware that we are the cause of our own discomfort, we blame past or present people or circumstances. I realized that with this inner war raging in me, I cannot help but teach war. I cannot be a source of peace. I remain part of the problem, unable to be part of the solution. Clearly the only way to be of service, the only way to bring peace to this world, is to set myself free. Staying focussed on my own liberation in the face of the enormous suffering of Auschwitz is the most generous thing I can do. Because freedom and enlightenment are not for oneself; they are the gift of all gifts that belongs to all beings.

> Our stressful thoughts victimize us, and it is we who perpetrate them on us. We are victim and perpetrator in one.

I cannot be free as long as I believe my stressful thoughts. One of them was, "People cause others enormous suffering." This thought appeared so unquestionably true to me that it came as a great surprise to realize I could question it. I realized it only because thoughts that are stressful—no matter how true they seem—belong into inquiry. And so I began.

"People cause others enormous suffering." Is it true? Yes. Stark evidence for it was all around me.

And can I absolutely know that it is true? Of course, Yes! I want to say, but experience stops me. I have learned to mistrust my stressful beliefs because they never seem to hold true when I question them, and so I open to some new insight. Although the evidence seems overwhelming, I have to say: No, I cannot *absolutely* know that it's true.

How do I react when I believe that "People cause others enormous suffering?" Terror arises in me, shame and deep sadness. Something painfully contracts in my chest. My breathing stalls. I do not want to be part of this in-human race, and yet there is no choice. I am inescapably one of these people, who in their blind demonic madness destroy themselves and each other. I feel despair and deep anguish. I am completely powerless in the face of this cruelty. I see these people as unfeeling monsters, against whom self-defense seems to be the only sensible options. I live in a forboding, unfriendly and harsh place. I don't want to be here because it seems impossible to find happiness, human kindness, and love when I believe this thought. I feel weak, condemned to a life of continual struggle, dominated by fear. It is a life not worth living.

Who would I be without this belief, "People cause others enormous suffering?" I pause. The last question caused the familiar eruption of fear and hopelessness and I wait until my emotions clear. Then I imagine myself without this belief. Without it I am free. I feel my posture change, my breath opens up. I can feel good about myself. There is no shame. I can love me, I can love this planet and its people. And I can recognize that I am universal, a soul inside this body, not bound to any tribe, nor to any label or past. If I am bound at all, I am bound to my divine origin. Without this thought I am free to live in the Now, unencumbered, humble, joyful, grateful for the countless gifts of my life that surround me on all sides. I can open my heart to the people around me, unburdened, and see in them my own love mirrored, in gratitude for the miracle of life that is Now.

A wave of relief washes through me and I move on to the turnarounds:

The first turnaround is, *"I cause others enormous suffering."* I let the thought sink in. And yes, it's easy to see as I look into my past: I caused others enormous suffering through my anger, my inability to love, my defensiveness, my depression. I allow specific examples to come up, a moment of rage at a friend, my mother's dissapointed face when I stayed distant from her, my father's pain when I dropped out of school. Looking at yourself that way is the bitter medicine of self-awareness. No one wants to look at their own failings, but unless we do, we are doomed to repeat them. So while the medicine may be bitter, the freedom it brings is sweet and it comes fast.

Then I turned the thought around to, *"I cause me enormous suffering."* That was obvious. My negative thoughts made me depressed, fearful and angry; they stifled my heart and took from me the happiness of being compassionate and loving to others.

The third turnaround was more difficult. *"People do <u>not</u> cause others enormous suffering."* I had to become very still to understand the truth of this turnaround. First the obvious examples came up, the way Buddha, Christ and countless great sages have benefitted us and shown us the way out of suffering. I thought of the immense goodness that occurs between people, the love between parents and children, between friend, lovers and siblings. I sensed the vastness of this love and it brought me peace. "But what about here?" I thought. "How can it be true here?"

I realized I had to look at different levels of reality. On the physical level, undoubteldly people cause others enormous suffering, suffering beyond comprehension. To find the truth of this turnaround I had to go deeper. I realized there are three levels of experience. In our constricted ego-awareness we identify with the body and we suffer. We are all familiar with that. But when awareness expands, we become aware that we are a soul, a reflection of God's light. With that our focus shifts. We realize that whatever suffering comes to us can have only one effect: it brings us closer to God, to enlightenment, to release from the cycles of birth and death. As a soul this is our sole aspiration. It gives peace to the mind and clarity to our actions. Our focus is liberation and no force on earth can divert us from this goal, rather, everything that happens brings us closer to it.

A metaphor for the awareness of soul is that each being is like the light of the sun reflected in a jar of water. When we identify with the jar (our body and personality), our sole concern is to defend its integrity and any harm that comes to it causes us pain. When the jar breaks we see this as the end of our existence, an absolute calamity, and we live in fear of that. But on the soul level, we come to realize that we are not the jar, but the sun's reflection and our aim is to realize our oneness with the sun, our true Self. Naturally we will take care of the jar, but we are less afraid about what happens to it. We know that it is transient and cannot be the sole cause of our happiness. Finally there is the level of absolute truth, where we realize that we are neither the jar, nor the reflection, but the sun itself, the divine presence that shines in us.

Realizing its true identity, the soul is one with its own origin—the sun in our metaphor—as Jesus said, "I and my Father are one." All the great realized beings have told us that our true state is this oneness and that seeking it is our purpose. It is the Ground of Being,[1] the *purusha, Ishvara*,[2] satchitananda. This cosmic awareness is a state of pure and total presence,[3] the majestic universal consciousness, which manifests universes. When we experience this state beyond hope and fear, all anxiety is transcended. When our awareness expands out of ego-bound smallness, we eventually reach the state beyond suffering. It is what we are. The experience of this state of absolute freedom is what yogis strive for and it can occur spontaneously to us at any time, especially during moments of rapture or pain. In such a moment awareness leaves its limited state and gives way to the realization of oceanic awareness. You realize you are the Great Ocean of Being in whom all beings exist like individual waves. When the body suffers and dies, this ocean of consciousness is not shaken in its vast peace. This is what we already are and always have been.

People can torture and kill a body, but they cannot touch our soul. Suffering is the necessary catalyst that provides the spark for spiritual awakening. Even now the lingering horror of Auschwitz inspires me in this way. When seen from this perspective, suffering leads to grace. Everything people do, both in their love *and* their cruelty, helps us to seek the realization of our true identity and the end of all suffering. And another turnaround appears, *"People cause others to realize the end of suffering."*

What does that mean here in Auschwitz? I remember the reports that among the prisoners were some few, who reacted to their horrific situation in a very different way to most others. They cared for everyone around them. Seemingly unconcerned for their body's welfare, they gave away their last piece of bread to help someone else before they perished. This greatness of soul has been reported many times. It is the recognition of the soul's true identity, the truth of our being.

Learning to live in that truth, with a clear mind and an open heart, has to be our answer to Auschwitz. The self-transformation that is required for that is always an individual choice, effort, and victory. It's up to us now. I don't see another way we can react intelligently to the pain in the world, but to end pain in us. This is the way we can end the pain of the world. It is the most important gift we have for each other.

The Watchtower

The following day our group meets in the central watchtower. Looking down from above, the camp sprawls before me, a maze of rusting barbed wire with the crematoria in the distance. I try to step into the mind of one of the SS men who used to guard the camp from up here. I find it difficult. These people and their actions have been the greatest source of pain in my life, and yet I feel no anger or animosity. I am simply unable to relate. Once more I ask myself, "How is it possible that human beings fall into such gross abuse of power? Into such unfeeling insanity?"

I look over the camp trying to imagine being one of them, holding a rifle, able to shoot and kill any prisoner on a whim or for sport. My well-honed ability for imagery eludes me here. Then I remember a story. One day in Auschwitz a rabbi asked his ragtag friends in the barracks to help him sing an ancient Hebrew song of gratitude. They looked at him, they looked at each other, and then they looked at him again. "Rabbi," they said, "what is the matter with you? Look at us! We are starving; we are desperate. Any moment we could go into the ovens. We are the walking dead. What do we have to be grateful for?" The rabbi looked back at them. Then he pointed outside through a window where some of the guards were standing and said, "You could be one of them."

After a while Bernie speaks to the group. He tells us that at a previous retreat he had suggested that the Nazis also deserve our compassion and our forgiveness, which riled the peacemakers so much that it almost came to blows among them. It doesn't surprise me. We may be less attached to our prejudices than the Nazis were, but we still have them. My own great prejudice had been against Nazis. I hated them as much as I feared what they stood for. I hated what they had done, how they had so devastated the world into which I was born. I blamed them for the pain in my life. I was completely committed to my conviction; I was totally oblivious to the fact that I was as narrow-minded as they had been. Then one day I was shocked to see how bound by prejudice I was; I saw what blindness truly is and how absolute it can be.

In my intolerance I had been exactly like them. I had believed that certain human beings were toxic and wrong. My thoughts were not different in kind from the Nazis' belief that the "subhumans" were contaminating the purity of their race. The Nazis had been my *Untermenschen*, my subhumans. When I realized that, relief and a deep sense of gratitude arose in me, for I had acted upon my prejudice mostly in my own mind and had been spared the temptation to persecute those against whom I was prejudiced. But it was a difference in degree only, not in kind.

So is it true that I cannot relate to the Nazis, the SS guards, the rapist, the thief, the murderer, to all the perpetrators of crimes in this world? No. I certainly can. Now I see that they are exactly like me when I'm confused, when I believe my stressful thoughts and do not examine them. Sometimes I don't know that my judgmental thoughts cause me stress. I am so sure that I am right that I gain a sense of power from my convictions, from the seductive assurance that I am the one who knows. It allows me to ignore my insecurity and confusion and gives me the pride that I am better than others. My friends all agree with me, "Yes, Nazis are wrong." We bond in our blindness. We have a common enemy—the Nazis, the Blacks, the Whites, the men, the women, the Jews, the Muslims, the gays, the straights, the rich, the poor—all those we see as different from us.

Every step I take is a step taken in freedom.

Can I recognize that the people I disagree with or dislike are part of the perfection of life? Can I accept them as they are, even while I do whatever I can to help them evolve, and keep those from gaining power, who don't have the wisdom to handle it? Can I see the face of Hitler in the picture of Maharajji without fear or hostility? Can I see everything as part of God? Can I become aware that the perpetrator, the abuser, and the terrorist need my compassion most because they are most confused? Can I find their confusion in me and clear it there first? Evil is another word for confusion. Can I free myself of confusion to the clear recognition that God is everything and God is good?

IN AUSCHWITZ

Thinking Mind – Wisdom Mind

Once more I sit at the selection site in meditation. I have to find a bridge between my perception of evil and the reality that the love of God permeates everything. How can I bridge these perceptions? How can that great love be found here? How can I dispell the hold my fear of evil has had on me? All I can see right now is profound suffering and the utmost brutality of man against man. I know what I have to do: in my mind I have to take myself through the experience of a prisoner while staying entirely in the now. I have to see if I can walk through this camp to my death with the mind of a Buddha, with the heart of a Christ, so completely open and present that fear will lose its grip on me. This inner experience, I know, could show me that even here in Auschwitz freedom could reign.

Obviously this is my own internal experience, not what a prisoner might have gone through. I cannot know what their experience actually was. I can only set myself free. And so, for the sake of my freedom, I go again and again through my internal ritual: As a prisoner I am getting out of the train, disoriented and afraid, and the Nazis line us up, women on one side, men on the other. For the last time I see my parents, my children, my loved ones. Then there is a man in uniform who points to the left or to the right. Accordingly I am led to a fast death or to a slow death after torture. Again and again I go though this ritual in my inner vision. I realize that my experience takes place in my mind. The whole world takes place there. Thoughts create suffering. If I know what's in store for me, I panic. Fear blinds me. I am overwhelmed by terror.

> In my true identity as pure awareness I am already and always completely safe.

How can I find the kindness of the universe as I am stepping out of the train? Only if I can find it here on this ramp will I be able to find it everywhere. I go through it again and again. The hundredth time I finally manage to step out of the train with no preconceived thoughts. I am completely open to the here and now. My mind has become peaceful and it allows me not to create a future or to look at a past. Whatever happens now, whatever that may be, *is* my path into liberation. With the thinking mind stilled, I move in the wisdom mind, in pure awareness. I embrace this moment, whatever it may bring. I am unconditionally open. In this state of mind I move without resistance and fear. Every step I take is a step taken in freedom.

In the turmoil of barking dogs, screaming men, and guns pointing at me, I am lined up with the others. As I am separated from my loved ones, the mind stays balanced and calm. I love them deeply and my love is not bound and shaken by attachments. We have been separated many times; it is part of life. Can I experience this parting openly, without fear and clinging, without wanting the moment to be different than it is? I move ahead in the line and there is a man in uniform; he looks at me and points to the right. They call him "the angel of death," the nickname the prisoners used for Dr. Mengele. It is true; he is that for me. I don't have to make a decision. I don't have to fear. I am going through hell and out of hell into the light of God, and every step I take brings me closer to my goal, my awakening. It strikes me how this is entirely true for everyone at all times. We are all going to our destiny with every step we take. We all don't know what the next step may bring. And the clear mind knows that there is no other place where we can possibly go but into merging with God. That is why we can move through life openly and in trust.

> Even here in the city of death, I walk in the glory of God. Every step I take leads me to enlightenment. All life is like that, whether I know it or not. We are always walking in the presence of God.

I walk along with the others. My heart is at peace. I walk on in deep wisdom, in the Buddha mind, the heart of Christ; I rest in the *Shekinah*.[4] I know I am completely safe because I am not this body; I am consciousness, I am immortal, I am the presence of God. No stressful thought disrupts this peace and, if one comes up, inquiry meets it and it dissolves. No emotion disturbs me. I am awake. I am one with my Beloved. My heart and my whole being are fully alive.

I have found the key. Ancient fear drops away. All my life I have been terrified of what might happen to me. I have assumed that suffering was inescapably real. I have lived in a treacherous world in my mind: "Look at the terrible things that can happen to people and therefore to me!" My life was marked by deep insecurity born out of fear. Again and again I have told myself the story of how unsafe I am. The world was poisoned for me, and now I see that the poison was in my mind. The concentration camps and the gas chambers appeared to be the ultimate proof that my fearful view was correct. My mind colored the whole world with that fear. Now I see there is a different choice. I can walk this mysterious path of life in inner freedom and peace. Without believing my fearful thoughts, there is no fear. I am free. I am free to love each step of my path as it is. In my true identity as pure awareness I am already and always completely safe. Like clouds cannot injure the sky, the turmoil of the world cannot touch me. Since I can walk in this clarity here, I walk in it anywhere.

I walk and I breathe, and I notice how the earth supports me, how my body moves, how the sun shines down through the trees. I am fully alive. I am in this form now; at any moment, I could be in another. But I am not form. I am soul, one with the Self, inhabiting form. Without a future to fear and a past to regret, I am at peace and my happiness is unshakable. Without fear, the world reveals its true face of absolute kindness.

Even here in the city of death, I walk in the glory of God. Every step I take leads me to enlightenment. All life is like that, whether I know it or not. We are always walking in the presence of God.

And we are always dying. We are always moving out of this world of appearances into the greater reality of what we are. For a moment we appear as precious individuals in this world, like snowflakes dissolving in the warmth of the sun.

Naked in the House of Love

Another day and I go deeper. I imagine all has been stripped from me—my possessions, my dignity, the meaning my life once held for the people who knew me, my education, my standing. They took my clothes, my hair, and even my name. I have been reduced to a number tattooed on my arm. In a moment my body can be the smoke in the chimney, a pile of ashes. Fear, hunger, and pain are my constant companions. But numbness devours even those, and I am nothing at all.

And then I can see it. Because I am absolutely nothing, because I have nothing left to hold on to, to build an identity of, nothing to defend, nothing to want, nothing to judge, and finally nothing to fear, I am free to know what I am, and it is my core—the Self in the cave of the Heart, the consciousness that creates this world every moment anew, in me. This is the view of truth. What I am is in the heart in all beings, the one heart that recognizes itself in the common plight we all share, the common, most ordinary, astounding miracle of what we are. In this connectedness of our one, universal heart we are alive. In our shared humanity, we come to know what we are: nothing and everything and the bliss of unconditional love.

This is the indestructibile human wisdom. Out of the greatest darkness, the unconquerable reality of the Self flashes forth like lightning from a black cloud. I don't know how many were able to see it back then; but when the darkness is overwhelming, we notice the light that much more keenly. For us the awakening to such an immense truth may take a while to be recognized, but it is as inevitable as spring follows winter.

Today, for an ever-increasing number of us, the realization of our indestructible diamond heart has become a matter of choice. As we pursue our liberation on purpose and master the lessons of Earth School, we reduce the need to evolve through pain. Voluntarily, we strip away our defenses, our desires, our self-importance and grief. As we question our stressful beliefs, the thoughts that blind us dissolve and we gradually come to realize the emptiness of all phenomena. Empty inside we can open to the fullness of life, brought to light by devotion, by the conscious practice of inner peace and emotional harmony. We see the truth beyond our thoughts, witness our emotions, dissolve our drama. Eventually, even the body is revealed as a nothing, as transparent, simply a momentary manifestation of the magnificence of the soul. In this peace we discover our indestructible heart.

No one said it more clearly than Nisargadatta Maharaj: *"When I realize I am nothing that's wisdom, and when I realize I am everything that's love, and between the two my life turns."* Wisdom and love are what we are, nothing and everything, and in that lies our promise and our truth.

24

Resurrection

IT IS A MOONLESS COLD NIGHT. I go to the children's bar-racks alone. The previous night, about thirty of us held a vigil here, lighting candles against the dark, huddling together against the cold as we sang songs of peace and compassion from the countries of our birth, in German, Hebrew, English, Swahili, Spanish, and French. It was an unforgettable night for all of us, coaxing such love from the darkness. Something drove me to come back here alone tonight. In the almost complete darkness, I feel my way along the rows of rough three-tiered wooden bunks where the children were housed in the most appalling conditions. There are small ladders on these bunks. The children who were kept here were used for pseudo-medical experiments. They were tortured by these experiments and when they were no longer of use, they were killed.

My heart opens to the point of breaking, further than what the mind can understand. These children are my children. I can do nothing but surrender as the mysterious spirit of Auschwitz operates on my heart. In the deep stillness I open, and it is painful and blissful at the same time. In the innermost chamber of the heart something new is born, a new ability to be present and to love. What remains is the sense of a larger heart, a compassion that appears to arise from beyond the center of time and space, much larger than what I could feel as a separate being.

I go on to the women's barracks. In the near total darkness, I carefully move from building to building. Here the women who were too weak to work were kept until it was their turn for the gas chamber. They were sick and starving, imprisoned here without food for many days. When the building was full, more were kept outdoors in an enclosed yard, even in the dead of winter. Many did not survive long enough to be gassed.

> We can see in the darkness the bright, eternal light of the soul. It rises as the sun of a new consciousness, and love is born out of fear.

In the silence inside the building I feel my way into what happened here. To my mind the suffering of the past is still all too tangible in these walls. It is a rough energy, violent and forceful. It makes me shudder and I sink into stillness, into deep prayer. In this prayer I have nothing to say. What happened here is beyond words, beyond the capacity of my mind to understand. All I can do is to give myself to the presence of what I sense. It is so vast I cannot encompass it. It appears dark and immensely threatening. It drives me deeper into stillness, here in the black of the night.

In the space of my chest it forms an immense weight, a weight that has a violent, tearing quality. Wordlessly I hope for a resolution, for even the slightest light to appear in the darkness, but nothing comes. Nothing comes. Too great is the recognition of how immense suffering can be. How human cruelty and insanity can blot out seemingly everything else.

I seem paralyzed here in the women's barrack and unable to say how long I have waited, focused on this tremendous weight on my heart. Then there arises in my mind's eye the image of the black Goddess Kali with Her necklace of skulls, blood dripping from Her long sword. Here She is, the majestic Goddess of Transformation, the divine force without which nothing new could be born. She is the Power of Time, the transcendental wisdom that destroys the delusion that we are not eternal and beyond the reach of death. She is dancing wildly over this vast cremation ground. Her presence reveals that beyond all cruelty and madness there is always a divine force at play.

The dance of Kali is not personal. It is a cosmic force, a divine dance, the liberating destruction of all attachments and all that is untrue in order to reveal the Self, the all-pervading Reality, the Ocean of Bliss. Whether we sense it in the image of Jesus on the cross or in the symbolic form of Kali, we all encounter destruction with a divine purpose many times in our lives. It happens when our ego-based hopes and plans are disrupted, sometimes violently, by events we could not foresee. Then we complain that life is unfair and cruel. We cannot sense the greater plan the divine has for us in awakening us to higher and higher levels of understanding into the transcendent peace of the soul. The purpose of fear and destruction is to awaken us. Kali is a tough teacher, but always a divine force. When we have a solid commitment to enlightenment, she becomes our friend, our Mother, even our lover. Then we can welcome all forms of transformation and realize that what we actually want is *reality as it is,* and in this unconditional acceptance we are free.

As I sit here in the deep silence of the women's house, I feel a shift. A new awareness enters my heart. Here, concretely now, what could be the higher purpose of this destruction? What higher order reality is born out of this darkness? And I see how the vast suffering of this past century has been followed by a spiritual awakening the world has never seen. Slowly at first, but gaining increasing momentum, millions of souls are reaching up for a life of greater meaning, for an end to their suffering, for the liberation from bondage. Wisdom teachings proliferate, innovative teachers arise, new skills are born. If anything can change human consciousness on this planet, this is it. Suffering inspires the search for liberation. Unconsciousness comes to a crescendo and it leads us into freedom. Can I know for certain that the mass killings and the enormous human-caused suffering of this past century laid the seed for today's spiritual awakening? No, I cannot, but somehow it feels true to me. And the monument for this awakening out of death into freedom is this dark place of Auschwitz. Here, if we look deep enough, we can see in the darkness the bright, eternal light of the soul. It rises as the sun of a new consciousness, and love is born out of fear.

Once the razor-sharp power that destroys illusion has done its work, it can show its hidden face: the same universal force reveals itself as deeply compassionate, the transcendent healer, the life-giver. Looking from this awareness, I see the gigantic sacrifice of millions of humans in our past. In both our roles, as victims and perpetrators, we have suffered through senseless destruction until at last, at last, an awareness arises that has the power to end all war inside and among us. With that vast insight, a gentle and powerful presence floods my heart.

A great softness flows through me. It is the all-encompassing love of God, the Self, the guru who lives in the heart. It is the love we all share. Beyond even the greatest deprivation and pain, this love is there. The heart can never die; it takes us to freedom. Deeply nurtured and peaceful, I walk back through the darkness to join my friends.

Hitler and Ravana

It was of great value to experience Auschwitz in the company of a group of experienced meditators. We held each other in a safe space of introspection, compassion, and release. We came together from many countries around the world to bear witness to this dark moment in our human history. There were among us some whose families had been murdered here, as well as the children and grand-children of Nazis and officers of the *Waffen SS*, the Nazi storm troopers who were responsible for the majority of the crimes of the Holocaust. There were Israelis and Germans, French and Americans, people from Africa and Asia, all drawn by the desire to put an end to fear, anger, and pain. When we sat in meditation together, when we read from endless lists the names of the dead, when we walked along the rusted barbed wire fences to the crematoria, when we sang and cried and spoke what was in our hearts, we pulled each other deeply into the space of forgiveness and understanding. Once more I realized the importance of *satsang*, the priceless support of the companionship of seekers after the truth.

On the last evening we shared a formal meal to celebrate our deep inner work. At that occasion I had the opportunity to share a lit-tle-known aspect of the story of Ravana, the great demon whose destruction is the theme of India's great epic, the *Ramayana*—the fundamental tale of our human condition and its resolution. The evil ten-headed demon king Ravana, has overtaken the world; ignorance and ego have overtaken the mind. In response, the forces of good assemble to bring about balance again. Rama, the divine incarnation of Lord Vishnu, assisted by his brother Lakshman and the monkey-god Hanuman, engages the demon king in battle and eventually kills him.

In the mystical interpretation of this story Ravana stands for the ignorance of the Self; all the forces of darkness emanate from this primal delusion. Rama, on the other hand, is the Supreme Self that dwells in each heart and delights the whole world. The Self, in incarnation as a soul, plays out the illusion of separation and seeks to reunite with its higher intelligence. This cosmic intelligence is symbolized by Rama's wife Sita, who was kidnapped by Ravana. In this formidable adventure the soul is assisted by willpower (Lakshman) and the enormous strength that accumulates from deep devotion and faith and the invincible power of sadhana (Hanuman).[1]

> We so often fail to remember the magnificent beauty and the profound goodness we are.

Around the table that night, the figure of Ravana could be interpreted in only one way: the ten-headed monster was the perfect metaphor for Hitler and all negativity in the world and in us. But everything is not as it seems. There is a story that tells how Ravana came to be the great enemy of the Gods. Long, long ago, the great Lord Vishnu, the upholder of the universe (our very own Self), had a gatekeeper in his heavenly realm, a highly evolved celestial being who was enormously devoted to Lord Vishnu. But he developed some subtle pride and failed to recognize the identity of a group of sages who arrived to pay homage to Lord Vishnu. He barred the gate and didn't let them enter. The sages recognized his pride and cursed him, saying that he had to incarnate ten times on earth so he could learn humility.

In despair, the doorkeeper threw himself at the sages's feet, asking them to lift the curse because he could not bear the thought of separation from his beloved Lord. Moved by his pleas, the sages reduced the curse and told him that he could choose either ten incarnations as God's greatest devotee on earth, or three incarnations as His greatest enemy. Motivated by his fervent devotion, he chose to be separated from the Lord for only three times. Ravana was one of the three incarnations of this powerful and sublime divine being.

When Rama killed him in battle, he was released from the curse and again realized his oneness with God.

As everyone connected the story of the doorkeeper to Hitler, silence fell around the table as they considered the implications. We judge others (and ourselves) from our human viewpoint, but what do we really know? Could it not be that there is a divine purpose behind everything, a supremely divine design that will remain hidden from us as long as we believe our fearful, small thoughts?

Rebirth into the Light of the Heart

On my return flight from Auschwitz, I had a four-hour layover in the Atlanta Airport. It was an ordinary day, nothing special. I walked through the crowd of thousands of people with my eyes and heart open. What I saw was amazing. Everyone in the whole airport was filled with a deep and abiding love. I could feel this usually hidden reality; it was everywhere, completely tangible, completely real. I realized that this is true for all of us all the time. We are just not aware of it. When we are not present in our lives, we don't know the unshakable love that dwells in our hearts, but it is always present and it is always true. It is in the women who laugh in the coffee shop. It animates the family hurrying to their next flight, the man speaking angrily on his cell phone, the baby crying in the stroller and the big sister who tries to console her.

> Now we can choose to remember who we are and systematically open our minds, eyes and hearts when they are closed by confusion.

I sat in the waiting area next to a young couple. The mother played with her baby, making the wonderful gurgling sounds only mothers and young babies can make. The sullen and worried father, in his early 20's, sat next to them, so unaware of the great happiness right in the next seat and the bliss hidden in his own heart. And yet he too existed within that bliss; he was simply asleep to his real nature.

We so often fail to remember the magnificent beauty and the profound goodness we are. That's why we suffer, because we are estranged from ourselves. None of us can ever be guilty of anything more than confusion. The deeper our confusion, the greater our suffering. But now we can choose to remember who we are and systematically open our minds, eyes and hearts when they are closed by confusion.

HEARTSOURCING

25

The Cave of the Heart

A YEAR AFTER MY TRIP TO AUSCHWITZ, I was in Kainchi, Maharajji's ashram in the Himalayas. After an absence of 30 years, I was again sitting next to the takhat, on the small porch, in the very spot where he filled me with his astounding love. When I arrived at the ashram, I had been greeted by Siddhi Ma, the woman to whom he entrusted his ashrams, the perfect devotee. She must be in her 80s now, living an extremely simple life of pure service to the ever-expanding family of Maharajji's devotees. In the evening we met in the back of the ashram, just five of us, sitting outside in the mountain air, watching the blue light among the pines change to grey. After a few questions about my travels, Ma said, "Ram Giri, tell me about the marble plate with the Hanuman Chalisa that is in the wall of the temple."

I was speechless. How could she have known about this? By this question, she showed me to what extent Maharajji is present in her, in the awareness of knowing all things through the power of love. Through her profound surrender, his presence has come completely alive in her, and not for a single moment would she claim the gifts she holds as her own. Her being shows us the fulfillment of the path of devotion, where the heart has melted all its obstructions, and lover and Beloved have become one and the same.

I however, was not in a placid state. I had returned here to this mountain ashram because it was time for the next step. Ever since I had given my life to passing on the gifts of this great love, I had been in a state of preparation. I was being trained and I had a great deal to learn. Now, however, I knew it was time. It was time to find the key to sharing Maharajji's great gift. And once more, as had happened so often, I had no clue of what it could be. I had collected the best Skills for Awakening, but something was still missing. Somehow I sensed that there was yet another piece to the puzzle, and I began to demand it. After all, it was not alone my reponsibility to ready me for this work. It was Maharajji's work, it was his gift, and I felt it was time for him to deliver. For three days, the intensity of my demand increased until it had reached an unyielding level of intensity.

At six o'clock the next morning, pitch dark and cool in the mountain air, I was silently reciting the Hanuman Chalisa, all 40 verses of it, again and again. There were just a few other people out at this time, all deeply immersed in their morning devotions. And as my body swayed slightly to the rhythm of the song, my attention was drawn powerfully inside, into the innermost chamber of the heart. Deeper and deeper I went. The chant became like a drill, the words penetrating past all distractions into deeper and deeper layers of my being. The world disappeared, and I was taken deeper and deeper still. Then the internal space opened up, I entered into it like through a gate and realized for the first time the inner reality of the Spiritual Heart.

In this interior dimension of the heart, I fell into a state of absolute wonder and awe. I found myself in what I can only describe as the manifest space of the absolute Self, the world of enlightened sages, a Buddha realm, alive with layers upon layers of limitless, absolute, divine love, shining with a wondrous internal light, an infinite world that is completely unforgettable. It was a direct perception of the infinite Reality hidden in all of us, a perception where seeing and feeling, hearing, smelling, and tasting, duality, and non-duality were all one in all-encompassing love. I went as deeply as I could into this miraculous state of being, the real world, of which our universe is but a shadow. And as I gazed at this truly indescribable reality around me in wonder, the wish arose to share its essence with others here on this lonely planet. Words formed in my mind:

Within us there are uncounted dimensions upon dimensions of pure, unconditional love without end!

Indeed, our innermost reality is the most sacred space. It is the Source of everything we truly long for, everything that makes life what we want it to be: solidly peaceful, fulfilled, secure, and filled with unwavering love. It is the cause of all healing, the true foundation of wealth, the limitless well of infinite joy. And we have missed it. We have looked for its gifts everywhere else. What a marvel, that we have searched for it for thousands of years, have written countless books about it, forever yearned for it, and yet we have missed its life-giving presence, accessible right here in our heart. It is the most sought-after secret hidden in plain sight!

We can learn to tap into this Source to enjoy its unimaginable gifts, the secret of secrets, now no longer hidden at all.

Out of that inner space of wonder, the cosmic heart is pouring itself continuously into our world and we have not seen where our

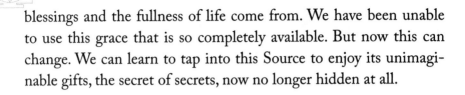

blessings and the fullness of life come from. We have been unable to use this grace that is so completely available. But now this can change. We can learn to tap into this Source to enjoy its unimaginable gifts, the secret of secrets, now no longer hidden at all.

26

7 Steps To Unconditional Love

HEARTSOURCING IS OPENING TO ENLIGHTENMENT THROUGH the power of love. It is tasting the unsurpassable delight of the nectar of the heart, as it flows into us and out from us into our world. It is a complete life-giving practice of self-nurturing to substantially elevate our well-being and bring us to the point of spiritual awakening. It entirely eliminates the fear of love and it activates the great healing power of the Self. What we have most deeply yearned for—unconditional love, healing, deep happiness, peace, and security beyond fear—is now available to us as we discover that in our core we are the Lover and the Beloved in one. With HeartSourcing, we can overcome problems of mind, emotions, behavior, body, and relationships. The essence of the heart is the direct manifestation of grace, which is absolutely abundant and accessible to us.

As it is, our mind is conditioned to suffer by a world that has turned away from grace in its confusion. As long as we identify with our personality we are emotionally disoriented and filled with the fallout of fear. The amount of stress we experience is an exact measure of our lack of authentic self-love. Like Narcissus[1] we are enamored with our reflection, but afraid to love genuinely. We expect to be hurt. We have built walls and protections around the heart that imprison us. Our behavior and the social world we co-create match our thoughts and emotions. And—hidden by the distractions in our minds—in the center of all shines the heart with its gifts, like a diamond of infinite brilliance and power.

Underneath our many desires and fears, what we truly yearn for is groundless happiness, the absolute love of the Self, as it alone is freedom and lasting fulfillment. We have searched for it in vain by looking for its reflection outside of ourselves, and even inside the mind it cannot be found. We have been hungry ghosts, unhappy with us while hoping to receive fulfillment from other people, from situations, from a purely external image of God, or from inadequate spiritual practice, but we have been disappointed. As long as we remain engrossed in desires and fears, we live a peripheral life and remain disconnected from Source. This confusion can now come to an end.

When we understand where the Source really is, that *it is what we are*, we can turn inside and begin to practice the most obvious truth that we haven't been able to see: this love and this freedom are here, inside us, available for the asking. This is the invitation to HeartSourcing.

HeartSourcing

HeartSourcing is the way to open the heart, transform our life, and realize the Self, the bliss of God, the Supreme Reality. HeartSourcing is both a process of healing and purifying and tasting our already existing, absolute purity and completion. It is the path and the taste of the fruit of the path in one. Its purpose is to remove confusion, self-doubt, and self-hatred, to experience the abundance of the inner Source and to develop fervent devotion to the Self, which helps us to dissolve obscuring ego structures. With this love alive in us, we will naturally engage in compassionate action, and realize our inborn wisdom and peace.

The Practice

A formal daily practice will enable you to deepen your access to your heart more and more easily. Take your time with HeartSourcing. Be very gentle with yourself and yet determined to open the heart to taste its rich essence. Nothing you do to allow the heart to awaken is ever wasted. Keep practicing, because *any effort you make is cumulative.* To create a regular habit of HeartSourcing it is best to reserve a regular time for it every day. Sit in a quiet and peaceful place with your body erect, your spine and head straight, but not rigid, so the internal energies can flow freely. The basic instructions for meditation apply here. Practice a certain amount of time daily, not too much and not too little, and allow it to become as natural a routine as brushing your teeth. Be aware when the pain body makes attempts to disrupt your practice.

The following are step-by-step instructions for opening yourself to the core of your being. Consider these instructions like a menu and choose what works best for you.

1. **Bring your attention into the here and now.**

   ❧ Slow down. Come into the present. Bring yourself to your senses. For instance: feel your body; notice how the weight of your body presses down into your seat; notice the weight of your arms and hands, of your head. Take your time. Notice your breath and follow it in and out. Repeat, "I am aware I am breathing in; I am aware I am breathing out." Listen deeply to the sounds around you without labeling and without judgment. Be fully present.

   ❧ Become still. In that stillness repeat your mantra in your innermost heart. Choose as your mantra any sacred word or short phrase that represents to you the presence of the highest reality. For example, you can use the word Ram (pronounce: Raam). Ram Ram Ram Ram.

   ❧ Breathe in and out with the mantra going. Notice how the mantra calms and centers the mind.

2. **Visualize the sun in your Heart.**

   ❧ Direct your attention to the innermost center of your chest, the heart cave. It is always interior to any tension and stress, a non-local reality, forever pure, peaceful and perfect; it is boundless as space.

   ❧ In inner stillness visualize a brilliant point of light in this deepest core of your being. Let it be like a beacon, attracting your attention. Let the mind become fully focused on that single point of light.

- After a while, let the light expand and become a radiant, brilliant sun. Hold that image in your mind; settle into it, enjoy it.

- To enable you to tune into the essence of the heart more easily, use any of the following options (use one at a time):
  - Visualize how the sun in the heart radiates its life-giving power into you.
  - Picture yourself descending into the depth of your heart.
  - Breathe in and out of the Heart Cave. Increase the intensity of the light with your breath, like fanning an ember.

3. Feel the Heart Essence.

- Sense the inner presence. Let it come to you as you become still and settle more deeply into the heart. Notice the sensations that spontaneously arise, the feeling essence that emanates from the Heart Cave. Tune into whatever positive, peaceful and nurturing sensations you can perceive. Let that inner comfort nurture you.

- Notice the most fundamental sensation, completely pure and uplifting, the sacred tremor of the heart (spanda) that can open to you a never before imagined aliveness and depth of love. It is there. It is waiting for you. Open up to it.

- Center your attention even more deeply in the heart by using a mantra of your choice. Imagine the mantra repeating itself effortlessly within the heart.

ॐ If you notice stressful sensations in the chest, remember the Heart Cave is always interior to any stress or disturbance. Open to it there. Become very curious and receptive to feel the Heart Essence. It may be subtle or powerful and is always good. Become even more still.

ॐ Tune into the very core of your being by using one of the following visualizations:
- Name the pure sensation that arises in the heart and feel it deeply.
- Feel the life-giving warmth of the sun in your heart.
- Evoke a memory of being loved unconditionally and let it radiate through you.
- Evoke a specific memory of loving someone or something deeply.
- Remember a moment when you were able to accept and love yourself fully. Step into that memory.
- Evoke a memory of experiencing peace in nature.
- Picture an infant in his/her mother's or father's loving arms. Be the parent and be that infant.
- Picture a wise and enlightened and fully loving person. Sit with them.
- Visualize in your Heart Cave the presence of your Beloved, the outer or inner teacher or guru. Feel that devotion.

4. Keep focusing the mind on the heart and go deeper.

ॐ If the mind carries you off into a stream of thoughts, say to the mind in a kind voice, "Not now." Make your mantra stronger and gently but firmly return your attention to HeartSourcing. (Distractions will happen, so try not to judge your mind; simply notice and come back to the heart.) Again and again, let the mind dissolve into the heart.

- Focus your mind more deeply on your mantra.
- Appreciate the mind for doing its job, and come back to the heart.
- Use kirtan or any devotional music of your choice, repeated silently in the mind, to focus the mind in the heart.
- Deepen your sense of stillness.

5. Allow the heart essence to radiate throughout your whole being.

෴ Fill yourself from this infinite Source. Become the radiance of the inner sun.

෴ Mentally guide the flow of the heart essence into every cell of your body, into every part of your mind, into every emotion. Realize that you are now both the giver of love in the heart, and the receiver of love in the rest of your being. You are the lover and the Beloved at the same time.

෴ Notice when you are the lover and the Beloved in one, loving is completely safe. There is no one here who can hurt you or abandon you. Therefore you can give yourself fully to this loving. Dissolve yourself in this love. Practice with passionate commitment so this inner union can blossom and become increasingly stable. Again:

- Experience that sun-like radiance in every part of your body. Bask in that radiance. Let it shine from you.

- Enjoy the rich flow of the Heart Nectar. Let it nurture every part of you fully. Let it flow into your relationships.
- Set a strong intention to be that radiance, or that flow of Heart Essence permanently.
- Allow your individual identity to merge with the divine Beloved.

6. Open to HeartSourcing repeatedly during everyday activities

- ∾ Take any opportunity, at any moment you remember, to bring your attention into the heart.

- ∾ Identify daily recurring situations (waiting at a red light, riding an elevator, doing the dishes, etc.) and infuse them with the spirit of HeartSourcing. In this way they will become automatic reminders to open the Heart.

- ∾ Serve others anonymously. Do something loving without the other person finding out.

7. Share the love that you are.

- ∾ As you discover this love in you more and more deeply, you will increasingly realize that you are this love. When your heart is wide open you will naturally love everything as it is, because it is all part of God, part of life, part of you. Then you are at peace. You have become what you are: love.

- ∾ Love spontaneously wants to share itself and it reveals to you the secret of secrets, what a great privilege and joy it is to share this love. As genuine compassion arises, you appreciate the gift to be able to serve and love other beings. Every time you do that, your love multiplies. Therefore you will naturally seek the active expression of love and compassion.

∾ Open your heart in relationships; do not wait for situations where caring can be expressed, but create them proactively; speak and act from the Heart with sincerity.

∾ Love never forces itself. If it is alive in you, it is an invitation to others. Let it live in you and watch it do its work. The love in you has a supreme intelligence of its own. Awakening your heart is the key.

Please see Appendix V for an example of a comprehensive daily practice of HeartSourcing Yoga.

For most of us, access to the heart is blocked by a crust of fears and defenses. But it's not difficult to slip through a crack in this armor and enter the wide space of the heart. At times you may feel locked out by stressful thoughts and emotions. But you can always visualize a light in the innermost heart, beyond the reach of stress and worry, a small sun radiating its pristine purity into the rest of your being. Imagine the heart essence shining its light wherever it is needed. With some practice and greater stillness it will become more tangible to you and you will begin to feel the heart essence.

Spanda

This sensation of subtle vibration is known as spanda, the sacred tremor of the heart. You may notice it first quite faintly as a joyous, peaceful and nurturing feeling, attractive but delicate, or perhaps it will come as a sensation of stillness. Let it draw you toward it like a magnet; follow it into the heart where it will become increasingly ecstatic and peaceful. This is your very heart-essence, the force that lives you. It is the opening of your soul to grace. Spanda is grace. It is the background and center of all the vibrations of life. Let it return you to the joy of life; let it awaken you. After a while the feeling of the heart will flow into your actions and you will find it reflected in your relationships with people and the material world. With ongoing practice, your being will be permeated by the vibrations of love. You will take on the perfume of the loving Self. In this process the crust of fears and defenses will completely evaporate. This is how you can transform you and your world.

When true insight dawns and you discover that love is present everywhere, even in the deepest darkness, that the world is indeed the very "body" of God, then a deep joy begins to permeate your life; a sense of oneness begins to spread. It is a profound, unshakable peace, arising from the realization that anything that can happen—anything at all—is always for your ultimate good. Through your commitment to awakening, whatever happens can have only one effect: to bring you closer to the true Self, to freedom from confusion, and the realization that *you are boundless love.* Then you will understand what Catherine of Siena meant when she said: "All the way to heaven is heaven."

Call it by any name—God, Self, the Heart, or the seat of consciousness—it is all the same. The point to be grasped is this: that Heart means the very core of one's being, the center without which there is nothing whatsoever.

--Ramana Maharshi

Your pocket guide to HeartSourcing:

The 7 Steps of HeartSourcing

1. Bring your Attention into the Here and Now
2. Visualize the Sun in the Heart, or Feel the Heart Essence
3. Become Still and Go Deeper
4. Keep focusing the Mind in the Heart and Go Deeper still
5. Allow the Heart Essence to Radiate into your Whole Being
6. Open to HeartSourcing repeatedly during everyday activities
7. Share the Love that you are

27

Living from the Heart

PRACTICING HEARTSOURCING IS BENEFICIAL ANYTIME, ANYWHERE, for anyone. This is not just because it feels good, but because it is a direct way to access the Self, the inner guru, the Supreme Reality. The good feelings that come from HeartSourcing are an emanation of the bliss of God in us.

Through HeartSourcing we can have a fearless and open heart in all our activities. This is the direct experience of the reflection of the Self. The more we are able to feel the heart nectar, the more it will attract us. Spanda is the most delicious and liberating sensation and we can give ourselves to it completely because it is completely safe. The first benefit is that we feel good in the moment, but it does much more than that. With practice, the ego becomes more subtle as we identify increasingly with love. This dissolves the heavy burden of the pain body.

The more the heart opens, the more grace we are able to receive. HeartSourcing is a delightful path because we quickly begin to taste the fruit of our efforts, and its blessings follow us everywhere.

We can practice at any moment. Focus on your heart while washing the dishes, while speaking with someone, while working, playing, or resting. Do it in the middle of an argument or when you are sick or in pain. Moment by moment, make your life come alive with your love. Meditation will assist you in that by deepening your inner stillness. The Work and Open Attention can help you quickly remove the thoughts and emotions that keep you a prisoner of your conditioning. Use them to peel away suffering layer by layer.

Whether we know it or not, we are always tithing our time and effort either to the Self or to the ego. At any moment, we strengthen one or the other. By doing nothing and simply continuing to live as a conditioned ego, we call suffering into our life, because the essence of ego is suffering. The love of the Self is the most powerful medicine to prevent such a waste of potential.

Dissolving into Love

To live with an open heart, to experience the world through the heart, in friendliness, harmony and genuine caring, is the most natural way to live because it expresses what we are beyond the veils of thoughts, emotions and ego. It bears the fruit of lasting happiness without cause.

One day I met Katie in a crowded conference hall where Eckhart Tolle was going to be on stage in a few minutes. We hadn't seen each other in a while and we were thrilled to meet again. We hugged and plopped down into two empty seats, still in our embrace, wordlessly touching forehead to forehead. A great rushing river of love flowed between our hearts. This love was all that existed. Still forehead to forehead, Katie pointed to her heart and to mine, back and forth, and gave voice to what we both knew. "You know, Ramgiri," she said, "this love is what it's all about! This love is what it is all about!"

With practice we come to realize that all our fears and shame have never been real and can never be real, and that exactly the opposite is actually true. Then we see that all the other quarrelling thoughts we have taken so seriously also aren't real. They are all actors, demons and gods appearing on the screen of the mind, posturing in alluring or threatening forms, shouting "take me for real, take me for real!" And we have been hypnotized by the movie of what can never be true. We have created a role for us, a fabricated ego, and we have been taken in by the drama we have enacted. Now, one by one we unmask all the actors and discover that they are nothing but smoke and mirrors and it dawns on us that we're not a pawn in the movie of life. Our mind is the projector, and we are the empty screen on which the never-ending movie continues to play.

Within the drama of life there is a deeper current that sustains us. It is the heart-essence that comes alive as we unmask the actors—our demons and gods. This great love will enrapture us and permeate everything on the screen of the mind. It is the pure love of God. It is our love. It is ecstasy, the true taste of freedom.

In this state of freedom we know we are the ocean of bliss. To the world we look to be just an ordinary individual, a little wave on the surface of the limitless ocean. Internally, however, we are one with Infinity. And we continue to participate in the drama of life for one reason alone: because love wants to share itself. It's called compassion, but it's not something we do; it is all that is left of us, the intention to share this love out of gratitude.

Thank you for coming on the journey of this book with me. It is my sincere hope that I have been able to share with you some insights about what opening the Source of the heart can do for you. As Maharajji said, *Love is the best medicine.* It does not only cure what is ailing us at the moment, it can end all our suffering and confusion in the realization that *we are Love.*

Of course there is more to this journey than can be put into a book. For this reason we have created a website—www.ramgiri.com— where we are offering free instructions in the skills, as well as courses and mentoring for those who want to overcome the obstructions in their life by taking up a regular practice. Through our website you can also connect with like-minded individuals—HeartSourcing yogis and yoginis—for satsang, or spiritual companionship.

The world is filled with the presence of God, and this presence can be most readily accessed in your very heart. You are therefore already in possession of the most important ingredient to an enlightened life: the Source of grace within you. This Source wants to guide you. All you need to do is open to it.

With my very best wishes for your great journey home.

–Ramgiri

*Cleansing the mirror of the heart
is the most important thing you can do.*

—Siddhi Ma

Appendix I

MEDITATION

IF YOU'RE NEW TO MEDITATION, YOU probably shouldn't do what I did when I first started out. Don't sign up immediately for an intensive two-week retreat. Step into it slowly. If you're trying to learn playing piano, you would not start by practicing twelve hours a day for two weeks; your enthusiasm might burn out and you might never go back to it. Build your meditation practice carefully, step by step, so it can gradually replace the harmful habits of the unruly mind. If you do that, meditation can be a lifesaver, a crucial skill to dissolve pain and come to know your true nature. When you begin to practice, know your limits; try to maintain a consistent daily practice of 5-10 minutes and gradually expand your practice from there. Don't overreach. You may get discouraged and give up because you're trying to do too much too soon.

> By holding still and observing whatever arises, your mind will become transparent and stress-free.

Here is one way to meditate: Sit still in a solid and erect

pose. Quietly, or mentally, repeat a mantra of your choice, for instance *Ram, Ram, Ram*[1]... or *Om (Aum), or Jesus, or Sita Ram, Sita Ram, Sita Ram, Jai Sita Ram.* You can use a mala or rosary to help steady the mind. Imagine that the mantra is repeating itself in the cave of your Heart, the innermost place in the chest, and notice how your attention is gradually drawn away from the ever-changing thoughts into the peace of the Heart. Rest your attention there. Maintain this focus for a certain period every day. Observe every state of mind you experience.

> Meditation is like a clear mirror in which you can see the mind's empty nature. It enables you to recognize that you are not the ever-moving thoughts and desires, but the clear, vast, and peaceful field of stillness in which thoughts arise.

In your practice, you may encounter all kinds of thoughts and emotions: blissful and stressful, interesting and mundane, boring, scary, alluring and shameful, infuriating, and nasty. Try your best to put up neither resistance, nor to run after your thoughts. Simply watch them arise and pass away; they are just thoughts, not necessarily the truth. Yes, thoughts can have a great deal of power, but soon you will be able to distinguish them from reality. Regular practice will begin to free you from the terror and pain that thoughts can evoke. Learn not to give in to these thoughts and feelings; don't let them control you. By holding still and observing whatever arises, your mind will become transparent and stress-free.

There are three phases to meditation: concentration, meditation, and samadhi. It is as though you are trying to kindle a fire with a magnifying glass. First you must find the right position for your hand holding the glass. That is concentration. When you have found the right position and the sunlight is focused on some combustible material, such as dry leaves and twigs, then you simply have to hold it still over some time and let the light do its thing. This is the steady practice of meditation. As a result, the leaves will catch on fire. That is *samadhi,* the inner intuitive experience of advanced states of consciousness, an entirely new dimension of experience. It happens as a function of concentrating your attention and holding still for the necessary amount of time.

Meditation is like a clear mirror in which you can see the mind's empty nature. It enables you to recognize that you are not the ever-moving thoughts and desires, but *the clear, vast, and peaceful field of stillness in which thoughts arise.* That insight changes things quite dramatically: You are not the waves on the surface that push you around, but the vast, peaceful ocean. As you identify less and less with your stressful thoughts and feelings, they lose their power to control you and you find peace.

Aaaah.

Additional resources for training in Meditation:

Sharon Salzberg **sharonsalzberg.com**
Zen Peacemakers **zenpeacemakers.org**
Spirit Rock **spiritrock.org**
Online courses by Ramgiri at **ramgiri.com**

THE FIVE STEPS OF OPEN ATTENTION

T HE FOLLOWING ARE STEP-BY-STEP INSTRUCTIONS FOR liberating stressful emotions so you can find inner balance and harmony. Nothing is needed for Open Attention except inner awareness.[1] This inborn awareness has the power to spontaneously liberate anything that obstructs the pristine and blissful reality of the Self. When first learning this skill, it's helpful to find a quiet place for your practice. Please remember that the purpose of this skill is to learn self-love! Understand also that the ego will interfere with this practice and don't berate yourself when that happens, but persevere. Learn to open to what you have rejected in you for so long. Through this you will discover your courageous heart and over time it will free you of doubts and bring you joy and happiness. If an emotion should become too strong, stop the exercise and come back to it later. If you meet a strong emotion even for a second with Open Attention, much is gained. Deep patterns change through continuous practice. Long-standing negative emotional habits can be replaced by positive habits. Habits are built by repetition. Every stressful emotion offersus an opportunity for practice. The more often you practice Open Attention, the more spontaneous and effortless it will become.

The Five Steps:

1. Tune in to the body sensation of a disturbing emotion or physical tension.

    ∾ Focus on a present negative feeling or recall a past event where you experienced a stressful emotion. Get as close to the memory as you can tolerate (always remember to be gentle and kind to yourself).

    ∾ Turn your attention to the physical sensations the emotion triggers in your body now. Stay in the observer position. Take your time. Be gentle and kind with yourself.

2. Identify the exact location of the body sensation.

    ∾ Mentally scan through your body to identify exactly where the sensation arises. If there are several different sensations in the body, focus on the one that is strongest.

    ∾ Remember that the sensation is not a threat or an enemy, but a part of you that needs help. Do you approach it with hesitation, fear, or rejection? Just notice. Don't try to change your inner experience in any way. Let it be what it is and see how it progresses.

3. Open to this part of yourself that needs help. Hold your mental focus steady.

    ∾ Notice any impulse to flee, fight, indulge, or complain. Your attention may have an unsteady quality at first; it may be dull, afraid, bewildered, or cloudy. It may be difficult to maintain your focus because you have trained the mind for such a long time to avoid these sensations.

ᕗ Use the breath to steady the mind. Imagine that your breath streams through the part of the body where the sensation is, carrying your mental focus into that place. Settle into the body. Relax. Be a friend to yourself, to this a part of you that needs help. Be kind, open, and pay close attention. Use your natural sense of curiosity to study how the sensation manifests.

ᕗ Repeat a mantra inside the location of the body sensation. This can help you further focus and steady the mind.

4. Bring your Attention deeply into the body sensation in the Here and Now.

ᕗ Normally the mind is like a light bulb, sending its light (attention) in all directions. When you focus your attention strongly in one direction, your mind becomes like an X-ray machine, capable of looking deeply into the body sensation. With even more concentration, the mind can become like a laser, sending forth a powerful stream of attention without any distractions. Let the laser beam of your attention flow exclusively into the body sensation, using your breath to deepen your concentration. Get absorbed in this unwavering attentiveness and maintain it as long as you can.

5. Notice what happens to the body sensation.

ᕗ Simply by applying your attention, the body sensation may begin to change on its own. Like an unbiased witness, just notice what happens. There are many different changes and experiences that can occur. The following are the most common:

A. The sensation dissolves. When exposed to the light of awareness, darkness is dispelled, negative feelings dissolve. Congratulations, your work is done for now. Or you can choose to go even deeper by becoming more still and focusing on more subtle aspects of the sensation.

B. The sensation moves from place to place. If the "darkness" of stressful feelings dissolves in one place, it may become noticeable somewhere else. Follow the wisdom of the body. It will guide you perfectly to where your Open Attention is needed. Move your attention through the body, always focusing on the strongest sensation.

C. The sensation does not change at all. When that happens, your first reaction may be, "Oh darn, it's not working!" This is an understandable reaction but a mistake—you just fell once more into the trap of fight or flight. Remember, the aim is never to "get rid of it," but rather to bring your attention to this part of you that needs help. When the sensation does not change, it may mean that you have come across a particularly strong emotional pattern that may take a while to dissolve. Train your mind to become even more focused, calm, and patient. With a strong sensation to focus on, go deeper to discover and free new layers of your being. When its time has come, it will dissolve. Darkness cannot stand up to the light. Meanwhile, use your practice to train the mind to be open (relaxed and receptive) and able to pay attention (focused, active, and creative).

Open Attention Summary

1. *Tune in to the body sensation of a disturbing emotion or physical tension.*
2. *Identify the exact location of the body sensation.*
3. *Open to this part of you that needs help. Let your mental focus become steady.*
4. *Bring your Attention deeply into the body sensation using imagery or breath, fully in the Here and Now.*
5. *Notice what happens to the body sensation. Does it dissolve, move from place to place, or stay steady? Stay with it. Relax. Find the peace behind the emotion.*

Additional resources for the generation of emotional harmony:

The Chapters on Presence in Eckhart Tolle's books
　　"The Power of Now" and "A New Earth."
The Sedona Method **sedona.com**
Online courses by Ramgiri at **ramgiri.com**

Appendix III

THE WORK OF BYRON KATIE

I F ANYTHING, THE WORK IS SIMPLE to do:

Identify a stressful thought, write it down,
ask four questions and turn it around.

Here are the 4 questions; we'll deal with the turnarounds in a little while:

1. Is it true?
2. Can I absolutely know that it is true?
3. How do I react, what happens, when I believe the thought?
4. Who would I be without the thought?

Lets jump right in. Here is a thought: "Joe hurt me." To make it personal, please replace "Joe" with someone who you feel hurt you, someone whom you have not yet forgiven 100%. So for you it may be Rachel, or Dad, or Max, the neighborhood bully.

1. *Is it true that Joe hurt you? Yes or No?* Take your time with this. This is a treasure hunt for your truth, the truth that will set you free. You don't want to miss any clues.

2. *Can you absolutely know that it is true? Yes or No?* notice the key word: "absolutely." And both a Yes or a No are good here. Remember, you are looking for your truth.

3. *How do you react, what happens, when you believe the thought* that Joe hurt you? Now go into detail, into depth. Go slow. What feeings come up with that thoight? Where do you feel them in your body? How do you treat Joe when you believe he hurt you? How do you treat yourself? Are there any benefits the ego derives from holding on to this thought? When you feel you've fully explores what happens when you believe this thought, move on to:

4. *Who would you be without the thought?* See yourself in your mind's eye, hanging out with Joe without the thought. What's that like? Can you feel it?

Okay, now you have given yourself a thorough education about what happens when you hold that thought. That is important, but it will not yet liberate you from its effect. For that we need the turn-arounds. They are simple changes to your original thought, which bring you to a different, but closely related thought. There are three primary turnarounds, sometimes more, sometimes less, depending on the complexity of the thought we are examining. In our case they are:

1. I hurt Joe.
2. I hurt me.
3. Joe didn't hurt me.

Working with each turnaround is a short meditation. It requires of us to become still inside and to listen to the voice of the heart. And it is always about our search for our truth, never about self-judgment or self-criticism. We are looking for a deeper truth so the heart can open. Remembering that prevents any tendency of the conditioned mind to come in with its old habits of judging.

So here we go: "I hurt Joe." Can you find at least three valid examples of when and how that has been true? Go to real situations, even if they just occurred in your mind or imagination. Take your time. Feel each example. It may not feel good to realize that you hurt Joe, but in the search for truth we look at everything, not to judge, but to become self-aware. Once we are self-aware, negative patterns of thoughts, emotions and behaviors will leave by themselves. As long as we are blind to them, they will rule us.

Then repeat this exploration with "I hurt me." How many times and in how many concrete situations have you hurt yourself? I would not have any shortage of examples here. For too long have I been my worst enemy. Let each insight sink in. Feel it. Be loving and compassionate enough with yourself to stop the insanity. And finally, can you see the truth of "Joe didn't hurt me?" First, how many times has that been true? And then: did Joe's actions or words hurt you, or was it the way you reacted to them? The deeper you can look at this, the more you can set yourself free.

And we can go even another step? What is the opposite of "hurt?" Maybe "help?" Another turnaround can be "Joe helped me." Can you find concrete proof of that thought? Maybe you can see how Joe even helped you to clear your head through this inquiry. You hear me say it: in the world of spiritual awareness, everything helps us. Everything brings us closer to the end of pain, and all pain begins in our mind.

Additional resources to clear the mind with The Work:

Byron Katies excellent website: **thework.com**
Online courses by Ramgiri at **ramgiri.com**

Appendix IV

SETTING THE MONSTER FREE

HOLDING A NEGATIVE SELF-IMAGE IS A collective human phenomenon. Whether we know it or not, we are all infected with it. The outer manifestations of that shadow—from genocides, terror, wars, and atrocities to hurtful behaviors of all kinds—continue to be perpetrated by individuals, families, corporations and governments. In the subconscious mind this specific manifestation of our shadow becomes the archetype of the monster. Because of their history it is present in Germans in a particular form. It has been the source of tremendous pain. I honor the Germany people greatly for the way they have undertaken a cleansing of the collective mind. In the media and in public discourse, the shadow cast by the Nazi-era has been proactively addressed for decades. Many Germans are consciously dealing with their painful inheritance and setting themselves increasingly free. Through this effort, the nation has transformed itself to a great extent. Today Germany is by most accounts the most peace-loving nation on earth. This has much to do with their courage to face the past. A true *joie de vivre*, a clarity of mind, and—imagine!—a sense of lightness are replacing the former negative national characteristics. The nation has set an example other countries could follow and it gives us reason to hope that we, humanity, will be able to avoid the trauma of collective suicide that the German past has so desperately demonstrated.

The reason why the Germans have engaged in this collective turn-around was certainly because they have been so relentlessly burdened by their monster. Although many may deny it, the collective mind carries the secret fear that somewhere in them lurks this threatening force and they need to be very careful that it doesn't emerge again. The intensity of this shame—the sense that there is something deeply wrong with them—is one factor that has caused Germans not to brush the past under the rug, but to deal with it with much self-honesty and awareness. Of course the inner monster is a toxic presence in the collective mind of all humans because we all share the repressed traumas of thousands of years. Continuing to deny this means to remain blind to our hidden dark side. To overcome it, we need to face it. The monster expresses itself in many ways; for instance, we allow 15 million children to starve to death every year. And this is only one of the many hidden holocausts we allow to continue while we look away.

Here are some facts about the planetary reality we are creating at present: Every seven seconds, a child under 10 years of age dies from the direct or indirect effects of hunger. In the Asian, African, and Latin American countries, well over 500 million people are living in what the World Bank has called "absolute poverty." One in twelve people worldwide is malnourished, including 160 million children under the age of five. (United Nations Food and Agriculture). Nearly one in four people, 1.3 billion, live on less than $1 per day, while the world's 358 billionaires have assets exceeding the combined annual incomes of countries with 45 percent of the world's people. (UNICEF). Three billion people in the world today struggle to survive on US$2/day. One out of every eight children under the age of twelve in the U.S. goes to bed hungry every night. For the price of one missile, a school full of hungry children could eat lunch every day for five years.

We don't like to hear it, but most of us still do what the Germans once did so well. We pretend not to know. We look away. But the subconscious mind does not have this ability; everything gets registered there. Everything! And so we remain paralyzed by our hidden fears, separated from our inner Source, trapped in chasing after superficial distractions, and the heart remains blocked. But you can break out of this state of inner imprisonment. In your multi-faceted diamond heart lies the true reality of what you are. And you are entirely good.

To liberate the internal monster is an individual task. Only you can dissolve your own demon. Its presence in thoughts and emotional patterns can be identified and dispelled. It is nothing but an illusion, but it is an illusion that creates enormous amounts of damage and pain.

The metaphorical monster may appear in many guises, but it is primarily the shame and fear we carry about our more or less hidden anger and hatred, our mean or murderous impulses, our depression, dullness, and indifference to others' suffering, or our pattern of victimhood. It takes form in beliefs like these: *There is something terrible in me, I am rotten to the core, I am not worthy to be loved, If they knew who I really am, they would reject me,* and many more. Trust your inner wisdom to set you free. The healing intuition in you will guide you safely, step by step, to your freedom—if you ask for that guidance. Simply take one step at a time and *keep moving forward* through that internal birth canal out of your darkness into the light.

To permanently dissolve this deep dread is not a psychological ploy to help you live more comfortably in your illusion of separateness. No, it is true yoga, true religion, an important step in the practice of uniting with the absolute Self. The secret lies in the hearts' intuitive intelligence and unconditional love. By dispelling the internal monster, you will find *the friend*, a term the Sufis use to describe God. Then the painful lessons of Earth School will not have to be repeated and you will gain access to the unimaginable gifts of the Self.

Meditation to Dissolve the Inner Monster Archetype

This meditation combines HeartSourcing with Open Attention.

Find a quiet and undisturbed place. Settle down. If possible, sit in meditation pose with your spine erect but not stiff. Notice how your mind and body calm down.

Recall your resolute intention to free yourself of negative impressions in the subconscious mind. Remember that you are moving from the illusion of fear to the reality of love. Any negative experience you may encounter is <u>what you are not</u>. This is illusion. It is insubstantial like a dream. Like darkness it will dissolve in the light of awareness. <u>What you are</u> is the infinite consciousness and the unconditional love of the Absolute Self, the presence of God, in the heart. This is reality.

Soon the stressful and negative impressions will dissolve and you will gradually but <u>inevitably</u> gain access to the nurturing presence of the heart. It is not something you lack and have to get; it is what you are. A clear mind is like an open window into the heart.

Now let your attention rest on the breath. Feel it flow in and out on its own. Notice how the breath is breathing you... Let yourself be breathed that way...

Become aware of the quality of your mind. Is it calm or jagged, sluggish or peaceful, or is there a sense of aggravation or restlessness? Picture the mind like a glass of muddy water. Let the mud settle down. It happens through stillness. There is nothing else to do but be kind to yourself...

As you become centered and peaceful, notice how your mind interprets your physical presence as an "I," an ego, as "me." Sense that ego presence, the sense of I-ness in your physical body. It's your habit of experiencing yourself in that form. Settle into that...

Ask yourself with deep kindness: "Am I ready now to open myself and pay attention to some of the unpleasant thoughts, feelings, and images in me? Listen to what answer arises from your heart... The voice of your deep heart-intuition is already there. Become still and listen deeply... In stillness you can detect a yes or a no response to your question. Resolve to follow that answer...

If you receive a no, realize that your inborn kindness and wisdom tell you this is not the time. Trust your inner knowing, relax and try again another time. If you receive a yes, proceed with a sense of profound kindness and courage and open yourself to grace. Remember that what is in you cannot ever be a threat or an enemy. Instead it is <u>a part of you that needs help</u>, and you are the one who can provide what it needs. You have the most powerful medicine in the world in your heart.

Again, mentally check throughout your body for any aggravated or nervous sensations and allow them to calm down before proceeding...

Now gently call into your mind what you are afraid or ashamed of, what disturbs you, what robs you of peace. Invite a specific trauma, pain, or negative impulse to show itself. Let the mind become an empty screen and simply wait. Look with your inner eye, listen, feel until you notice what comes up...

What comes up may be a memory, a single picture, or a scene of a memory movie; it could be something you witnessed, or completely imaginary, an emotion, a body sensation, or a thought or belief. Simply open to whatever may come...

If anxiety or fear arises, this could be it.

Whatever arises, notice it. Breathe... Be aware of your body reactions. If a stressful sensation appears, observe it closely. Go slow...

You may notice that the mind runs away from the sensation, or becomes distracted or fearful. Continue observing. Stay with it. If the mind goes into other thoughts, say to the mind softly but firmly, "Not now," and return your attention to the body sensation... Let the mind become completely focused on the area where the body sensation appears...

Continue focusing until your attention on the negative sensation has become stable... Now leave the sensation where it is, and bring your attention to the heart. Evoke the heart essence.

- Imagine a brilliant point of light in the heart that expands to become like the sun, then let the light powerfully radiate from the heart into the negative sensation.

- Or feel the heart nectar like a tangible substance and cause it to flow from the heart into the stressful sensation.

- Become completely giving in the heart and completely receptive in the area of the body sensation.

Whether as a light or as a stream of nectar, observe how the heart essence flows into the area of the stressful sensation. Open to it. Receive it fully. Notice the continuous flow of heart essence into the part of you that needs help.

You are now the <u>giver of love</u> in the heart ... and the <u>receiver of love</u> in the place where the negative impulse arises.

Feel yourself giving... And feel yourself receiving...

Because the power of the heart shines by itself, focus on becoming completely receptive. Allow the heart nectar to saturate you in the place of the pain; then let it spread everywhere. Delight in the unlimited healing power of love...

Give yourself to it with complete abandon...

<u>You are now the Lover and the Beloved in one.</u> Enjoy this profound inner embrace.   Let it heal you and disperse all confusion...

Let it guide you home to yourself…

Let the light and the essence of the heart be what you are…

Stay in this space of inner-focused attention as long as you can. Know it to be the most direct expression of compassion for yourself. When it is time, return your attention to the breath, then to your body awareness. Become centered and grounded and resolve to make time again to enter this space of inner healing. Then gently open your eyes again. Create a daily practice with the intention to reach complete enlightenment for the sake of all beings.

Repeat this meditation as often as you want. Expand it. Find anything in you that causes you suffering and expose it to the healing power of the heart. Exchange all inner darkness for the light of your soul. Awaken yourself to the immense glory of what you are.

You can trust the practice of HeartSourcing to keep you moving out of darkness into the light. As you awaken the great Heart in you, you will eventually see it reflected everywhere in all guises: friendly and grim, divine, sometimes appearing demonic, and often quite humorous. You will see it everywhere because your eyes are clear. There is a sublime joy in living with an open heart right here on earth, held in the arms of your supreme lover, who turns out to be none other than yourself!

Appendix V

A Daily Practice Routine

WHAT IS A GOOD DAILY PRACTICE routine? The following is a description of my own practice at the time of this writing. This is not how you should do it; it is simply an example. Please adjust it to fit your particular habits and needs. Our needs for practice change and soon my routine may be different. What will be the same is that I will continue to practice with as much single-minded devotion as I can, taking myself deeper into my heart until all obstructions are gone. Your intuition can guide you safely in this.

After waking early in the morning, I stay in bed a while longer and practice Open Attention. Because I am very relaxed before starting my day, the practice is usually rich and rewarding. It puts me directly in touch with the internal Beloved, as Open Attention effortlessly flows into HeartSourcing. It is very enjoyable. I get out of bed and sit in front of my altar for a formal HeartSourcing practice. This is how I connect deeply with my heart and the external beloved. This is Maharajji for me, both in his personal form, as well as seeing him in everyone, everywhere. This sets the tone for the day.

When I notice stressful thoughts about someone or something, I question some of them in writing with The Work. This is quickly done in about 10 to 15 minutes. If needed, I take The Work deeper and devote more time to it. Devotional practice is woven throughout the day: I listen to devotional music, practice my mantra, and at home I am surrounded by pictures and photographs of Maharajji. At night I meditate, and once in bed I use Open Attention again to deepen my peace before going to sleep.

This is not a rigid schedule. I may feel inspired to do more or do it differently. What is important to me is that I am always tuned to the source of my happiness. I go through periods where one or the other skill predominates for a while, as needed. This allows me to live and breathe my sadhana, and it prevents me from forgetting to practice when tensions are high. This routine does not at all interfere with a busy lifestyle; on the contrary, it supports and enhances my life. It clears the mind and makes me more aware, focused, and productive during the day. It is time gained, never lost.

Notes

Introduction

1. The word 'love' is often extremely misunderstood. When I speak of love I do not mean a state of ego-driven desire, attachment, or romantic infatuation. I refer to the absolute love that is the unity of our being, the expression of oneness, the bliss of the Absolute. It is an unlimited state of being, pristine, and complete, and present in the inner core of every heart. This love is never tainted by suffering. It is the state of the liberated soul.

Waking Up

1. Playing In Bomb Craters

1. "To millions of Germans the loss of the Fuehrer...was not the loss of someone ordinary; identifications that had filled a central function in the lives of his followers were attached to his person...he had become the embodiment of their ego-ideal... Through the catastrophe not only was the German ego-ideal robbed of the support of reality, but in addition the Fuehrer himself was exposed by the victors as a criminal of truly monstrous proportions. With this sudden reversal of his qualities, the ego of every single German individual suffered a central devaluation and impoverishment."
Alexander Mitscherlich and Margarethe Mitscherlich, *Die Unfaehigkeit zu Trauern*; *The Inability to Mourn*; *Principles of Collective Behavior*, trans. Beverly R. Placzek (New York, Grove Press, 1975).

2. One of the most telling documents of the depraved insanity of the time is documented in a speech by Heinrich Himmler, the second most powerful man in Nazi Germany, to SS officers in a secret meeting on October 4, 1943, in Poznan, Poland: *"I also want to mention a very difficult subject before you here, completely*

openly. It should be discussed amongst us, and yet, nevertheless, we will never speak about it in public… I am talking about the "Jewish evacuation": the extermination of the Jewish people. It is one of those things that is easily said. "The Jewish people are being exterminated." Every Party member will tell you, "perfectly clear, it's part of our plans, we're eliminating the Jews, exterminating them, ha!, a small matter."

And then along they all come, all the 80 million upright Germans, and each one has his decent Jew. They say: all the others are swine, but here is a first-class Jew. And none of them has seen it, has endured it. Most of you will know what it means when 100 bodies lie together, when there are 500, or when there are 1000. … And to have seen this through, and—with the exception of human weaknesses—to have remained decent, has made us hard and is a page of glory never mentioned and never to be mentioned.

… We have the moral right, we had the duty to our people to do it, to kill this people who wanted to kill us.… We have carried out this most difficult task for the love of our people. And we have taken on no defect within us, in our soul, or in our character."

2. Waking Up In Heaven One Day

1. Psychedelic drugs are marijuana, peyote, ayahuasca, LSD, and others. Even though they were important for my initial awakening, I do not recommend the use of drugs. In our present culture we have no established "sacred container" or positive spiritual tradition for the use of these substances, nor do most people have access to elders who can serve as experienced guides for journeys into states of expanded consciousness. In addition, the illegality of these drugs, impurities in their chemical make-up, indiscriminate use, and many other factors can lead to harmful effects. Today, safer means of consciousness expansion are available. Love is the best drug.

2. Primarily from pre-1970 publications by Aldous Huxley (*The Doors of Perception*), and Timothy Leary, Ralph Metzner, and Richard Alpert (*The Psychedelic Experience*).

3. The word God means as many things as there are people using it. What I mean by it is a state of absolute fulfillment and wholeness. "God" to me can be both personal and impersonal; it is certainly not a God of good vs. evil, but the *Ground of Being* which encompasses all opposites in their natural oneness. It is that which we cannot know (because it transcends the rational mind), but what we already are at our core, the mystery, and the totality. It becomes personal and intimate through the compassion of sages and saints and in the core of our heart.

4. To complete this personal mandala, to find a stable inner harmony of masculine and feminine forces, took more than 3 decades of focussed spiritual work The completed mandala, with the shakti triangle, can be seen at the end of the HeartSourcing chapter

5. From the novel *Don Quixote de la Mancha* by Miguel de Cervantes

3. Earth School

1. *Ashtavakra Gita*

The First Skill: Stillness

5. Meditation

1. *The Collected Works of Dilgo Khyentse, The Heart of Compassion.*

6. The Ego

1. *Tao Te Ching*, Stephen Mitchell, tr.

2. For more on the pain body, see Chapter 16 and also Eckhart Tolle, *The Power of Now* and *A New Earth*.

7. The Messenger Appears

1. More at **maharajji.com** and **nkbashram.org**.

The Second Skill: Love And Devotion

8. Opening The Devotional Heart

1. *Ashtavakra Gita*

2. *Shakti* is a complex term with many layers of meaning. In this context it means sacred force, the primordial cosmic energy that can be activated in a human being through spiritual realization, the combination of power and love.

9. Under The Blanket

1. For an account of many of Maharajji's miracles see *The Divine Reality of Sri Baba Neeb Karori Ji Maharaj*, by Ravi Prakash Pande "Rajida." Available from: Sri Kainchi Hanuman Mandir & Ashram, Kainchi, District Nainital – 263132, Uttaranchal, India.

2. Jnana Yoga. In living memory Ramana Maharshi was the greatest proponent of this yoga of knowledge through self-inquiry. See **sriramanamaharshi.org**

10. The Universal Self

1. Shiva, the archetype of the perfect yogi, is one of the three primary emanations of *Brahman*, the formless ground of all being. Along with the creator (Brahma) and the preserver of the universe (Vishnu), Shiva is the destroying, renewing principle. This represents the ability of the

mind to destroy what is false, remove illusion, and open access to enlightenment in non-dual awareness.

11. Devotion

1. Matthew 18:20

2. God is One and this One Ultimate Reality can manifest in countless forms. We therefore best turn to the form of the divine that attracts us the most and then devote ourselves to that form with single-minded purpose. God, in essence, is beyond all name and form. The form we worship is like a doorway through which we enter the immensity.

12. From Molehill To Mountain

1. Saffron or orange clothes are worn by most sannyasins or Swamis.

2. From *Miracle of Love, Stories about Neem Karoli Baba*, compiled by Ram Dass.

3. Many years later movie technology created the effect of faces 'morphing' into each other. As usual, Maharajji was ahead of his time.

4. Shankaracharya, or Adi Shankara, was a great reformer of Hinduism. While reestablishing the ancient Vedic religion after a period of Buddhist dominance, he founded the present day monastic system of *dasnami sannyasins* or Swamis.

5. The Kumbha Melas are enormous gatherings of holy beings and pilgrims, numbering in the millions, which are held in four specific sacred places in North India every 12 years.

6. Recordings of the Hanuman Chalisa are available from Sounds True: Krishna Das, "Flow of Grace," and "Hanuman Chaleesa, Songs in Praise of Hanuman." For a YouTube video tutorial on the Chaleesa, see: http://tinyurl.com/63vl6pv

The Third Skill: Emotional Harmony

13. Spiritual Community

1. http://www.youtube.com/watch?v=9QC7r6CvVm0&feature=related

2. http://www.kashiashram.com/egg_on_my_beard.pdf

3. see www.kashi.org

14. The Emotional Rollercoaster

1. *Tapasya*, "purification by fire," the practice of austerities leading to the Self-realization.

16. The Pain Body

1. For more on the pain body, see Eckhart Tolle, *The Power of Now* and *A New Earth*.

The Fourth Skill: Peace Of Mind

20. Clarity Of Mind

1. Instructions in The Work are available at www.Ramgiri.com, and as
   a free e-book: *The Little Book* available at www.thework.com. All you
   need to clear your mind of stress is here, including audio and video
   clips of Katie doing The Work with people as they struggle with various
   problems.

The End Of Fear

22. Finding The Light In The Darkness: Auschwitz

1. The inner guru can be experienced in one of three different ways. When
   we think of ourselves as separate beings, it is the presence of a deep
   sense of safety and a connectedness to love that can be present even
   while we encounter fear or other emotions. When we're aware of the
   soul level, we sense that we are a reflection of the presence of God, or
   the light of the Self in all things. And on the level of truth, we realize
   that what we really are, the Self, guru or God are one and the same.

2. According to one study, in this past century, "Most probably near
   170,000,000 people have been murdered in cold-blood by governments,
   well over three-quarters by absolutist regimes." R. J. Rummel http://
   www.mega.nu/ampp/rummel/power.art.htm

3. *Yad Vashem* is the Jewish people's living memorial to the Holocaust:
   http://www1.yadvashem.org/

4. *"Hustled by truncheons and kicks we creep into a dark, damp and stinking hole 90 to
   90 centimeters big*
   There are four of us, we stand
   We inhale our closeness
   Urine, excrement, the unbearable stench of festering phlegm, hostile hatred
   We breathe helpless anger, and fear
   To creep out in the morning – with the help of beating
   *-- into your labour commando running and to work yourself down running and in
   the evening to come back into the nightmare of the night…running…"*
   -- Marian Kolodziej

5. The average life expectancy of these prisoners was about three months.

6. *The Liberation Through Hearing During The Intermediate State* or *Bardo Thödol*,
   composed in the 8th century by Padmasambhava and recorded by his primary
   student, Yeshe Tsogyal. Carl Jung commented in his introduction: "The *Bardo
   Thödol* began by being a 'closed' book, and so it has remained, no matter what
   kind of commentaries may be written upon it. For it is a book that will only
   open itself to spiritual understanding, and this is a capacity which no man is

born with, but which he can only acquire through special training and special experience."

23. *The Doorway Into The Light*

1. The expression "Ground of Being," coined by the Christian philosopher Paul Tillich, beautifully resonates with the Vedantic concept of sat-chit-ananda

2. In Vedantic philosophy, *Ishvara* is the supreme cosmic consciousness, the cause-less, perfect, omniscient, omnipresent, incorporeal creator, ruler, and eventual destroyer of the world.

3. I am paraphrasing the words of the Tibetan master Longchenpa (1308-1363); see Longchenpa,
You Are the Eyes of the World, Ithaca, NY: Snow Lion Publications, 2010

4. *Shekhinah*, the Indwelling, is the Divine that resides within the life of the world, the inner glory of existence.

24. *Resurrection*

1. For an in-depth interpretation of the mystical meaning of the *Ramayana*, see Swami Jyotirmayananda, *Mysticism of the Ramayana*, Yoga Research Foundation, at www.yrf.org.

Heartsourcing

26. *7 Steps To Unconditional Love*

1. Narcissistic traits are a mental disorder characterized by a lack of em-pathy, a willingness to exploit others (including using them to get their affection, acknowledgement and attention), and an inflated sense of self-importance. When it manifests at an extreme we call it a disorder, but it is a general quality of the unenlightened state.

Appendix I Meditation

1. Pronounce: *"Raam"*

Appendix II Open Attention

1. Guided practice sessions of Open Attention and related resources are available at www.RamGiri.com.

Glossary

Abhyasa: regular and constant spiritual practice over a long period of time. Along with vairagya—detachment—abhyasa is essential to control the mind and to gain moksha or spiritual liberation.

Ahamkara: the "I-making facility," often loosely translated as "ego." It is the tendency of the mind to create the perception of a separate entity out of our experience. This is a state of illusion. Paradoxically, the ahamkara has to be powerful, clear, and harmonious enough for us to engage in spiritual practice so we awaken from the illusion of separateness.

Antaryami: the timeless witness of all things and the knower of all Hearts, the origin of universal intelligence and all-embracing, unconditional love. This non-dual consciousness is present everywhere, and accessible to us in the core of our Hearts. The true guru is the antaryami, the all-knowing inner witness, controller and lover of all things.

Avadhuta: a completely free being without egoic motivations and beyond the dualities of attachment and detachment, right and wrong. One who lives in the awareness that he is the infinite, immortal Self. Such beings "roam free like a child upon the face of the Earth."

Bardo (Tibetan): The intermediate state between death and rebirth. Since we are constantly "dying" to each moment of life that passes away, we have the opportunity of liberation at each moment if the individual soul has matured to the point of merging into God, of recognizing its oneness with the universal soul, the clear light. Or it can be a way-station to further incarnations, the quality of which are determined by the balance of the purifying effects of suffering and meditative awareness, and by the contamination of negative actions.

Bhakti or **bhakti yoga**: the path of devotion. In *Glimpses of Divine Vision*, Swami Ramdas says, "Devotion to God who is seated in the hearts of us all is the one path that leads the struggling soul to the haven of perfect peace and joy.... Devotion sweetens life.... Devotion means loving remembrance of God. Blessed indeed is the heart which adores the Lord and are the lips which utter His nectar-like name."

Bodhisattva: a spiritually committed being, motivated by great compassion, who has a great desire to attain enlightenment for the sake of all beings and decides to intentionally reincarnate for the upliftment of all beings.

Brahman: the eternal, unchanging, infinite, immanent and transcendent reality that is the Divine Ground of all matter, energy, time, space, being, and everything in and beyond this Universe.

Burning ghats: wide steps by a river where the bodies of the dead are burned in open fires in India.

Chela: the student or, better, devotee of a guru.

Dakini: female deities in Hindu and Tibetan Tantra, also known to manifest as spiritually awakened women. Of volatile and wrathful temperament, dakinis act as a spiritual muse or guide. Their function is to transform the energy of negative emotions into the energy of enlightened awareness. They point out the insubstantial nature of all things which contains their pure potentiality and power in everyday experience.

Dhuni: a sacred opening in the ground symbolizing the *yoni* (or vulva) of the Goddess in which the Mother Goddess is worshipped by Indian sadhus. The dhuni holds a sacred fire, representing the linga (or phallus) of Shiva, which burns uninterruptedly. Keeping a dhuni is a sacred practice of return from the physical to the spiritual level, a ritual of merging with the oneness of ultimate reality.

Durvasa: a mythological sage, known for his short temper. Encountering Durvasa is a metaphor for encountering the numerous hardships and challenges of life. He teaches patience and the ability to see the divine hand in anything we encounter.

Five limbed yoga: the humorous description of the activities of a bhakti yogi in the state of divine intoxication—aimlessly walking about, telling stories of the Beloved, eating, drinking, and letting your love flow into song.

Gargoyles: grotesque, at times demonic figures on the outside of medieval European cathedrals. They are a Western form of the guardians of the gates of some temples and shrines in the East.

Gopi: a lover of Krishna. In the stories of Krishna, the gopis are enlightened sages who incarnated as women at the time of Krishna's birth to enjoy the taste of passionate love for God in physical form.

Hanuman: a Hindu deity, who is a central character in the Indian epic Ramayana. He is a symbol of humility and the singular motivation of mind in true selfless service.

Hanuman Chalisa: a hymn of forty verses in praise of the God Hanuman, the symbol of humility and perfect service to God.

Heart Cave: an imaginary place in the innermost part of the chest. It is the Source of everything, beyond space and time, and contains the potential of all wisdom and love, the wellspring of life, the immortal Self. It is always interior to any disturbing sensations that may be present in the chest.

Heart-mind: wisdom mind, the Source in the heart center with which we can guide our lives and decisions in the realization of compassion and wisdom.

Jnana Yoga: the yoga of knowledge. Its most well-known proponent in recent memory is Ramana Maharshi, the sage of Arunachala, India.

Karma: the law of cause and effect of positive and negative actions.

Kirtan: Hindu devotional chanting of the names and glories of God.

Klesha: suffering or affliction; by some counts, there are five kinds of kleshas: (1) ignorance of Reality, (2) the perception of separateness of the ego, (3) desire or attachment, (4) aversion or hatred, (5) the fear of death or the clinging to life, which is the fear of losing one's mistaken identity, the ego.

Lila: the divine dance. The entire universe is the blissful dance of divine consciousness.

Mantra: a sacred sound, word or phrase, or a name of God, repeated silently or in a low voice, which is capable of creating transformation. As vehicles of adoration, mantras are repeated to provide protection and to center and calm the mind and open the heart.

Moksha: spiritual liberation, release from the patterns of ignorance and delusion and realization of the soul's oneness with the Absolute Self.

Mudra: a symbolic or ritual gesture expressed by the hands or the whole body.

Namarupa: name and form; *nāma* describes the spiritual or essential properties of an object or being, and rūpa the physical presence that it manifests. The distinction between nāma and *rūpa* in Hindu thought explains the ability of spiritual powers to manifest through inadequate or inanimate vessels, such as the physical body of a saint or the presence of the divine in images that are worshiped through puja.

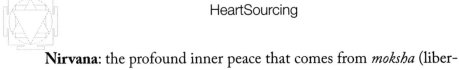

Nirvana: the profound inner peace that comes from *moksha* (liberation), the realization of oneness with *brahman*, the Absolute.

Pain body: a term coined by Eckhart Tolle (in *The Power of Now*) that explains the unconscious addiction of the ego to create pain for itself. It is the emotional part of the ego that identifies with pain.

Parabrahman: the Absolute, the Ground of Being, the cause of all causes. The Upanishads say: *"Whoever realizes the Supreme Brahman attains to supreme felicity. That Supreme Brahman is Eternal Truth (satyam), Omniscient (jnanam), Infinite (anantam)."* It is Eternal, Conscious, and Blissful (sat-chit-ânanda). *"The One is Bliss. Whoever perceives the Blissful One, the reservoir of pleasure, becomes blissful forever."*

Persona: the mask; the patterns of thought, emotion, and behavior we imbue with an identity, an ego. The roles we play in society.

Prasad: blessed food; the term is also used to describe any form of tangible blessing.

Pujari: priest in the Vedantic (Hindu) religion.

Purusha: pure consciousness, the non-manifest substratum of all existence, out of which Nature, or Prakriti, is born.

Sadhana: spiritual practice, a process by which bondage becomes liberation.

Sadhu: renunciates who have left behind worldly attachments and concerns, and live devoted entirely to spiritual liberation in forests, caves, and temples all over the Indian subcontinent.

Samsara: the world of illusion.

Samskaras: impressions of past negative or positive tendencies in the unconscious mind.

Sanatana Dharma: the "eternal path'" or "eternal law"; the Hindu philosophy and religion.

Sanyasin: a monk living in the final stage of life, one who has renounced attachment to the world to be fully dedicated to his or her spiritual pursuit. Most sanyasins are Swamis wearing orange or ochre cloth, connected with an order but roaming the country freely, teaching and aiding the people in their spiritual quest. In Chapter 5, verse 3 of the *Bhagavad Gita*, Krishna says: "… that one who neither disdains nor desires the fruits of actions is always a renunciate; certainly that person being free from all dualities is easily liberated from bondage."

Satchitananda: an expression used to describe the nature of Brahman, the unified state, as pure Being or Truth (*sat*), all-encompassing consciousness (*chit*), and eternal bliss (*ananda*).

Satguru: an enlightened or fully realized saint capable of guiding a *chela* or devotee to the realization of Brahman, or unified consciousness.

Satsang: the company of seekers after the truth, or the community of disciples of a guru. Satsang may include devotional practice, study of scriptures, meditation and more. Satsang is of central importance in the quest for spiritual liberation. The company of like-minded souls gives us the strength, stability and help we need for the path. It allows us to know that we are not getting lost in confusion. In the words of Sri Shankaracharya: *"Satsang leads you to detachment, detachment destroys delusion. Free of delusion you become rooted in God within you, unaffected by the world. That state then leads you to jivan mukti, liberation in life."*

Shakti: the primordial cosmic power that creates all appearances. Shakti manifests as creation, and within creation as the form of the Goddess or Divine Mother. All women are a concrete representation of shakti. The interplay (or *lila*) of Shakti and Shiva (the unmanifest Ground of Being), is the divine dance of the totality of existence and non-existence, form and formlessness, wisdom and love. Shakti, as the combination of divine power and love, is a personal liberating force that can be activated in a human being through sadhana and spiritual realization.

Shoah: Hebrew for "calamity" or "destruction," an alternative word for Holocaust.

Spanda: the sacred tremor of the heart; a term used in Kashmiri Shaivism. It is the ecstatic vibration, or shakti, of consciousness, arising in the heart of the divine. *"Spanda is the pulsation of the ecstasy of the divine consciousness"* -Abinahavagupta (975-1025 c.e.)

Swami: a title for sanyasins that points out their learning and mastery of yoga, their devotion to god, and to the Swami's guru. Swami means "He who knows and is master of himself" or "free from the senses."

Takhat: a simple piece of furniture, like a small bed, covered by a firm pad wrapped in coarse brown woolen fabric.

Tantra: An approach to spiritual practice that exhibits a world-embracing rather than a world-denying attitude and is oriented more to householders than monastics. It teaches that the whole of reality is the self-expression of a single, free, and blissful divine consciousness. One of the maxims of Tantra is that "Nothing exists that is not divine."

Tapasya: "purification by fire," the yogic practice of austerities with the goal of spiritual liberation.

The Tibetan Book of the Dead, also called *Liberation Through Hearing During The Intermediate State* or *Bardo Thödol*, is a manual for the guidance of a soul from death through the "intermediate state" or bardo, into liberation or a rebirth.

The Way of the Cross: here refers not to the devotions of the "Stations of the Cross" as practiced mainly by Roman Catholics, but rather to accepting one's suffering as a process of atonement and salvation. This is related to the expression of "taking your cross upon you" in humility and surrender.

The Way of the Heart: bhakti yoga, the yoga of devotion.

Vairagya: detachment or renunciation, essential in the pursuit of *moksha*, spiritual liberation.

Acknowledgements

THIS BOOK HAS BEEN BIRTHED OVER many years and so many kind and amazing souls have assisted its creation that it is impossible to list them all here. At first therefore my apologies to anyone I neglect to mention. The heart doesn't forget!

HeartSourcing of course is the gift of my guru, Neem Karoli Baba Maharajji and all credit for this work belongs to him. He has been the inspiration, the guide and the substance of this book as well as of my life. There is no way to express the gratitude I owe to you, my Beloved.

Next I must mention my teachers who in their kindness nurtured, guided and challenged me, H.H. the 16th Karmapa, Ma Jaya, Byron Katie, Swami Jyotirmayananda, and Eckhart Tolle. No less important are the teachers whom I did not meet on the physical plane: Ramana Maharshi, Baba Nityananda, Sai Baba of Shirdi, Dilgo Khyentse Rimpoche, Nisargadatta Maharaj, Papaji and Mooji and many more.

A very deep gratitude belongs to my family, Ram Jyoti, Bhagavati and Ganga Devi, who supported me unconditionally and over long periods of time missed their father and husband who was buried in his book. And to Durga (Julia Sanchez), you are a miracle.

Satsang is essential and I have been blessed with an amazing spiritual family. I want to thank especially Ram Dass, Rameshwar Das, Raghu, the two exquisite Mirabais and of course Parvati, the private secretary, who had a major hand in shaping this work. Your presence and support have been invaluable.

Then there are countless friends, who over many years supported this project: Jean Houston, along with Ma Jaya, provided the initial push by telling me in no uncertain terms that I had to write. Ram Dass generously provided the foreword despite the challenges with his health. Rameshwar Das, his right hand man, was forever helpful. Roshi Bernie Glassman took me to Auschwitz and so opened the door to deep forgiveness and understanding. Ken Druck sparked a new beginning as if in a trance. Dan Nevel keeps the machinery going. And Sol Borchardt and Federico Cerdeiro stepped forward and made it happen. Rosemary Ravinal, Nancy Campos, Barry and Leslie Rosen and our Miami satsang are continuing to serve this project in wonderful ways.

Most importantly I owe enormous gratitude to my students. Through your aspiration for freedom and love you have made Heart-Sourcing real. You proved its effectiveness. May your awakening help others to follow in your footsteps.

Credits

GRATEFUL ACKNOWLEDGMENT GOES TO THE FOLLOW-
ING photographers for the use of their work in this
publication:

Page xv: Ramgiri and Ram Dass in Maui. Photo by Dasi Ma.

Page 7: Ultimatum. Original WWII flyer, air-dropped by US forces over Halle. From family archives

Page 16: Ramgiri with Dad. Family picture.

Page 24: Landscape in Bavaria. Photo by Ramgiri.

Page 32: Yantra design process. Design by Ramgiri

Page 55: The Path to the Mountains graphic. Design by Ramgiri

Page 68: The Human Structure and Stillness. Design by Ramgiri

Page 79: Siva, The Lord of Yogis. Sculpture and photo by Ramgiri.

Page 89: Maharajji. Photo credit: Balaram Das

Page 98: Maharajji. Photo credit: Balaram Das

Page 107: Vishnu Digambar and Ramgiri by Maharajji's tucket. Photo by Durgamayi Ma.

Page 112: Maharajji with westerners, Kainchi Ashram, India. Photo by Roy Bonney

Page 115: Maharajji with westerners, Kainchi Ashram, India. Photo by Roy Bonney

Page 118: Ramgiri at Maharajji's Funeral Pyre, Vrindaban, India. Photographer unknown

Page 121: Maharajji. Photo credit: Balaram Das

Page 140: Ramgiri in Kainchi Ashram, India. Photo by Rameshwardas

Page 157: Ma Jaya. Photo credit: Kashi Ashram

Page 218: Painting by Marian Kolodziej, with permission

Page 236: Ramgiri in Auschwitz. Photographer unknown

Page 271: Yantra design by Ramgiri. All graphics by Julia (Durga) Sanchez